LUXURY AND CORRUPTION

Challenging the Anti-Corruption Consensus

Tereza Østbø Kuldova, Jardar Østbø,
and Thomas Raymen

I0136033

B BRISTOL
UNIVERSITY
PRESS

First published in Great Britain in 2024 by

Bristol University Press
University of Bristol
1–9 Old Park Hill
Bristol
BS2 8BB
UK
t: +44 (0)117 374 6645
e: bup-info@bristol.ac.uk

Details of international sales and distribution partners are available at bristoluniversitypress.co.uk

British Library Cataloguing in Publication Data
A catalogue record for this book is available from the British Library

ISBN 978-1-5292-1241-9 hardcover
ISBN 978-1-5292-3633-0 paperback
ISBN 978-1-5292-1243-3 ePub
ISBN 978-1-5292-1242-6 ePdf

Cover design: Liam Roberts
Front cover image: iStock/knape

Contents

About the Authors

Tereza Østbø Kuldova is Research Professor at the Work Research Institute, Oslo Metropolitan University. She is a social anthropologist and the author of six books and numerous articles, including *How Outlaws Win Friends and Influence People* (2018) and *Compliance-Industrial Complex: The Operating System of a Pre-Crime Society* (2022). She is the founder and editor-in-chief of *Journal of Extreme Anthropology* and of *Algorithmic Governance Research Network*. She leads the LUXCORE project *Luxury, Corruption and Global Ethics: Towards a Critical Cultural Theory of the Moral Economy of Fraud*, funded by the Research Council of Norway.

Jardar Østbø is Professor and Head of Programme for Russian Security and Defence Policy at the Institute for Defence Studies, Norwegian Defence University College. He is author of *The New Third Rome: Readings of a Russian Nationalist Myth* (2016) and his articles have appeared in numerous journals. He is the leader of the international project RUSECOPOL (2019–23) and a core researcher of the LUXCORE project *Luxury, Corruption and Global Ethics: Towards a Critical Cultural Theory of the Moral Economy of Fraud*, funded by the Research Council of Norway.

Thomas Raymen is Associate Professor of Criminology at Northumbria University. He is a co-founder of the Deviant Leisure Research Network, author of *The Enigma of Social Harm: The Problem of Liberalism* (2023), and the founder and editor-in-chief of *Journal of Contemporary Crime, Harm, and Ethics*. Raymen is a core researcher of the LUXCORE project *Luxury, Corruption and Global Ethics: Towards a Critical Cultural Theory of the Moral Economy of Fraud*, funded by the Research Council of Norway.

Acknowledgements

This book springs from a research project funded by The Research Council of Norway, *Luxury, Corruption and Global Ethics: Towards a Critical Cultural Theory of the Moral Economy of Fraud (LUXCORE)* [project no. 313004], which investigates the global governance of corruption and the dynamics between compliance and defiance through the lens of luxury. We would like to thank all our colleagues who are involved with or who have engaged with this project. For all the inspiring conversations, special thanks go to Petr Kupka, Cris Shore, Bitten Nordrik, Audrey Millet, Davide Casciano, Joanne Roberts, Steve Hall, Kristin Reichborn-Kjennerud, Aleksandra Bartoszko, Simon Winlow, Daniel Briggs, and to The Research Council of Norway for enabling and supporting this research and lasting collaborations. This book would also have not been possible without another parallel research project funded by The Research Council of Norway, in which both Tereza Østbø Kuldova and Jardar Østbø participate, namely, *Algorithmic Governance and Cultures of Policing: Comparative Perspectives from Norway, India, Brazil, Russia, and South Africa (AGOPOL)* [project no. 313626]. We therefore also acknowledge this project and express our thanks to The Research Council of Norway for enabling these important synergies across research groups. Within this project, we would in particular like to give special thanks to Christin Thea Wathne, Helene O.I. Gundhus, Shivangi Narayan, Tomas Salem, Ella Paneyakh, Dean Wilson, Ursula Rao, Paulo Cruz Terra, Kjetil Klette Bøhler, Veronika Nagy, Ashwin Varghese, Tessa Diphoorn, Mikkel Flyverbom, and Simon Egbert. This book has also greatly benefited from the discussions with the members of the *Algorithmic Governance Research Network*, and from many years of conversations and encounters with numerous brilliant colleagues from across anthropology and critical and ultra-realist criminology, special thanks here go to Simon Winlow, Steve Hall, and Alexandra Hall.

Preface: Luxury, Corruption, and the Assumption of Harmlessness

There are several obvious reasons for writing a book about the relationship between luxury and corruption. For starters, there is a longstanding relationship between the two. The idea that luxury is a corrosive force on individual morality and politics has endured since antiquity, when it was seen as cultivating an effeminacy and softness that corroded masculine virtue and corrupted moral wisdom (Berry, 1994). In today's culture of consumerism, luxury is fulsomely embraced, and its legitimacy more generally is not in question. The ability to purchase luxury goods and pay for luxury experiences are a marker of one's success in life, a deserved reward for working hard and earning a sufficient income for luxury spending. However, the sense that there is a pernicious element to luxury nevertheless persists, with the desire for luxury lifestyles seen as corrupting politicians, public officials, and other professionals and drawing them away from the duties and responsibilities demanded of their office or role (Kuldova, 2021b). This is particularly the case in an era of leaks and scandals, where in the past 7 years alone we have had the Panama Papers, Pandora Papers, Paradise Papers, Suisse Secrets, FinCEN Files, and a host of other cases such as the Malayasian 1MDB scandal among others. Each of these leaks and scandals laid bare the financial secrets and luxury lifestyles of political and business elites. They were avalanches of information that merely empirically confirmed what we already knew: namely, that corruption, tax evasion, money laundering, and kleptocracy are commonplace among the world's political and economic elite, and that luxury commodities and industries are one of the key ways in which such elites both enjoy and launder their illicit wealth. Since February 2022 this relationship between luxury and corruption has been cemented in the popular imagination, as Russia's full-scale invasion of Ukraine cast the global spotlight onto Russia's oligarchs. Particular attention has been paid to their luxury assets dispersed across the world such as real estate, superyachts, fine art, classic cars, vintage wines, jewellery, and jets. Quite simply, corruption more generally, and its relationship to luxury in particular, is firmly on the agenda.

Therefore, we could quite easily write a book exposing all the gory details of the relationship between the world's corrupt actors and the luxury industries. We could look at how these elites have looted, embezzled, bribed, and muscled their way to billionaire status and bent the rules to their own ends. We could then provide a blow-by-blow account of how their illicit wealth is enjoyed, laundered, and stored through real estate in London, superyachts in Monaco, auction houses in New York and freeports around Europe. We could discuss how our political-economic system provides the legal and financial infrastructure to move illicit wealth freely throughout the global financial system and cast aspersions on the complicity of banks and luxury industries who act as 'enablers' in facilitating this activity. We could detail the lavishness of these luxury assets, complete with the staggering sums of money involved in their purchase and maintenance. We could present this material in such a way as to make the reader gasp and shake their head in despair, furrow their brow as they try to comprehend the truly mind-boggling sums of money involved, and seethe at the impunity with which these elites seem to thumb their nose at all forms of law, authority, and ethics.

Certainly, there will be a small dose of this throughout the book. Indeed, when writing a book on luxury and corruption, it is difficult to avoid this. But shocking our readers and inspiring their outrage, or simply adding empirical detail around the relationship between luxury and corruption is not the primary purpose of this book. There are a few reasons for this. Firstly, the extent of the relationship between the luxury industries, corrupt actors, and money laundering is by now quite well established, as are the mechanisms through which this is performed, with other academics and investigative journalists doing outstanding work to cast greater light on this world of shadows (Bullough, 2018, 2022; Michel, 2021). For us to do the same here would not add much in terms of value or knowledge. Secondly, while it is fascinating to voyeuristically peek into the nefarious machinations and luxury of the world's wealthiest and most powerful individuals, and while there is equally a perverse enjoyment in raging at the injustice of their luxurious lives and the gaudy sums of money spent on luxury assets, the production of this voyeuristic enjoyment belongs more to the genre of popular non-fiction. Academic work can inspire anger. But inspiring outrage – even for the dubious goal of 'raising awareness' – should never be the primary *aim* of intellectual endeavours. Instead, our job as academics is to advance not just empirical knowledge, but also *thought*, and it is our contention that recent developments in the relationship between luxury, corruption, and anti-corruption demand a great deal more critical thought. Simply documenting, in an empirical and material fashion, the ways in which corrupt actors launder and enjoy their illicit wealth and the ways in which the forces of anti-corruption try to stop them is not going to lead us to any higher truths or deeper insights. Instead, we must step into the broader ideological narratives surrounding luxury, corruption, and anti-corruption that inspire various new forms of action, policing, and decision-making.

To take one example that we discuss in Chapter 1 and other places throughout this book, US President Joe Biden has elevated corruption to a core national security issue for the US. Some might write this off as mere political rhetoric, a PR exercise that makes it appear as if the administration is getting truly 'tough' on corruption. While this may be partly the case, we should be wary of being too hasty in our dismissal, as such cynicism can cause us to fail to ask important questions which might yield more prescient insights. From an ideological perspective, Biden's declaration of corruption as a national security issue is a novel and highly interesting development, one that is generating very real forms of action, however ineffective those actions may be in ultimately tackling corruption. We must ask *why* corruption has been upgraded to a national security issue. Exactly what kind of threat is imagined here? The kind of corruption with which the Biden administration is concerned is primarily the kleptocracy of foreign political and business elites, rather than the more nuanced forms of corruption that pervade US and Western political economy more generally (Wedel, 2014). This kind of corruption is undoubtedly a serious issue, but it arguably does not pose either an *immediate* threat to the life of US citizens, US sovereignty, or to the viability and functioning of the domestic US or global economy. For all of the hyperbole around the consequences of corruption, if we are being truly honest, we know that money laundering by Russian kleptocrats is not going to directly kill people in West Virginia, collapse the US economy, or disrupt its normal functioning in ways that generate negative consequences that are directly experienced by people living in Oklahoma or Colorado. So why then, has corruption been upgraded to a national security issue? What is understood as being under attack or so vulnerable from the threat of corruption that President Biden demands it to be spoken of within a language of national security that is usually reserved for mortal threats from terrorists or other nation-states? What deeper purpose does his declaration serve for the US, for the compliance industry, and for the wider political-economic system over which the US has presided as the global hegemon for at least the past 50 years?

Similarly, there has been an explosion of efforts in recent years to cleanse – at least on paper – financial systems, industries, and supply chains of 'bad money' and associations with bad people that include, but are not limited to, corrupt actors, kleptocrats, and organized crime groups. As we discuss in Chapter 3, even objects such as artworks or artifacts must have their purity verified, as their histories are checked for any dark and troubling associations that may 'taint' the object at hand. When luxury art dealers perform due diligence and provenance checks on artworks and artifacts, what ideological fantasies are at work? When anti-corruption practitioners and compliance professionals seek to close all the gaps and loopholes in the global financial system, what do these actors imagine themselves to be accomplishing? The luxury industries, who have been seen as 'risky' perpetrators full of suspect enablers, are now being enlisted as a frontline force in the battle against corruption, tasked with identifying and purging the 'dirty' money, 'dirty' buyers, and 'dirty' objects that pollute their markets. Through the tools of compliance which make up the architecture of anti-corruption, these industries can exist simultaneously as both the suspect and the detective, the polluter and the purifier, the regulator and regulated. What purpose does this have for contemporary liberal capitalism? What function does it serve? What methods, tools, and instruments are used in the production of moral purity, and who and what are the primary beneficiaries of this production? Is it 'the people'? Democracy? The anti-corruption and compliance industries? Or is it liberal capitalism and the political and economic elites themselves? It is upon these kinds of questions that this book will focus.

Some might argue that this is all a little 'old hat'. Critical scholars of corruption, it could be argued, have always interrogated the ideological function that corruption and anti-corruption plays for contemporary liberal capitalism. There is an element of truth to this. After all, it has become commonplace to read how corruption's definition as 'the abuse of public office for private gain' (or the more recent 'abuse of entrusted power for private gain') has always been, in truth, a neoliberal ideological ploy to demonize the public sector, encourage greater private sector involvement in the economy, and definitionally exclude the forms of corruption driven and perpetrated by the private sector from the purview of anti-corruption efforts. Why else would the major institutions of global capitalism and liberal democracy – such as the World Bank, IMF, OECD, UN, and World Economic Forum – demonstrate such a marked enthusiasm for anti-corruption efforts unless it served some purpose in furthering their broader political and ideological projects?

However, this critical engagement with ideology is scarcely – if ever – extended to the whole gamut of anti-corruption tools, instruments, technologies, and logics themselves, which have been developed over the past half-century and proliferated in their volume, complexity, and importance over the past 20 to 30 years. Things such as the dizzying array of ever-shifting rules and regulations around financial conduct; know-your-customer (KYC) and due diligence checks; anti-money laundering (AML) compliance; and the hybridized forms of fast-swelling regulatory and supervisory technologies (RegTech and SupTech hereafter) that are being employed to manage the increasingly complex compliance sphere (Verhage, 2011; Kuldova, 2022a). When these things are critically scrutinized for their failures, it is the efficacy and efficiency with which they have been implemented that is called into question. Industries, financial institutions, and individual people, it is held, are simply not performing KYC and due diligence checks *correctly*. Perhaps their software is flawed or lacks sufficient computing power. Maybe there is a knowledge deficit within a corporation around fraud, money laundering, business ethics and compliance that is to be corrected by the installation of a more rigorous compliance regime and the purchase of an accompanying set of regulatory and supervisory technologies. But the legitimacy of these tools, strategies, and instruments themselves are never called into question. Their deeper ideological purpose and function is never considered. After all, how can something like AML software have an ideological function? Is it not just an inert technocratic instrument?

But if such anti-corruption technologies, instruments, and strategies were truly just technocratic tools designed to successfully perform a function, then they surely would have been dispensed with by now. Technologies that are truly utilitarian and purely functional in nature persist in time and space only insofar as they successfully perform a useful material function and remain in good working order. But as we are at pains to stress throughout this book, these tools, instruments, and hybridized modes of regulation and governance which constitute the architecture of anti-corruption and compliance are most notable for their routine failure, as their supposedly impenetrable fortifications are breached time and again. Despite this continuous failure, the response to these scandals (as seen in Chapter 1) is to double-down on the same tools, instruments and strategies that have already failed us. The unwillingness to abandon these failed strategies suggests that there is a fetishistic attachment to their underlying logic and to the imaginaries and fantasies that they produce, an attachment that indicates a far deeper purpose that is fundamentally *ideological* in nature, and that the 'compliance-industrial complex' (Kuldova, 2022a) for all of its other failures – arguably fulfils very successfully.

Similarly, we seldom hear scholars in this field critically consider why, in Western policy circles and academia more generally, issues such as corruption, bribery, money laundering and fraud are seemingly all tackled through the lens of anti-policy (Walters, 2008a). Questioning this can be incredibly difficult. After all, how can anyone be opposed to anti-corruption, or AML, or any other anti-policy? If one is against anti-corruption or anti-racism, does this not logically mean that one is *for* corruption and *for* racism? Not necessarily, but the prefix of 'anti-' makes such misrepresentations easy to perform. Upon facing criticism, advocates of anti-policies can cynically dismiss constructive criticism as a Trojan horse that has been sent to derail their efforts on behalf of their enemies. In the face of this kind of distortion, it is often easy to set such questioning aside and join the chorus of those who are against the bad things, lest one risk their humanitarian and social justice credentials being called into question. The nature of this seemingly innocuous prefix of 'anti-', therefore, has the dual effect of both establishing consensus around how to tackle a particular issue, and closing down debate and prohibiting more substantive critical reflection on the consensus that has formed. The purpose of this book, as the subtitle suggests, is to resist such prohibitions and create a space wherein the consensus that has formed around anti-corruption can be challenged by critically considering its deeper ideological functions.

So, what are these deeper ideological functions of the anti-corruption consensus? One of the major purposes of the book is to explore this proposition, so we obviously do not wish to give too much away here. But an overarching function ties into what one of the authors has described elsewhere as liberal capitalism's assumption of harmlessness (Raymen, 2021, 2022). Capitalism – and indeed the enterprise of money-making more generally – has never been considered to be entirely innocent and benign, even by its advocates. During capitalism's nascent period in the 17th century, the rationale of political arguments in favour of capitalist markets was that it could cure the ills of a society plagued by civil strife, religious tension, and foreign wars (Hirschman, 1977; Dupuy, 2014). While economic self-interest and the desire for profit was seen as an extremely strong and powerful drive, it was also understood as calm, calculated and predictable in comparison with the more violent passions associated with military and political conquest or religious fervour; what Frances Hutcheson described as the 'calm desire for wealth' (Hirschman, 1977). Economic avarice was still seen, to a certain extent, as a vice; but it was felt that such passions could be harnessed for the wider social good, exemplified in Bernard Mandeville's notion of markets as being capable of turning 'private vices' into 'publick benefits' (Mandeville, [1732] 1988), or Adam Smith's 'invisible hand', whereby everyone acting in their own self-interest unintentionally served the common good. This is perhaps the earliest manifestation of the assumption of the harmlessness, in which the symbolic violence inherent to market relations is put in service of the good, and thereby transformed into the good itself (Dupuy, 2014), with philanthrocapitalism being perhaps the most enduring expression of the assumption of harmlessness (McGoey, 2012, 2015). Alas, it is to be noted that this assumption originated and developed under very different socio-economic conditions, prior to the industrial revolution, but this ideology, divorced from the reality of contemporary capitalism, continues to persist (Anderson, 2017).

Today, however, there seems to be a drive not just to harness the vices of capitalism for a greater good, but to try and purify capitalism of its ills altogether. The likes of Bloom have argued that capitalism has always sustained itself through various non-market ethical principles, viewed by its advocates as a flawed but perfectible political-economic system whose ethical shortcomings could ultimately be fixed with a few technocratic tweaks (Bloom, 2017). Therefore, while not entirely novel, in recent years there nevertheless seems to have been a further intensification of efforts to (formally) cleanse capitalism of the various kinds of dirt under its fingernails. Customarily, all corporations and financial institutions now have anti-modern slavery statements; equality, diversity, and inclusion (EDI) targets; and environmental, social, and governance (ESG) portfolios which demonstrate how they are embedding environmental, social, and governance concerns in all of their investment strategies (Kuldova, forthcoming). Similarly, they also have AML, anti-bribery, anti-fraud, and combating the financing of terrorism (CFT) processes and procedures in place, all of which are to be ensured through rigorous compliance regimes which are supplemented by various forms of RegTech and SupTech. On the surface of things, we might be seduced into thinking that 'tackling' the corruption and luxury of economic and political elites through a raft of compliance measures is, in a small way, taking aim at and challenging the dominant political-economic order. Why then, as Kuldova has observed (Kuldova, 2022a), are corporations, banks, and financial institutions so eager to embrace anti-corruption and compliance regimes?

In truth, as we intend to argue in the pages that follow, such measures are in many respects the ideological servants of capital. One of the functions of ideology, as we discuss in Chapter 2, is to transform problems and contradictions that are *internal* to a particular social order into *external oppositions* that can ultimately be overcome without altering the core of the system itself (McGowan, 2019). This, we argue in various places throughout the book, is precisely the purpose of the various tools, technologies and compliance strategies employed and advocated by the anti-corruption industry. While corruption is not unique to capitalism, the forms of corruption that take place within global capitalism are undoubtedly internal to this system, generated by its economic imperatives and the various desires it cultivates. Instead of confronting this internal contradiction, the tools and technologies of anti-corruption allow corruption and its actors to be transformed into an externality which have no relation to capitalism. Rather, the corrupt actor is positioned as an external 'Other' that is in opposition to 'true' capitalism, polluting and corrupting its functioning, and which can be eradicated and ultimately overcome through a perfected regime of compliance that will close all the gaps and holes in the financial system, thereby achieving a pure, fair, and thoroughly meritocratic political economic system. We see this in the language used to describe corruption, which casts it in medical terms as a 'virus': an external infectious agent which penetrates and transmits illness to an otherwise healthy host (Forsberg & Severinsson, 2015). In doing so, current anti-corruption measures reproduce the ideological assumption of capitalism's essential harmlessness. Of course, given that this corrupt 'Other' is also the means through which capitalism evades its internal contradictions, its externality (and the promise of overcoming it) must continually be reproduced with the manufacturing of new threats and enemies to defeat. Perhaps, as we explore in Chapters 1 and 3, this is one of the reasons for the repetitive expansion of compliance tools and anti-corruption measures which fail to address the problem of corruption.

This argument holds true for the luxury industries in particular, even if the relationship between luxury and the assumption of harmlessness is slightly more complex. As Kuldova has argued, all luxury is predicated upon an enjoyment of its underlying 'dirt' (Kuldova, 2016). We enjoy luxury not merely because of the quality of the luxury experiences and commodities we consume, but because there is an acceptable transgressiveness to this consumption. What luxury transgresses is the ethos of utilitarianism, and while this transgression has now been thoroughly mainstreamed, enjoyment is nevertheless found in the superfluousness of the commodity and the wastefulness of the excessive expenditure. With artisanal luxuries, there is even an enjoyment in the 'painful expropriations' the underpin this luxury (Kuldova, 2016: 6) – the hours of labour that have gone into creating the luxury commodity and its surplus value. In this regard, it could be argued that the drive to purify and cleanse the luxury industries of its dirt undermines the very logic of luxury itself. But the transgression that is enjoyed through luxury must remain either an innocuous transgression that does not intrude too keenly on the conscience, or must be transformed into some form of ethical good. For example, we enjoy high-end jewellery not just for its beauty, but for the frisson of transgression that is experienced through indulging in an item that is opulent and superfluous. But this enjoyment is ruined if we were to learn that our prized possession was made up of blood diamonds mined by forced labour and children under the thumb of warlords in conflict zones. The decline in the luxury fur industry is another example where the innocuousness of our transgressive indulgence can no longer be maintained and enjoyed. Within Indian luxury fashion, the ruthless exploitation of artisans and craftspeople is transformed into an ethical good, whereby the luxury fashion industry is positioned as lifting the otherwise impoverished artisanal embroiderer or dyer out of destitution as a form of philanthrocapitalism (Kuldova, 2016, 2018a). With the luxury industries reliant on the enjoyment of innocuous transgression, but becoming more publicly embroiled with corruption, kleptocracy, terrorism and dictatorship, there is a clear vested interest in maintaining an assumption of harmlessness by purifying luxury markets of these sources of income.

This book is made up of four substantive chapters. Chapter 1 offers a novel theoretical approach which looks at the centrality of *enjoyment* to anti-corruption efforts. Specifically, an enjoyment of the ideological fantasies of wholeness, purity, and a world rid of informality and holes. These ideological fantasies contain within them a promise of a better world, a world of pure enjoyment in which what is lacking within global capitalism – namely ethics – is finally filled in through the eradication of dirt, of luxury and wealth in the wrong hands. Of course, the satisfaction promised by these fantasies is never forthcoming, and in truth the promise of these fantasies can only be enjoyed insofar as they are never fully realized. It is through the repeated failure of anti-corruption measures – and the repeated emergence of corruption scandals – that such fantasies can remain a yet-to-be-realized ideal in the future, their promise of ultimate satisfaction intact. The chapter therefore looks at the role of scandals in reproducing and proliferating these fantasies, and contributing to the growth of the anti-corruption industry and compliance-industrial complex in turn. As this chapter concludes, the war in Ukraine, more than any scandal, has injected new life into anti-corruption and the enjoyment of these fantasies. Stealing the enjoyment of Russia's oligarchs through the seizing of their luxury assets has been positioned as a crucial – albeit unclear – facet of the effort to stand with Ukraine against Russia's perceived expansionism, with the war in Ukraine not merely about protecting Ukrainian sovereignty, but eradicating kleptocracy and corruption and expanding democracy and liberal capitalism's 'rules-based order'.

This leads us nicely into Chapter 2, which shows how the image of the dissident, exemplified by Aleksei Naval'nyi, the imprisoned Russian anti-corruption activist, serves a crucial function in the reinvigoration of the moral superstructure of capitalism. We argue that in the context of crisis for the liberal or 'rules-based' world order, Russia – a monster with three heads: corruption, authoritarianism, and expansionism – has returned to become the West's constituting Other. The persecuted anti-corruption activist, on the other hand, represents a positive rallying point devoid of any content except being the opposite of evil. In this sense, corruption has become the new Communism, and Aleksei Naval'nyi has become the new Andrei Sakharov. The twin image of totalitarian Communism and the humanistic, anti-Communist dissidents formed the central moral theme to institute neoliberal reforms in the late 1970s and 1980s. Today, a similar binary – that of corrupt authoritarianism and the morally pure anti-corruption activists – forms the central moral theme of regulatory capitalism, of the eradication of evil through technologically driven anti-policies.

In Chapter 3, we give more attention to the compliance and defiance industries and the fantasies they produce, with a particular focus on luxury art and antiquities. The international art, antiquities and luxury markets are often described as among the last of the unregulated markets, easy to exploit by criminal and corrupt actors, oligarchs and kleptocrats. Scandals in relation to these markets, such as financial frauds and money laundering through art, the looting of antiquities to finance terrorism, forgeries of both artworks and provenance, tax evasion, 'abuse' of freeports, offshore tax havens, and methods of 'creative compliance' have abounded over the past decade. These scandals have attracted public attention and scrutiny, and spurred more (self-) regulatory action. This chapter zooms-in on the fight against crime *through* art, antiquities, and luxury markets as it manifests in AML, CFT, sanctions, and related regulatory regimes that extend the logic of banking regulations and compliance into the art and antiquities markets – a move aligned with the financialization of art, framed by issues of national security, foreign policy, cultural diplomacy, and transnational organized crime. The chapter sheds light on the ideological fantasy of compliance and defiance and shows how this fantasy serves to both disavow and evade the problem at the core, while stimulating the massive proliferation and growth of neoliberal regulation and control apparatuses that not only fail, time and again, to control what they set out to control, but also result in new forms of uncontrollability.

These regulations have to be understood as 'anti-policies' (Walters, 2008a) that aim to eliminate the *negative* (for the lack of a positive vision) and that enlist public and private organizations in the fight against crime, effectively delegating not only intelligence gathering but also policing powers to these organizations (thus expanding rather than undermining corporate sovereignty). Building on previous research on the 'compliance-industrial complex' (Kuldova, 2022a), we track its expansion into the art and antiquities markets and unpack two regulatory ideas that appear to have become hegemonic in these technobureaucratic approaches to crime fighting. The first is the desire to close various holes and gaps that are identified as *the* problem. It is the holes that are seen as being exploited by nefarious and criminal actors and must therefore be closed, be these regulatory or legal loopholes or gaps in data and knowledge. The second is the desire to tackle crime and other unwanted scenarios *through* others (rather than directly), in this case by enlisting the regulated (the same actors often revealed to facilitate crime) in crime fighting while relying on the logic of 'pre-crime', pre-emption (Zedner, 2007; McCulloch & Wilson, 2016; Arrigo & Sellers, 2021), intelligence gathering and private investigations, resulting in the pluralization, hybridization and privatization of policing under the guise of 'compliance' and 'due diligence'. We contrast these desires framed within the fantasies of compliance, purity, transparency, and disinterested objectivity with the fantasies of defiance embodied by the oft-cited nature of the art world as 'opaque', 'private', 'informal', 'discretionary' and 'secretive'. In doing so, we endeavour to shed some light on the ideological fantasy of compliance and defiance and show how this fantasy serves to both disavow and evade the problem at the core, while stimulating the massive proliferation and growth of neoliberal regulation and control apparatuses that not only fail to control that which they set out to control, but also result in new forms of uncontrollability.

The question is twofold: firstly, what kind of world does this regulatory fantasy of compliance and defiance effectively create, and secondly, how are we to traverse this fantasy and break its ideological hold?

Chapter 4 critically interrogates the moral philosophical underpinnings of anti-corruption and compliance, namely that of Kantian deontological ethics. As is demonstrated in great detail in Chapter 3, the compliance-industrial complex and anti-corruption strategies now involve a form of regulatory hybridization, whereby the luxury industries – seen as full of risky enablers and facilitators of corruption and therefore in need of regulation – are enlisted as collaborators and a frontline privatized police force in regulating, investigating, and reporting corruption, fraud, and money laundering. On the surface of it, this situation where luxury industries are simultaneously suspect and police officer, regulator, and regulated, seems like a *perversion* of ethics. But in interrogating the structure of Kant's deontological ethics which implicitly underpins anti-corruption and compliance, this chapter demonstrates that this perverse situation is in fact entirely in conformity with Kant's ethics. The chapter unpacks the flaws of this underpinning moral philosophical framework that, particularly in the political-economic context of neoliberal capitalism, is doomed to fail. It is argued that the very structure of this Kantian moral philosophical underpinning actively cultivates the gaps and loopholes that anti-corruption seeks to close in the name of the categorical imperative. Moreover, it is argued that Kantian ethics generate neither moral character and virtue or a sense of duty and a culture of compliance, but a manipulative and relativistic emotivism that is the diametric opposite of what Kant conceived as ethical conduct. Consequently, anti-corruption and compliance is actually just a means of moral encasement, a protective sheath that is a mere extension of the wider neoliberal order.

The epilogue closes the book by providing a theoretical thread which ties together the seemingly disparate chapters, topics, and actors discussed in this book, and looks at them collectively through a single theoretical frame. That theoretical thread is the analytical lens of the death drive. It is argued that all of the actors encountered throughout this book – from corrupt oligarchs and kleptocrats, luxury industry professionals, and the anti-corruption and compliance industries – are similarly subjects of the death drive. What they collectively share – albeit manifesting in different ways – is an underpinning emptiness and lack, a lack that they all seek to address in ways that routinely fail – and are, in truth, designed to fail – in ways that are redolent of the death drive's repetition compulsion, and that they all share an unconscious enjoyment in this repetitious failure. The death drive sabotages and undermines every attempt to move toward the realization of our ultimate desires, irrespective of whether these desires are progressive or corrupt. This, it is argued, is inescapable because we are all unavoidably subjects of the death drive. We cannot simply stop being subjects of the death drive, since it is only through the death drive that we can become human subjects. So, what are we to do? We must, it is argued, first recognize the influence of the death drive, and in doing so change our relation to it; and that if we fail, then we are doomed to remain trapped in the endless cycle of corruption, compliance, and surveillance until it has destroyed everything of value in human civilization and culture.

Luxury, Anti-Corruption, and the Fantasy of Wholeness

In March 2022, in response to the war in Ukraine, the United States Department of Justice (DOJ) established Task Force KleptoCapture. This hybrid team of experts in sanctions, anti-corruption, money laundering, asset forfeiture, national security, and tax enforcement, was tasked with the enforcement of sanctions, export restrictions and, most spectacularly, seizing the luxury assets of Russian oligarchs, corrupt senior officials, and other high-ranking elites. In his remarks on 28 April 2022, the US president Joe Biden consecutively announced a comprehensive package targeting the Russian oligarchs' luxury assets – superyachts, private jets, luxury mansions and real estate, artworks and more. The official transcript retrieved from The White House website reads as follows:

> In addition to this supplemental funding, I'm also sending to Congress a comprehensive package of – that will enhance our underlying effort to ~~accommodate~~ [hold accountable] the Russian oligarchs and make sure we take their – take their ill-begotten gains. Ha, we're going to 'accommodate' them. We're going to seize their yachts, their luxury homes, and other ill-begotten gains of Putin's kleptoc – yeah – kleptocracy and klep – the guys who are the kleptocracies. [Laughs.] But these are bad guys. This legislative package strengthens our law enforcement capabilities to seize property linked to Russia's kleptocracy.[1]

While Biden's repeated stumbling and fumbling over the word kleptocracy went viral on Twitter – both mocked and cherished, interpreted either as an alarming sign of failure or an agreeable sign of the president's humanity – Task Force KleptoCapture was busy putting these words into action. On 5 May 2022, the Fijian law enforcement, acting on a request from the DOJ, seized the $300 million luxury yacht of Suleiman Kerimov, a sanctioned oligarch who, as the press release stated, was 'part of a group of Russian oligarchs who profit from the Russian government through corruption and its malign activity around the globe'.[2] The Director of KleptoCapture, Andrew Adams, remarked that 'this seizure of Suleiman Kerimov's vessel, the Amadea, nearly 8,000 miles from Washington, D.C., symbolizes the reach of the DOJ as we continue to work with our global partners to disrupt the sense of impunity of those who have supported corruption and the suffering of so many'. Deputy Attorney General Lisa O. Monaco echoed Adams' sentiments. Monaco argued that the seizure sent a message, one that 'should tell every corrupt Russian oligarch that they cannot hide – not even in the remotest part of the world'.[3]

These statements and the hybrid nature of Task Force KleptoCapture already reveal a great deal about how the West thinks of corruption and security threats, about punishment and sanctions; but they also point us to the legal and regulatory instruments that were developed over the past half century and have grown especially in the past 20 to 30 years. They point us to the hegemonic *anti-corruption consensus* that has emerged in Western policy circles, and much of academia, and that has, despite its repeated (and widely acknowledged) failures (Johnston, 2012; Johnston & Fritzen, 2021), only strengthened its hold and stimulated the proliferation of more of the same solutions. This book, rather than being yet another study of corruption along the same lines, seeks to analyse and challenge this anti-corruption consensus, making it its object of study. With this said, we can return to the matter at hand.

While there was widespread scepticism as to the efficacy of such sanctions and seizures in mainstream media and political commentary (Chellaney, 2022; Constable, 2022; Haslam, 2022; Wright, 2022), which was proven right a year later (Constable, 2023), there was nevertheless a palpable sense of *enjoyment* in this elite form of retributive justice. Mainstream media, social media, and political figures alike revelled in the circulating images of luxury seizures, while the gaudy amounts of wealth estimated to have been lost by Russian oligarchs were reported in the news like Hollywood box office results. Arguably it was always fanciful to think that seizing the oligarch's luxury yachts, their super-prime real estate and artworks worth tens of millions of dollars was going to influence Putin's decision-making or help the Ukrainian people, but the seizures were enjoyable all the same – and, as it turned out, they were eventually legally speaking far harder to seize than one imagined, costing tax payers billions in maintenance (Baker, 2022). But maybe both points are beyond the point. After all, at the time we could read that the 'Images of impounded yachts and shuttered mansions of Putin cronies prompt Schadenfreude in Russia, too. Ordinary Russians like to see "the rich also cry", said Kalachev, citing a Mexican soap opera Russians watched in the early 1990s.'[4]

This same enjoyment was present in the UK and US. The UK Transport Secretary Grant Shapps was cited in the same article as saying that the sanctions are indeed intended to hit where it hurts by denying them 'access to their luxury toys', luxury toys being evocative of both irrational excess and infantile pleasures. *The Washington Post* reported on 'a growing group of online spectators watching and reporting as governments around the world seize Russian oligarchs' assets' (Lerman & Kelly, 2022), indulging in the pleasures of open-source intelligence and voyeuristically tracking luxury yachts and private jets across the internet, turning the surveillance gaze – for once – at the rich, powerful, and corrupt. The enjoyment or *jouissance* in the seizures of these luxury toys could not be more obvious.

The mission statement on the website of The Anti-Corruption Foundation, a non-profit established by Aleksei Naval'nyi, the famous Russian anti-corruption activist and opposition figure (whose modus operandi shall be discussed in detail in the next chapter), thus reads:

> Corruption kills. As Ukrainian cities are bombed by Putin, this has never been more obvious. Putin and his circle have done everything to stay in power – and steal, and steal, and steal some more. High on their own supply, they started a devastating war. *But we have the power to make sure that these murderers and thieves can't enjoy their ill-gotten gains.* We will find all of their mansions in Monaco, their villas in Miami, their riches everywhere – and when we do, we will take everything from the criminal Russian elite. We have been fighting Putin since 2011. We will fight him until we win. (Emphasis added)[5]

The goal of the popular investigations by Naval'nyi and his team, uncovering and evidencing corrupt networks of elite individuals, and their luxurious lifestyles, is thus, in a self-proclaimed manner – the robbing of these individuals of *enjoyment*.

Theoretical psychoanalysis tells us that we are all subjects defined by a sense of lack (Žižek, 2000; Lacan, 2001). We spend our lives trying to fill in this sense of lack, be it through money, consumer commodities, politics, religion, fitness regimes and so on. These things carry a certain promise of satisfaction that lies in the future, an ultimate enjoyment that will be attained once we have enough money, once we have achieved a certain body image, realized a particular political vision, accomplished a career goal, or died and gone to some heavenly paradise. But we cannot enjoy these things directly. Rather, we have to enjoy them indirectly through their prohibition. Once we have the consumer commodity, the job promotion, or some other object of our desire, we are forced to confront the relative emptiness of the ideal. We enjoy the *promise* of the thing more than we enjoy the thing itself. Which is to say that we enjoy our own lack, or the illusory prospect of a future of ultimate enjoyment (McGowan, 2013).

The corrupt oligarchs and kleptocrats are imagined in precisely the opposite way. They are the ultimate figures of *non-lack* who, through their kleptocracy and corrupt dealings, are perceived as possessing a direct, unimpeded, and immediate access to enjoyment that 'we', collectively, do not have, and which perhaps even impedes our own access to enjoyment. There is no doubt that these luxury toys are symbolically central here, not just as symbols of wrongdoing but as material representations of this excessive non-lack and direct and immediate access to enjoyment. They stand for the 'sense of impunity' that the DOJ seeks to 'disrupt'. They stand for the oligarchs' 'special liberty' to disregard and transgress all prohibitions – be they laws, rules, regulations or normative customs – in the name of their own self-interested enjoyment irrespective of their harmful consequences (Hall & Wilson, 2014). The luxury toys stand for *vice* and are a *proxy* for corruption, both financial and moral, and the sanctions targeting the illicit luxury of oligarchs, or luxury in the wrong and dirty hands, reveal the degree to which morality, politics, and enjoyment are deeply intertwined.

Corruption has a way of stirring popular passions and moral judgements, and when corruption pairs up with luxury, popular passions tend to be mobilized with even greater intensity (Lordon, 2014). A battle between the force of good and the force of evil materializes in the targeting of corrupt luxury. But this battle also creates the *promise* of a prospective future that will ensue should the forces of good prevail. A future that is unblighted by corruption, realizing a perfected mode of ethical capitalism and global good (neoliberal) governance by rooting out the corrupt oligarchs, kleptocrats, and business and governance cultures that stood in the way of such a world, thereby ushering in an era of bountiful global development. We are told that by rooting out and hunting down the corrupt *individuals*, and their *networks*, wherever they may be, and seizing their dirty assets, we will eventually reach a world free of corruption, free of evil – anti-corruption in this sense mirrors the logic of antiterrorism and manhunting as analysed by Chamayou (2015: 66–77). Anti-terrorism can be viewed as an anti-policy par excellence. As Chamayou argues, the politico-military logic of 'counterinsurgency' has been transformed into anti-terrorism driven by the logic of security and policing, which seeks to eliminate, hunt down and take out deviant, aberrant and evil *individuals*, dissolving any possibility of systemic and political analysis, and foreclosing alternative solutions (for more on this point, see Chapter 3). The apolitical and moralizing ideology of anti-corruption, too, seeks to achieve this state of bliss by mobilizing the logic of policing and security; alas, this is not resolving the issue, to the contrary, it seems to perpetuate it, ensuring instead that this state of bliss is forever postponed – the never-ending stream of corruption revelations and scandals testifies to it. The neoliberal status quo is reproduced, our attention diverted away from tackling systemic issues, and alternatives are foreclosed as we hunt for corrupt individuals and their enablers.

Among intergovernmental organizations, international financial institutions, anti-corruption NGOs, and anti-corruption crusaders alike, there is an immense libidinal investment in such a future and the enjoyment it promises. The mobilization, capture, and direction of popular and moral passions, despite widespread prejudice to the contrary, underlies the complex technocratic structures of global governance that are seen as the key to achieving this future, thereby fuelling their global expansion. Corruption, now embodied most forcefully in popular imagination by the Russian oligarchs and kleptocrats, is first and foremost viewed as a *moral* failing. Former UN General Secretary Kofi Annan saw corruption as 'evil and insidious' (United Nations, 1997), while Pope Francis stated that corruption is 'evil based on the worship of money and it offends human dignity'.[6] As Underkuffler argued (2013: 1), 'corruption, when used in law, is a troubled concept':

> The contemporary Western ideology of law assumes that law must operate within a universe of knowable and articulable standards, logical and demystified, that strive toward neutral content and operation. Corruption ... defies these limits. It is, in its essence, a pre-Enlightenment, intuitive, and emotional concept that relies on 'religiously' revealed ideas of good and evil, falsity and truth. It is, in philosophical terms, a 'degenerate' or 'incommensurable' concept. It contradicts the dominant theory or 'way of knowing' of law, and is something which that dominant theory cannot explain. (Underkuffler, 2013: 1–2)

The idea of corruption which animates public discourse and political speeches, shapes legal treatments, and fuels the frenetic regulatory activity 'is an explicitly moral notion, invoking notions of depravity and evil, human frailty and temptation ... it is the capture of individuals (and political systems) by corrosive, distorting, and decomposing forces ... it is ... the idea of the *capture by evil* of one's soul' (Underkuffler, 2013: 3–4; emphasis in original). Corruption is notoriously hard to define and quantify, and academic literature trying to do just that has ballooned over the last decades without much tangible success. This owes to the fact that corruption is a moral notion; which is why Wei would remark in a paper on corruption supported by the World Bank and IMF that 'like pornography, corruption is difficult to quantify, but you know it when you see it' (Wei, 1999: 4). This is precisely what lends the concept the capacity to *expand* and encompass new forms of breaches of rules, regulations and laws, making it both potent and dangerous. As Underkuffler points out, from a legal perspective, this 'idea of corruption as capture-by-evil in the design and enforcement of law carries many obvious dangers' (Underkuffler, 2013: 5), as it 'contravenes the idea that we should punish *acts*, and not *persons*', while inviting 'decision makers to implement subjective ideas of evil' which translate into 'invitations toward standardlessness, emotionally driven prosecutions, and other violations of basic guarantees of the rule of law' (Underkuffler, 2013: 106). While both of these key concerns appear over the course of this book, we will be more interested in what is done in the name of corruption as evil. What regulatory interventions and governance practices does the combatting of the evil of corruption legitimize, and what role does enjoyment play?

The remedies proposed against the unquestionable evil of corruption and which are to be implemented worldwide are also moralistic in character. They are the ethics of *transparency*, *accountability*, *integrity*, and *openness* (Garsten & Jacobsson, 2011), to be enforced through *compliance*. And as we shall see, this compliance is increasingly achieved through the expansion of digital and physical *control*, *governance*, and *surveillance* architectures (Kuldova, 2022a). In the name of anti-corruption, we can observe the growth of an expansive global system of formalized control, surveillance, monitoring, reporting and audit, which seeks to replace *informal* cultural norms with *formalized* and increasingly detailed regulations, guidelines, codes of conduct and risk assessments. This is overlaid by what the industry likes to call a 'culture of compliance' – a pseudo-culture reliant on formalized structures, procedures, and norms, typically with formal sanctions and rewards attached – that seek to infuse the technobureacratic solutions with morality. Informal economies in developing countries have been linked to corruption in the realm of policy for decades. But the compliance industry goes further, progressively conflating any form of informality with corruption, even in the realm of culture, with the result that all that is informal becomes by default *suspect* and risky, and hence in need of being subjected to formal regulation, risk management, monitoring, and various accounting techniques. Culture as such becomes suspect. But culture is precisely that, an informal form of regulation of our everyday lives; the function of culture is, among other things, to effectively function as a mode of informal social control and regulation, without being written down or attached to a formal regulatory authority or governing body. The informal and culture itself is thus increasingly recast as corrupt, dangerous, threatening, polluting, and potentially contagious in its vice (hence expressions such as 'toxic culture'), while the formal is recast as the pure and noble – an ideal. In effect, it is culture itself that is sought replaced by formal procedures and routines stemming from the corporate and managerial *form*.

The fantasy is one of a world rid of the impurities of informality, and by extension, of culture and its unwritten rules and modes of social control.

Where legal and formal regulations, law enforcement, and formal sanctions have throughout history been typically reserved and intended for serious breaches, we can observe now across contemporary Western societies a general tendency to regulate ever smaller breaches through increasingly formal means where they would have traditionally been taken care of informally (Campbell & Manning, 2014).

At the same time, while these formalized regulatory, compliance, and surveillance architectures are rapidly growing, they have been time and again declared an utter *failure* and profoundly impotent in achieving the professed goals. This heightens the perceived need for the creation and more fulsome embrace of a 'compliance culture' to buttress formalized rules and regulations, one that penetrates every nook and cranny of an organization and institution. But 'compliance culture', is often profoundly empty, asocial and shallow, as are its ethical codes; which is to say that it is culture only in its name; it is really the opposite of culture, an *anti*-culture. And hence it too, predicated upon the same logic as it is, fails. But this failure only sets into motion more and more refined attempts to create and even measure and benchmark this 'compliance culture'. Regulators, activists and academics have time and again, like Michael Johnston, asked: 'why do so many anti-corruption efforts fail?' (Johnston, 2012). There are numerous diagnostics out there which address 'why anti-corruption reforms fail' (Persson et al, 2013), many of which offer policy, compliance and various best practice improvements that are largely predicated upon the very logic that is to be found at the core of their failure. The solutions thus typically boil down to *more* of the same, only with new technological fixes thrown into the mix.

To return to the theme of enjoyment which opened this chapter, such repetitious failure does not inspire distrust or scepticism as to the efficacy of the compliance industry or compliance culture, but rather constitutes the means by which the future promised by these regulatory regimes is *enjoyed*. So long as the future promised by the compliance industry and compliance culture remains in a perpetual state of arrival, it is an ideal that can still be enjoyed. Failures and scandals, therefore, are simply confirmation that we are yet to achieve this ideal, that we are not 'there' yet (wherever 'there' may be), and that there is much more work to be done to establish a sufficiently satisfactory culture of ethics and integrity within individual corporations, institutions, and industries, with which individuals one day will comply. We need to root out one last nefarious figure or identify (in an increasingly granular manner) which areas of a particular business or industry require greater regulation. We need to develop better anti-money laundering (AML) software and collect more data. We need to establish more detailed metrics and integrity indicators. Upon discovery that institutions are 'gaming' these metrics and compliance regulations, we need to develop further rules, guidelines and metrics to try and mitigate and counteract this 'gaming' and make the metrics truly meaningful (Muller, 2018). And on and on it goes. When we have finally done all of these things, the Good imagined by anti-corruption activists, compliance experts, and advocates of 'good governance' can and will emerge. For us, this *failure*, its *repetition*, and the way it facilitates the continued *enjoyment* of an ideal future, constitutes the core driving force behind the expansion of anti-corruption regulatory regimes which, as we shall see, stretch well beyond corruption per se to encompass, merge, and hybridize with related and new regulatory regimes.

Consequently, our aim in this book is not to contribute to this type of literature that re-investigates the same while offering more of the same as a solution. We do not wish to contribute to this *more*, or fill imaginary gaps in knowledge. Instead, our goal is to subject this repetitive failure and quest for more of it to analysis and investigate what is at stake in this proliferation of *more*. What is at stake in the proliferations of solutions premised on the same logic, increasingly brought to its extremes? What is at stake here for society, for politics, and for the futures of how humans may end up being governed and even conceived? It is easy and even pleasurable to be against the forces of evil, to cast oneself as a champion of the good. It is easy to build consensus and collective action around the evil one is against. But the key question we need to ask is: what are we actually *for* when we are against the evils of corruption and financial crime? This question is at the heart of this book. The global anti-corruption governance and regulatory architecture now constitutes a global consensus and epistemic hegemony, one that is rapidly expanding in response to the ever-proliferating scandals, revelations, and leaks. But we must stop to ask: where is this architecture actually pushing us? Revelations of corruption and 'ill-begotten gains' are mobilizing our political and moral passions. But in service of what? What world will we get when bodies such as Task Force KleptoCapture keep on proliferating? What vision(s) underpin the global fight against corruption and how are these put into practice? What industries are fuelled by these visions and in response to ever proliferating regulations? What power do these industries gain in the process, and with what consequences?

Therefore, we attempt to break with the hegemonic knowledge on the subject, with what we deem the 'governance realism' – a variation of Fisher's 'capitalist realism' (Fisher, 2009) – that constitutes the horizon of the thinkable, and lift our gaze by painting a picture of key developments in broad strokes, while simultaneously attempting to bring to the fore the libidinal economy of the repetitious *emptiness* at the core of this form of governance. We will also argue that, rather than merely repeatedly failing at the self-declared aims of fighting corruption and other designated evils of financial crime, these hollow and yet powerful structures of governance turn out to be *criminogenic*, fuelling a moral economy of fraud rather than combatting it in any meaningful way. But it is precisely this failure that fuels their growth, the failure manifest in the scandal is a generative force: the mediated scandals that repeatedly capture our attention, the juicy revelations and leaks. With each new scandal, each new proof of failure, the governance architectures get a boost, only to fail again. If we are correct in our contention that the future ideal that is promised by the elimination of corruption can only be fully enjoyed so long as that future is prohibited, then might we be able to argue that within the anti-corruption industry there is actually an unconscious libidinal attachment to corruption itself, given that it is corruption that constitutes the prohibition which allows them to enjoy their ideal? We will delve into this further at various points in the book. But before we do, let us briefly return to the seizures of luxury yachts, a particularly revealing case that can shed some light on the latest trends in the global anti-corruption governance and regulation, as well as the dynamics of compliance and defiance.

Luxury, special liberty, and enjoyment

Luxury yachts, as an extreme point of consumption and expenditure, of excess and waste, speak to the articulations of sovereignty in a consumer society as first and foremost *consumer sovereignty*. This fantasy of consumer sovereignty and the pursuit of pleasure through consumption, this fantasy of sovereignty and enjoyment reached through the satisfaction of consumer desires, has been shown to fuel much of crime (Hall et al, 2012). The fantasy of consumer sovereignty reduces the quest for sovereignty to a perpetual and unrestrained pursuit of pleasure through excessive consumption and its displays, to an absolute right to consume and enjoy. But as we have already alluded to, and contrary to the false promises of commercial advertisements, one never reaches a point of satisfaction, one never has enough (Veblen, 1970; Tudor, 2018). The promise of consumer goods is always-already illusory, inevitably so, and yet it is pursued repetitively and with vigour. The quest for the empty lost object keeps the consumer in an eternal loop. Even an ultra-luxurious giga-yacht fails to satisfy. Over and over again, we repetitiously fail to identify the true locus of our enjoyment, locating it within the object of our desires, rather than in its prohibition.

At the same time, transgression of rules and the law appears as key to both enjoyment and sovereignty. As the Marquis de Sade or Georges Bataille would have it, there is neither pleasure, luxury, or sovereignty without *transgression*, without breaking the rules, without breaking out of the sphere of utility, necessity or household economy defined by limits and submission (Bataille, 1993; Kuldova, 2019; Featherstone, 2020). Criminal luxury, such as the luxury toys of the oligarchs, thus breaks not only with the realm of necessity and utility as any luxury does, but also with the law, being a result of corruption, fraud, and crime, the very manifestation of the 'ill-begotten gains' as Biden put it. Transgression is thus redoubled, not only does this luxury transgress the realm of necessity and utility, but also the criminal and civil law, as well as a host of anti-corruption codes of integrity and ethics, and the realm of technocracy. The luxury yacht of the oligarch provides us with an image of spectacular and luxurious *defiance*. As such, it stands in direct opposition to *compliance*, the key notion of contemporary anti-corruption governance. The luxury yacht is a materialization of defiance of laws, rules, and social norms that triggers both desire and admiration, and moral disgust, rage, anxiety, envy, and anger. The luxury superyacht is also an elite space of privacy par excellence in a world of governance driven by the imperatives of transparency – ownership hidden in offshore jurisdictions and equipped with the latest advances in security technology, high-end yachts promise 'absolute, complete, and total' privacy, as the CEO of Veritas, Simon Rowland put it.[7] This paradoxically augments and adds to the luxury superyacht's power mystique, making it both extraordinarily repulsive and seductive – or else, *sublime* (Kuldova, 2017b). The luxury yacht in the hands of the oligarch thus signifies an act of *defiance*, symbolic of the oligarch's special liberty. It becomes seductive to the spectator not despite, but precisely *because* of the criminal, illegal, or unlawful acts that may have gone into its acquisition.

But the hunt for the oligarch's luxury yachts also reveals the less spectacular acts of sidestepping of existing rules and laws: namely, the refined and often hidden techniques of evasion that rely on financial, legal, audit, and other types of expertise, on the 'evasion experts' and middlemen facilitating the establishment of complex networks of shell companies, money laundering schemes and more (Zucman, 2015). Evasion, carefully kept in obscurity and hard to trace, paradoxically manifests itself in luxurious defiance vis-à-vis national and transnational systems of regulation, and in visible refusals to self-regulate and to submit oneself voluntarily to the proposed code of global ethics of transparency, openness, accountability, and audit – and thus to the regime of compliance. It is therefore no coincidence that the spectacular luxury yachts and other luxury assets funded by illicit wealth have been designated as *the* target, as *the* pain point for the oligarchs capable of making them cry, and why luxury goods feature prominently in corruption scandals. Task Force KleptoCapture thus hits where it hurts because it strikes at the core of the oligarchs' enjoyment, targeting the very symbol of his or her special liberty, and (consumerist) sovereignty; this is also what makes it satisfying for the public to watch the seizures. Targeting criminal luxury makes the libidinal enjoyment in the realm of the political conspicuously evident (Hook, 2017). In seizing the yacht, the oligarch, whom we imagine as enjoying at our expense, as robbing us of our enjoyment, is finally himself robbed of his enjoyment – he, too, must *submit* to the force of law; and the reader can indulge in a righteous moral outrage, itself a powerful source of libidinal gratification (Hook, 2017). There is thus a dirty pleasure, a form of vicarious enjoyment, to be had in the acts of seizures, in the authorities' demonstration of power vis-à-vis those who have been living beyond the reach of the law. Media observed, too, that 'There's just something satisfying about watching online as a billionaire's luxury yacht moves around the globe – and then gets snagged by law enforcement as part of sanctions designed to crack down on Russia' (Lerman & Kelly, 2022).

The seizures of ultraluxury assets are almost *carnivalesque*, suspending for a moment the business-as-usual of the global economy built on inequality, exploitation, and a 'moral economy of fraud' (Whyte & Wiegratz, 2017), where the global 1 per cent own half the world's wealth – only to return to business-as-usual, possibly with even more vigour. After all, carnival rather than being disruptive preserves the status quo (Stallybrass & White, 1986). As the *New York Times* already warned, the spectacular seizures are the easy part, but the actual confiscation can take years of litigation and the result is unsure (Goldstein, 2022). If we were to go by the past track record, chances are that most cases will fizzle out in years of legal battles, culminating in settlements far less spectacular than the initial seizures would suggest, and far less satisfying. The seizures, it can appear, are more important from the perspective of *jouissance* than from an economic perspective; the seizure of criminal luxury translates into the ultimate act of snatching away the stolen enjoyment.

This can at least partially explain the widespread confusion around the actual aims of luxury sanctions, asset seizures, and freezes in the context of the war, where it is rather unclear what they are supposed to achieve in terms of realpolitik. When viewed from the angle of *jouissance*, however, it becomes clearer that we are dealing with a particular form of enjoyment organized and framed by a powerful *fantasy*, one that constitutes and revitalizes the social bond and collectivity through the carnivalesque action of the seizures (and no less through repetitive failures). We stand together, against the 'bad guys' as Biden put it, robbing them of their illicit enjoyment, of the enjoyment they stole from us and our allies. In the process, a collective *we* is constituted through shared *jouissance*. A *we* that is consolidated as it comes to stand against a shared enemy, this enemy in turn allows this *we* to cultivate its own sense of integrity, virtue, purity, and moral superiority and to disavow corruption, fraud, exploitation, and harm in its own midst. It can perpetuate the illusion that corruption proper belongs to the Other, while being a mere aberration among *us*, a one-time occurrence, the occasional bad apple. The repeated revelations and corruption scandals implicating Western companies in corrupt and criminal schemes do not appear to break this illusion. This, as we shall see, is a common feature of *anti-policies*.

Where the excessive consumption of the enemy Other is illegitimate, vulgar, and corrupt, our own consumer excesses acquire an appearance of legitimacy and even virtue. In a sense, we need the Other imagined in this precise way, to be able to enjoy and indulge ourselves. Throughout history, luxury consumption has been deeply connected to questions of morality and politics. Luxury was deemed corrupting for both the body and the soul, while luxurious decadence was linked to political decline and ruin. Luxury was condemned as evil and immoral; indeed, 'the concept of luxury is of the oldest and most consistently negative principles history has known' (Zanda, 2013: 2). Luxury was deemed dangerous, harmful, and threatening if left unchecked, hence the notorious sumptuary laws and regulations which demarcated the boundary between legitimate and illegitimate luxury consumption. The 'sumptuary ethic' deemed it 'the right and the duty of the government to regulate the consumption of its citizens ... justified in terms of a moral imperative' (Zanda, 2013: 1). While the passage to modernity was paved by a redefinition of luxury and consumption as beneficial to trade and development, and while mass consumerism has further loosened much of the moral strictures and liberated luxury from at least some of its negative connotations, enabling 'the rise of men of low beginnings into great opulence' (Godkin, 1868: 249), some of the anxieties connected to luxury consumption have persisted, in particular those concerning the suspicious 'luxury in the wrong hands' (T. Kuldova, 2020), the threat of those disrupting social hierarchies and consuming above their status.

Anti-policies and luxury in the wrong hands

As *anti-policies* of all kinds multiply, having in common that they are against the bad things nobody can be for, we are witnessing a return to the moralization of luxury consumption. This is possibly most visible in the realm of anti-corruption, where revelations of corruption scandals more often than not indulge in images of opulence and luxury goods in the wrong hands. The anti-luxury tropes used already in the Roman Republic, which have linked luxury and corruption, are resurfacing, albeit in new shapes and forms. We see obsessions with 'ethical luxury' (Kuldova, 2018a), 'sustainable luxury' and even 'minimalist luxury' – all more or less a contradiction in terms – while anti-luxury sanctions and export bans now form part of foreign policy. What is at stake is not only who deserves and gets to legitimately enjoy and who is punished and sought to be robbed of enjoyment, but also whose luxury consumption is deemed refined and sophisticated, and whose is deemed vulgar, corrupt, suspect, and illicit. In whose case is luxury consumption a proxy for corruption, and who is designated to be punished for stealing our enjoyment?

The boundaries between refinement and vulgarity and between legitimate and illegitimate luxury consumption are delicate. One can easily flip into the other and hence much effort often goes into the 'laundering' of reputations and moral purification of luxury consumption – be it through engagements in philanthropy, art-washing, or other means of making luxury excesses appear more noble. We can thus read of philanthropic luxury retail, of luxury businesses partnering with charities to relieve their customers of the guilt of luxury purchases and of the 'licensing effect in consumer choice' where luxury purchases are preceded by altruistic and charitable acts (Khan & Dhar, 2006). All this reveals that luxury is still potentially dangerous, threatening, and morally problematic. The dynamics of purity and danger is at play (Douglas, 2001); luxury is dirty and dangerous, in need of purification. Navigating the fine lines between purity and pollution, between purity and integrity and moral danger, is indeed central to foreign policy, anti-corruption, and compliance regimes at large.

There are a quite extraordinary range of quantifications, measurements, indicators, rankings, and risk assessments that perform this central function by assigning numerical values to countries' integrity or corruption levels and to the various risks connected to customers, third-parties, suppliers, and workers. These numerical values are presented as neat, objective, and apolitical, but despite all the seductions of evidence-based governance, what underpins these technocratic tools are moral, political, and interpretive judgments (Merry, 2016). These judgements mark and produce the boundaries between the pure and the dangerous, marking regions and bodies as more or less dangerous and risky, more or less threatening to spread the contagion of corruption.

The EU has thus imposed what could be called 'sumptuary sanctions' taking the form of a ban on export of luxury goods to Russia – including goods merely transiting through EU nations – over the value of €300. This includes fashion, jewellery, art, antiques, porcelain, champagne, truffles, cigars, and perfumes. These sumptuary sanctions apply to vehicles over €50,000 and musical instruments over €1,500. Details of the sumptuary sanctions can be found in *Article 3h of Regulation (EU) No 833/2014 as amended by Regulation (EU) 2022/428* and is explained in a separate FAQ.[8] But behind this ban, and behind the formal technocratic language of such EU regulations, lurks the same logic of *jouissance*, of robbing the Russian enemy of enjoyment. This libidinal element in politics and the fantasy that frames it is typically disavowed, overlaid by formalistic, legalistic, and procedural language of enforcement actions, of mutual legal assistance, of complex forensic and technical multi-jurisdictional investigations, of detailed technocratic regulation. In other words, this libidinal element is obliterated through a perfectly rational language of expertise and technobureaucracy. Other countries such as Canada, Japan, the US, and the UK have implemented similar prohibitions on the export of luxury goods to Russia, all allied in the aim of robbing their enemy of enjoyment. These luxury sanctions have a precedent in United Nations' Resolutions 1695 and 1718, which encompass sanctions on North Korea's luxury goods import and which were first enacted in 2006 in response to North Korea's missile and nuclear test; several other resolutions followed. While the effectiveness of these 'smart' sanctions targeting elites has been often disputed and there is enough proof of sanctions busting on the part of elites, with luxury goods continuing to be imported into North Korea, there is no doubt that these sanctions are an 'attempt to eliminate a source of pleasurable experiences for those who are well placed in the North Korean regime' (Jeong, 2019: 216).

Targeting kleptocrats' 'dirty' luxury toys

The EU sanctions are said to have 'frozen' the Russian oligarchs 'out of paradise'. Their ultraluxury villas in the Emerald Coast in Sardinia, worth $250 million in total, are now in the hands of the Italian state. It has disrupted the local economy which is dependent on the ultra-rich and caused job losses, while also presenting new headaches for the Italian state, which is required by law to take care of these empty, 'haunted mansions' and prevent them from falling into disrepair, but the maintenance is not cheap, as upkeep of such ultra-luxury assets typically run into six figures (Harlan & Pitrelli, 2022). This is not the first time such concerns have emerged. In 2018, for instance, we could read about the Economic and Financial Crimes Commission's (EFCC) car dump in Abuja, Nigeria, where luxury cars seized in the unit's anti-corruption campaign – such as Rolls Royces, Phantoms, Porsches, Ferraris and more – are 'caking with dust, cobwebs, bird droppings, and rodent infestation':[9]

> Some of the owners of the seized vehicles have been visiting the spot where the vehicles are parked to stare wistfully at the machines that erstwhile distinguished them as men of class and stature. Today, those expensive toys they acquired on a whim or out of desperation to be acknowledged as the rich upper class, are rotting away in EFCC custody.

Similar images of seized luxury cars rotting away have circulated in news from China and India, while in 2018 the Filipino president, Rodrigo Duterte, famously bulldozed and demolished seized luxury Porsches, Jaguars, and Corvettes among others in a display of his power to crush corruption and crime in Philippines.[10] Concerns about empty, frozen, and haunted luxury properties, yachts, and rotting luxury cars, reveal not only the extraordinary labour that is channelled into the perpetual maintenance of status, and the amount of power over labour power that sustains this status image, but also the proximity of luxury to decay. They also point to the emptiness, to the *lack*, at the core of luxury, to its haunted nature, to which we shall keep returning throughout this book.

Targeting the luxury toys of oligarchs and criminals, while possibly most spectacular thus far in the context of the ongoing war, is not a brand-new practice. Luxury goods and high-value assets have become the target of enforcement agencies and financial intelligence units (FIUs) across the globe in the last decade. We can read of anti-corruption raids in Bengaluru, Karnataka, seizing luxury watches, sunglasses, high-end cars, gold, and diamonds from the luxury bungalows of middlemen in a corruption scandal.[11] Or of the spectacular raids and seizures of luxury vehicles of Zandile Gumede,[12] former executive mayor in eThekwini Metropolitan Municipality in South Africa, and her co-accused, charged with corruption, fraud, and racketeering, following an investigation in 2018, leading up to a trial, still pending conclusion at the time of writing. The 1MDB scandal, one of 'history's most outrageous public-corruption scandals' that 'has shaken Malaysia to its core' (Gabriel, 2018: 69, 71), included the embezzlement of $4.5 billion in funds from Malaysia's sovereign wealth fund, implicating the Prime Minister Najib Razak and the investment banking company Goldman Sachs, who paid $2.5 billion to settle the Malaysian probe into its role in the scandal. Most notorious about the 1MDB scandal were the luxurious excesses revealed by the DOJ investigation:

> As the filings describe in detail, the money went to buy luxury real estate in Manhattan and Beverly Hills; paintings by Monet and Van Gogh; a chunk of one of the world's biggest music-publishing companies; a $35 million Bombardier Global 5000 business jet; a $260 million superyacht called Equanimity; and $8 million in jewels bestowed as gifts upon Australian supermodel Miranda Kerr (and since turned over by her to authorities). In addition, an estimated $85 million went to pay for Las Vegas gambling debts, while tens of millions more were sunk into a movie-production company co-owned by the prime minister's stepson, Riza Aziz. In an ironic twist, he used the money to make The Wolf of Wall Street, the 2013 hit film about financial criminality. (Gabriel, 2018: 69–70)

In a raid in 2018, the Malaysian police famously seized luxury goods worth $225 million from the home of Najib Razak.[13] In 2021, the Malaysian high court ordered the government to return the luxury handbags, jewellery, and other items to Razak, as well as the $3.6 million bungalow confiscated from the notorious fugitive financier Jho Low. The court ruled that it could not be proven that the funds used to purchase these luxury assets actually stemmed from the embezzlement case;[14] Razak was finally sent to prison in 2022, after years of legal battles.[15] What all these cases point to is the centrality of luxury in corruption cases, the desire to target this luxury, and luxury being seen as a *proxy* for corruption and crime, especially when vulgar and when in wrong, dirty hands.

But the dirty and vulgar luxury assets of the kleptocrats seized by Task Force KleptoCapture could also be said to lend some lustre and glamour to the enforcement actions, to the DOJ's and US national security apparatus's power demonstrations of its long and strong arms penetrating evermore remote jurisdictions (and disrupting traditional notions of national sovereignty). While on the face of it KleptoCapture pursues these luxury assets for their economic value, it is by now clear that these assets are *more* than simply laundered proceeds of corruption or crime, stashed in high-value assets. This *more* is what interests us here. Luxury is a potent *symbolic* and *moral* device, exploited in corruption scandals for what it is worth: images of obscene luxuries, golden toilets, price tags of high-end goods and more are used to convince us of the moral corruption of their owners. Throughout Western history, luxury has been associated with excess, waste, disorder, illicit desires, corruption, irrationality, eroticism, perversion, disease, informality, exuberance, sacrifice, monstrosity, the realm of unproductive expenditure, moral decay, secrecy, opacity, mystique, uncontrollability, the sacred, the ritual, sovereignty, and symbolic immortality. Luxury thus stands in direct opposition to the Western idealization of rationality, formalism, efficiency, economic limits, productivity, bureaucracy, technocracy, order, formalism, integrity, transparency, the rule of law, purity, health, and thus also visions of good governance and the cybernetic imaginaries of the world as programmable, controllable, and engineerable.

Anti-policies and the expansion of securitized global control architectures

The dichotomies of luxury and corruption on one side and good governance and transparency on the other can easily be traced across Western anti-corruption discourses and the global regulatory and governance architectures that have emerged as a result. What becomes immediately clear is their interdependence; the one cannot exist without the other. *Anti-policies* – anti-corruption, AML and so forth – cannot exist without the spectacular images of the evils they seek to combat. If anything, anti-policies depend for their very existence and legitimacy on the perpetual manufacturing of that which they seek to eradicate, on the growth – and not diminishing – of these threats, which simultaneously forever appear to escape and evade them. The governance structures of the forces of the good liberal order combat these evils in their multiplying iterations, growing in perpetuity as their ultimate goal is permanently deferred. The utopia of a liberal world order of good governance is forever postponed, always under threat, and consistently failing to deliver on its promises (Deneen, 2018). These failures and repeated scandals drive the expansion of the global control architectures designed in the name of these anti-policies to monstrous proportions. Indeed, in a perverse way, they do succeed – only not in the manifest goals they set out for themselves. As they grow and assert themselves more fully, as they embrace their underlying logic, they flip into their opposite, demonstrating the very irrationality and excess that they proclaim to combat (Deneen, 2018), creating a world that becomes more, rather than less, criminogenic. The Task Force KleptoCapture is merely the latest iteration of these global control architectures, one that is most manifestly *securitizing* and *weaponizing* luxury and anti-corruption.

Task Force KleptoCapture and the imposed sanctions are not unique in targeting luxury assets. What is new, is that they elevate the fight against corruption to a new *securitized* level, which, as we shall argue, is part of a much larger trend where luxury, corruption, 'securitization of moral values' (Østbø, 2017) and securitization of compliance intersect. Pre-dating the war in Ukraine, Joe Biden declared in his *National Security Study Memorandum/ NSSM-1* released on 3 June 2021, the fight against corruption a 'core United States national security interest'.[16] Corruption was framed in the familiar tropes of a 'cancer within the body of societies – a disease that eats at public trust and the ability of governments to deliver for their citizens'.[17] The *United States Strategy on Countering Corruption*, launched in December 2021 and widely deemed both aggressive and ambitious, promised an intensification of both national and global enforcement of anti-corruption, anti-bribery, and AML measures, countering the financing of terrorism (CFT), as well as sanctions regimes in years to come (White House, 2021b). Monaco stated that sanctions enforcement is the 'new FCPA' (Foreign Corrupt Practices Act) (Tokar, 2022a), thus promising aggressive joint enforcement from the DOJ and the Office of Foreign Assets Control (OFAC) of the sanctions regime, while suggesting that it expands upon and integrates into the regulatory architecture developed over the last decades to combat foreign corruption and bribery. Only now, this fight has become more aggressive, upgraded to a matter of *national security*. This aligns with Biden's anti-corruption strategy. Sanctions enforcement and anti-corruption have thus become integrated. The UK *Global Anti-Corruption Sanctions Regulations 2021*, are premised upon a similar logic of hybridization, expanding the powers of the UK Government, allowing it to enforce anti-corruption measures in the form of 'thematic' sanctions targeted at select perpetrators beyond the jurisdictional scope of the Bribery Act 2010.[18]

Anti-corruption increasingly serves as an umbrella structure that integrates the fight against a host of related financial and transnational crimes. Kleptocracy and the weaponization of corrupt practices as a tenet of foreign and national security policy were clearly identified in the strategy and were to be combatted through new hybrid bodies such as KleptoCapture, which incorporates experts from numerous branches of combatting financial crimes while also being supported by public-private partnerships (PPPs). The hybridization of regulation that integrates previously separate bodies and concerns, blurring of boundaries between the private and the public is worth noting here, and we shall treat it throughout this book in greater detail. For now, let us note that the fight against corruption takes a central position due to its ability to deliver a straightforward moral tale. It codes the global fight against corruption as a Manichean fight between the forces of good and evil, the pure and the dirty, between those with integrity and those corrupt, and between a healthy body politic and a diseased body politic that infects others like a virus, requiring political-economic, cultural, and ideological vaccination. It is precisely in this sense that it relies on the logic of securitization and policing, which turns complex, social, and systemic problems into new and ever more elaborate modes of (transnational) crime-fighting – into problems that we are told can be solved by more refined ways of intelligence and data gathering, by smarter regulations, and by the intensification of the hunt for bad actors. KleptoCapture translates this into concrete actions that seek to consolidate the fight against this threat and simultaneously enforce and give a boost to the liberal international world order erected after the Cold War.

This is taking place in a context where this order has in recent years been repeatedly deemed failing, and the era of liberal modernity proclaimed as coming to an end (Hochuli et al, 2021). It is thus not coincidental that the way we speak of the war in Ukraine, as an assault on the liberal world order, on rule of law and democracy (Fukuyama, 2022), is identical to that of anti-corruption discourses. It creates the same sense of 'we', underpinned by visions of moral superiority and righteousness, and by the surplus enjoyment to be derived in targeting the 'bad guys'. The *failure*, rather than being a problem, is thus *generative*.

Paul Massaro, a Senior Policy Advisor for counter-corruption and sanctions at the Commission on Security and Cooperation in Europe (CSCE) put this plainly in an interview on the KickBack podcast, when arguing that the war in Ukraine is really a war on corruption instrumental in the global anti-corruption fight, 'without any hesitation and very clearly the most impactful and effective anti-corruption measure':[19]

> Corruption is the manner through which authoritarian regimes operate, it's kind of the rails on which authoritarianism runs ... when it comes down to how do we build kind of the world that we are trying to build, it is all about fighting corruption. Without corruption we would not have this war, without corruption we would not have the Chinese communist party, without corruption we would not the Iranian mullahs. ... It's the basis, it's the foundation of all authoritarianism.

And you know, it has come into our society. The way I read it, the end of history happened reverse ... the Cold War ended, we integrated with these systems in the hope that our systems would triumph, we had definitely a very deep notion of triumphalism at the time, and over 30 years I think we have seen the opposite, we have seen a lot of dirty money, blood money *infect* our systems and impact our politics, and I have seen our politics become more like authoritarian politics and when I say our I mean the democratic world. ... This is the real war. (Emphasis added)[20]

The fight against corruption that has been at the core of the post-Cold War international liberal order and that has stimulated the growth of complex architectures of global governance, and that has been failing (which has already legitimized the need for its further expansion), is now positioned at the very core of US foreign policy and national security interest, the number one issue to be tackled if we are to preserve democracy and the liberal order. It is not only a matter spreading this liberal order, as it used to be, but also securing it: it calls for *securitization* as a solution (Buzan et al, 1998; Schuilenburg, 2011) – one that increasingly enlists and relies on (Western, large, 'clean' and 'legitimate') private actors and public-private partnerships for enforcement of these anti-policies.

Repetition, revelation, and the logic of the scandal

The growth of global control architectures and regulations is both mirrored in and stimulated by the perpetual stream of repetitive revelations. Be it Russian oligarchs, the 1MDB scandal, or the various leaks – Panama Papers, Paradise Papers, SwissLeaks, Pandora Papers, LuxLeaks, FinCEN Files, Dubai Uncovered, SuisseSecrets – time and again, in an almost ritual and repetitive manner, that which everyone already pretty much knew is being 'revealed'. Namely, that it is often Western jurisdictions and actors that facilitate tax evasion, embezzlement, and the laundering of proceeds from corruption. The purity of Swiss Alps, to take the latest example from the SuisseSecrets, appears to be matched only by the dirt and secrecy of its banking system, which is, really, no secret at all. Whistleblowers like the eccentric Bradley C. Birkenfeld, whose memoir *Lucifer's Banker: Uncensored* (Birkenfeld, 2020) documents his luxury life, obscene spending, and revelations on Swiss bank secrecy, illegal offshore accounts, and facilitation of tax evasion for ultra-wealthy American clients through UBS Switzerland, ensure that such activities are no secret. But they are really just confirmations of that which we either already knew without definitively knowing, or definitively knew and have consistently disavowed. Books from investigative journalists follow the same ritualistic and repetitive pattern. We can read Frederik Obermaier and

Bastian Obermayer's book on *The Panama Papers* (Obermaier & Obermayer, 2017), popular books like *Moneyland* (Bullough, 2018), *Kleptopia* (Burgis, 2020), *Secrecy World* (Bernstein, 2018), *Treasure Islands* (Shaxson, 2012), *The Enablers* (Vogl, 2021), not to mention the exponentially growing academic literature such as *Unaccountable* (Wedel, 2014) and others. Or we can just watch popular documentaries like *The Kleptocrats* (2018), *Plunder: The Crime of Our Time* (2009), *The China Hustle* (2018), or the Netflix Series *Dirty Money* (2018).

Financial crime clearly sells and makes for good entertainment, despite the repeated proclamations that nobody cares about it. Rather than being disappointed and frustrated at yet another scandal, revelation, or data leak, we seem to enjoy and crave them. This suggests that there is a kernel of truth to the claim that the collective 'we' who are against such corruption and ill-begotten luxury are actually libidinally attached to their continuation and revelation. Indeed, Frederik Obermaier, a German investigative journalist involved with initiating the Panama Papers, Paradise Papers, and Suisse Secrets leaks, recently commented on a prominent anti-corruption podcast[21] that he was, and we quote, 'addicted' to leaks and revelations. We are not suggesting disingenuous motives on the part of such investigative journalists and anti-corruption activists. We do not believe that these figures are twisting their moustaches, consciously and covertly sabotaging efforts to eliminate corruption. We are rather making the more nuanced point that there is a largely unconscious but powerful enjoyment of these scandals, revelations, and corruption. They serve as prohibitions to realization of an idealized future without corruption and an affirmation that we have not yet realized this ideal, and these affirmations and prohibitions allow us to enjoy the prospect of achieving the ideal in the future. But corruption scandals are also constitutive of a collective identity that we also enjoy; an 'us' that is defined by the existence of a 'them', and whose successful elimination would actually result in the dissolution of 'us', or at least require the collective 'us' to find a new enemy against whom we can define ourselves. This, we argue, is an enjoyment and a dynamic that is common to all anti-policies and anti-politics.

Therefore, we are flooded with a great wealth of details, analysis, and revelations. This ranges from the highly specialized and technocratic to the shocking and commercial, where luxury and obscene lifestyles are used in order to both elicit disgust and attract, where rule-breaking is the norm, and where the reader can vicariously participate, while indulging her own feeling of moral superiority. We do not lack knowledge, as the transparency advocates would like us to believe. To the contrary, we are *overwhelmed* by a deluge of leaks, data, revelations, and scandals. It is a luxury problem: an *excess* of detailed information, the scale and depth of which is impossible to for a single human to grasp. The increasingly frequent scandals, leaks and exposés produce gargantuan data and information dumps, replete with raw numbers, charts, spreadsheets, international comparisons, statistical analyses, and so on. Such dumps promptly generate a flurry of sound bites, incomprehensible regulatory updates, legislation, declarations, amendments, political and industry summits, and perpetually updated best practice. In short, an increasingly impenetrable maze of information overload, a problem of life in a *technopoly* (Postman, 1993).

This endless stream both paralyzes the public, numbing it on the one hand, and stimulates technocratic regulatory hyper-activity on the other, as we witness continued growth of compliance, regulation, and control architectures. Paralysis and acceleration go hand in hand, the one extreme prefiguring the other. If we only take the realm of the global fight against corruption and financial crime, we are dealing here with an exponential growth of global multilateral networked regulatory architecture. As these multistakeholder governance platforms proliferate, so does the power, market share, and profits of private sector actors who are effectively self-designating themselves as regulators. As standardization and industry bodies churn out voluntary regulation guidelines, private actors are also invited into this fight as partners and allies. Consultancy and audit companies such as the Big Four and Big Tech companies, and the rapidly growing compliance industry with its expert knowledge production, trainings and more, have an increasingly significant say in how anti-corruption and zero tolerance visions are to be translated into practice. Private actors – often ones with extremely chequered histories when it comes to corruption and other modes of misconduct (Garrett, 2014; Shore and Wright, 2018) – are thus inserting themselves into governance, effectively amounting to rentier landlords of compliance and political and business ethics. This is not to mention the charities, foundations, trusts, think tanks, lobbying groups, developmental agencies, and others active within this field.

The almost monstrous scale of networked bodies, more often than not blurring the boundaries between the regulators and the regulated, may have emerged in the name of transparency and accountability. But it has in reality resulted in the opposite: massive structures of opacity, delegations and evasions of responsibility and accountability, of governance by proxy and through (unaccountable) intermediaries, and through complex metrics and indicators – perfectly impenetrable for any ordinary citizen.

We see, time and again, the same pattern occur: leak/scandal – regulate – enforce new guidelines – embrace new products – rinse – repeat. The hope is *again*, like in 2014, that in light of the Credit Suisse leak that 'revealed that the bank held accounts for individuals involved in torture, drug trafficking, money laundering, corruption, and other serious crimes, over decades' (Makortoff, 2022b), Swiss bank secrecy will finally come to an end (Makortoff, 2022a). Only a scandal, or a leak, it appears, can push legislative change, and initiate a process of purification; another reason to have *more* of these. Despite all this, Switzerland ranks as number 7 on the Corruption *Perception* Index from 2021, as it is widely known for its brand of good governance, democracy, and freedom of speech – that is, provided one ignores minor details such as Article 47 of the banking secrecy law which can send any journalist or whistle-blower disclosing information about bank's clients, even when it is of public interest, to jail for up to 3 years. Corruption and its facilitation in the West is *disavowed*, time and again. The scandal, the leaks, and the repeated failures are perceived within the framework of good governance not necessarily as negative but rather as purifying, as healthy, as a form of periodic renewal, and opportunity for improvement (Miller, 2008). This mirrors the shift away from entrepreneurship as success to embracing failure in entrepreneurship at the precise moment when the revelations of fraud and failure could no longer be ignored and contained by the discourses of heroic entrepreneurial successes. Instead, failure has been recast as both productive and positive – a learning opportunity that contributes to economic growth; 'fiascos and frauds – become, through a general transformation of meaning, positioned as positive and potential events rather than as failures as such … these sublimations of fiascos and frauds turn them into something attractive and productive' (Olaison & Sørensen, 2014: 200).

> Whenever the abject 'speaks up' in unwanted breaks and leakages in the symbolic order, the hegemonic discourses in various ways rearticulate the disordered material as in fact part and parcel of already established truth(s) about entrepreneurship … when failure arose as integral to entrepreneurship, it had to be articulated as something positive, so that the negative aspects could continue to be abjected: fiasco becomes learning and an honest failure, the fraudster either becomes simple criminal, a false entrepreneur, a psychopath without the redeeming social qualities of the 'eccentric' (jobs) or 'nerd' (gates) or, on the other hand, a sign of the daring entrepreneur's extreme imagination and force of will against orthodoxies, someone 'ahead of his time'. (Olaison & Sørensen, 2014: 201)

The same goes for the anti-corruption discourse and the circles of financial crime specialists, which increasingly cultivate failure as productive – and indeed, these failures serve as a springboard to launch new and better products. Or as Paul Clandillon, the Practice Leader for Fraud and Financial Crime, IBM, put it during one of such sessions focusing on anti-corruption and AML:

> Well, I'm surrounded in this room by financial crime specialists who understand the detail of some of this and I don't think that anybody

22

would disagree with me if I were to say that we have failed so far in our attempts to interdict criminal funds coming into the money transmission systems. I don't think any one of us can be that proud of what we have achieved.[22]

This repetitious failure is also built into the way in which corporations involved in corruption scandals are prosecuted. As Brandon Garrett's *Too Big To Jail* explores (Garrett, 2014), since the turn of the century, prosecutors have overwhelmingly favoured the use of deferred prosecution agreements (DPAs) or Non-Prosecution Agreements (NPAs) against corporations suspected of corruption, fraud, and other forms of corporate misconduct. DPAs and NPAs are attractive to corporations because they enable them to avoid criminal charges and punishment that would likely be more severe and would ultimately amount to the death of the organization, and they are attractive to prosecutors because of the significant levels of difficulty, resources, and expense in securing a conviction at trial. For both sides, then, DPAs and NPAs are a form of risk and resource management. One of the ways for a corporation to avoid a prosecution altogether is to demonstrate that they have good compliance programs in place. But if such compliance programs are absent or found wanting, then DPAs and NPAs are used as a means of trying to *rehabilitate* the corporation, with the terms of the agreement usually demanding that such compliance programs are implemented, often to be overseen by an independent compliance monitor for a fixed period; much in the same way that a judge might require an individual offender to undergo anger management therapy or rehabilitation programmes for substance misuse. The point to be noted here is that corrupt corporations and large institutions get to have their cake and eat it too. As Garrett asks, 'one wonders whether companies can have it both ways: good compliance programs convince prosecutors that no prosecution is necessary, while bad compliance programs earn the company a lenient agreement aimed at fixing them' (Garrett, 2014: 74). The combination of scandal and failure serves to maintain the illusion of corruption and fraud as an aberration from which one can learn, in the end even improving one's reputation.

This is in distinction from countries deemed systemically corrupt. These countries do have scandals but typically only in so far as Western jurisdictions are involved, and only in so far as these can be put to work, so to speak, to implement what are deemed to be *universal* principles of good governance and fuel the transnationalization of anti-corruption law and regulation. Corruption scandal thus becomes a vehicle for the spread of the global governance architectures developed by the West, a vehicle for the spread of neoliberalism which takes the more concrete and intersecting forms of 'regulatory capitalism' (Levi-Faur, 2017), 'surveillance capitalism' (Zuboff, 2019), and 'philanthrocapitalism' (McGoey, 2012, 2014) where in the latter doing good far too often translates into crime-fighting (Kuldova, forthcoming). Corruption scandals and leaks, typically involving luxury goods in one way or the other, have turned luxury and high-value assets into a key *risk indicator* within these architectures – especially when detected in conjunction with transactions with countries ranked low on the Corruption Perception Index (CPI) and are therefore perceived as high-risk. Combined together, these risks then structure the suspicious activity reports (SAR) provided by financial institutions to local FIUs, which serve as possible intelligence for their enforcement actions. Luxury, therefore, has moved from the investigative realm into the *anticipatory* and *pre-emptive* realm of risk management and 'pre-crime' compliance programs (McCulloch & Wilson, 2016; Arrigo & Sellers, 2021).

The tools of the compliance industry, and the regulatory architecture of anti-corruption and AML endeavour to bring order to the world, to standardize it, and to make it comparable – and thus make it controllable and governable. Nations are ranked and compared according to various metrics, the very existence of which induces nations to behave in ways that can help them climb such rankings. Moving up always involves an ever-deeper commitment to good governance principles of transparency, accountability, and audit (Marquette, 2003; Shore, 2003; Sampson, 2005, 2015). But as we have alluded to earlier, such good governance programmes are often driven by *anti-policies* (Walters, 2008a). They are negative visions that, while explicit on what they are against, lack a substantive positive vision of what they are *for*. They seem to lack a conception of the world they want to create. Often, it seems that what the advocates of good governance want is to simply preserve and even spread what we already have further and further across the globe, while removing that which they are 'anti-'. The problem that this vision encounters is that it must pre-emptively reject any recognition that things such as corruption and fraud are systemically embedded into that which already exists. It views these things as external aberrations that can simply be removed from the system without fundamentally altering the system itself.

The fantasy of a world without holes

In this sense, the regulatory architecture of compliance, good governance, anti-corruption, and AML are trying to achieve the impossible. As the likes of McGowan and Žižek have argued, all social orders are predicated upon a gap, a missing signifier (or signifiers) that 'drops out' and whose absence constitutes the social order (Žižek, 1989; McGowan, 2013). For example, in a patriarchal society the missing signifier would be gender equality. One cannot have a patriarchal society *and* equality between genders. Therefore, in a patriarchal society, gender *in*equality is an irreducible gap that constitutes the patriarchal social order itself. One can make steps toward closing or narrowing this gap, but fully closing it would spell the end of patriarchy. Global capitalism's missing signifier, on the other hand, is arguably ethics. Despite all the proclamations of a new age of 'ethical capitalism' and trends in ethical consumerism, a true and unconditional commitment to ethics is a structuring impossibility within capitalism. Ethics implies a limit, a line that one will not cross. But as Marx taught us in the *Grundrisse*, capital cannot abide and will not recognize absolute limits to its own growth and accumulation (Marx, 1973). Instead, capital turns such absolute limits into barriers that are to be overcome or circumvented, as indicated by the defiance industry which grows and evolves in lockstep with the compliance industry. It can also be noted that the logic of risk management and endless risk assessments is precisely the opposite of the logic of limits: instead, it seeks to negotiate ways around limits, subjecting them to a cost-benefit and probability analysis, generating a world of trade-offs and mitigation strategies where no limit is absolute. In practice, almost anything can be done so long as one has a thorough risk assessment filed and documented, ready for an internal audit or investigation. The zero tolerance visions and the utopias of corruption-free societies are, paradoxically, to be achieved by practices that directly undermine them (and by doing so fuel the demand for more of such measures) – if they were ever achievable in the first place. This repetitious circling around the hollow core, which can never be resolved, not only fuels the industry that proclaims to fight corruption and all sorts of misconduct, but precisely also generates it as it fuels moral confusion.

It is in this regard that the vast regulatory architecture of anti-corruption, AML, and good governance has arguably set itself an impossible task. It sees corruption, fraud, money laundering, and so on as strictly empirical problems that can be resolved. They are seen as gaps that can be closed, rather than as representative of an irreducible gap that is necessary and constitutive of capitalism as a political-economic and social order. This is precisely what is behind the incessant and repetitious calls for *more* good governance, *more* transparency, *more* accountability, *more* integrity, *more* audits, *more* checks and balances, *more* monitoring, *more* control, *more* surveillance, *more* policing. This *more* is imagined as filling the holes in the protective walls, the loopholes, and cracks in the regulatory architecture. Nothing is to escape, all is to be under control, all is to be auditable and traceable – hence the drive towards total surveillance architectures and real-time forensics. For regulators, corporations, and researchers alike, the fantasy they share is a world *without* holes. For the regulators, this fantasy world is one in which there are no more loopholes, where regulation encompasses the whole complexity of the world in all its detail, where nothing that happens can escape it. For the corporations, theirs is a fantasy where no holes are in its control architecture, where no *leaks* are possible, where all scandal is anticipated and prevented through its surveillance architectures. For the anti-corruption activists, it is a world filled with sunshine and total transparency where there is no dark hole left. For researchers, there is a peculiar view of holes in knowledge, better known as knowledge *gaps*, that are imagined as fillable in the hoarding and accumulation of knowledge.

It is thus no wonder that the notion of *integrity* is key in anti-corruption and good governance discourses. Despite integrity being an 'elusive expression', it 'clearly implies, however, the idea of the *wholeness* of a particular substance' (Pasculli & Ryder, 2019: 6). The word integrity, from Latin *integer* (intact) refers to both the state of being *undivided* and whole, while the *lack* of integrity signifies this wholeness being corrupted; and in the contemporary context, lack of integrity is synonymous with corruptibility. Scholars of public integrity have thus attempted to distil key integrity norms from the very concept of integrity to be implemented in integrity programs (IPs), proposing: 'intentional wholeness; organizational wholeness; societal wholeness; and processual wholeness' and operationalizing each of these 'into three subnorms and six indicators, which results in an evaluative framework for assessing and advancing the integrity of IPs' (Hoekstra & Kaptein, 2021: 130), which are strikingly empty, formalistic, and processual, and can be read instead as a promise of manufacturing integrity or wholes through quantification. The same ideology underpins the OECD's *Public Integrity Indicators*, which aim to 'bolster global efforts against corruption by providing actionable data ... on the quality of public integrity and anti-corruption strategies'.[23]

What is peculiar to this fantasy of wholeness and to the search for it – and what is arguably fundamental to the logic of all anti-policies – is that they are never satisfied with their elimination of the negative and in their attempts to close the ever-proliferating holes. The indicators proliferate, but never capture the whole, their lack is gaping, nagging, and obvious. Focused on negativity – be it the thing they are *anti-*, or the *lack* and holes in integrity architectures – they strive constantly towards *more control*. As Buyng-Chul Han correctly observed, a society of transparency is a society of control (Han, 2015). What is also striking, is that as these architectures grow, they tend to focus on smaller and smaller transgressions, on issues such as 'micro-aggressions', on that which has for the most part of history been regulated informally, through culture *as* a mode of social control. The logic of criminal law underpinning even the voluntary codes of conduct and regulations, is applied to an ever greater spectrum of phenomena, in line with the fantasies of zero tolerance. With the advance of technology and big data analytics, which afford the possibilities of regulation in granular detail, the fantasy of total transparency (through total surveillance) appears a bit closer.

Promises are thus made by political leaders that the regulatory loopholes will finally be closed and the fight against corruption and illicit finance intensified, more aggressive (Tokar, 2022b). The vision of *zero tolerance* is a vision of total eradication of corruption, of total control. Zero tolerance, it has to be remarked at this point, is first and foremost a *policing* strategy, and what grows through these visions, as we shall see later on, are massive architectures of pluralized and privatized policing (Verhage, 2011; O'Reilly, 2015). This is not accidental, we are dealing with nothing else than global governance of crime (Nieto Martín, 2022). Despite this, the link between the calls for good governance and the actual control architectures which take the form of privatized and pluralized policing, implemented precisely to achieve good governance, have often been missed.

But the vision of zero tolerance is interesting also as a *fantasy* of a world in which we have eradicated the scourge of corruption and the bounty that it will bring – an imagined future of perfect satisfaction (Žižek, 1997). Zero tolerance of corruption may be the most repeated mantra in anti-corruption. From Uganda's *Zero Tolerance to Corruption Policy, 2019*[24] to the corporate compliance programs of the likes of Siemens[25] that has been working hard over more than a decade to clean up its reputation following its well-known corruption scandal through its Siemens Integrity Initiative, funding collective action against corruption, and even supporting the United Nations Office on Drugs and Crime (UNODC) with $4 million, 'the largest single contribution by the private sector to UNODC's anti-corruption work'.[26] The same zero vision appears in endless corporate Codes of Conduct and Anti-Corruption Policies essential to compliance programs across the globe. Or as Transparency International puts it: 'Our vision is of a world in which government, politics, business, civil society and the daily lives of people are *free* of corruption.'[27] Rich Russians are no longer to be a protected species in *Londongrad* (Hollingsworth & Lansley, 2010), Britain no longer the *Butler to the World*, 'the servant of tycoons, tax dodgers, kleptocrats and criminals' (Bullough, 2022). The US is to finally attempt to burst the secrecy bubble of the luxury real estate where the Russian oligarchs have been hiding their wealth in plain sight for decades.[28] Switzerland is to clean up its banking sector – or at least, this is the renewed hope of the anti-corruption activists: the political rhetoric finally materializing, these revelations and scandals finally delivering the desired transparency, accountability, and integrity that are the key ingredients of the fantasy of good governance.

The regulatory excesses of compliance culture mirror the excesses of criminal luxury. Both crave more of that which fails to satisfy because what they seek is an impossibility. The criminal actor's desire for luxury circles around the discovery of a phantasmic lost object that does not exist, whereas compliance regimes seek to preserve and rehabilitate capitalism by eliminating the gap of ethics which is constitutive of the entire political economic and social order. This impossibility, and the failure to recognise it, is what feeds both the insatiable growth of the compliance industry's vast regulatory architectures, and their opposite, the defiance industries utilized by corrupt elites.

The pattern is clear, it takes a scandal, a revelation, a cause to spur regulatory and enforcement actions, new guidelines, new agreements, new collective actions, new programs, new standards, and first and foremost, new products by accounting firms, the compliance industry and RegTechs (regulatory technologies). The war in Ukraine, more than any leak, has reinvigorated these hopes of anti-corruption activists and given a boost to anti-corruption enforcement which, up to now, has time and again been declared a failure. Or as the Forbes headline summed it up: *Oligarch Yacht Hunting is Energizing the Battle Against Financial Corruption* (Hyatt, 2022). Both the war and criminal luxury are symbols of senseless and irrational waste, destruction, and harm. Outrage against Russia's invasion of Ukraine has gone hand-in-hand with the indignation over the ill-begotten luxury of corrupt Russian oligarchs, thereby serving as complementary forces that can re-energize and revitalize the perpetually failing fight against corruption. Waste and destruction appear, paradoxically, to add life force and purpose to the anti-corruption fight. In USAID's *Dekleptification Guide*, launched in response to the Biden Administration's Anti-Corruption Strategy, we can not only indulge this neologism but also read that:

> The Ukrainian people have shown the world that dekleptification can be the most intensive form of anti-corruption. It requires innovation and perseverance. Ukraine's resolute defense against Russia's brutal attempt at recolonization and rekleptification shows how the governing capacity and public morale that flow from successful dekleptification can be the key to preserving democracy and protecting national sovereignty. Relying upon and building on the anti-corruption institutions Ukraine has erected over the past eight years will be key to a successful recovery and reconstruction process.[29]

It is truly remarkable that this fight against corruption and financial crime, comprising a massive global architecture of regulations, acts, laws, agreements and more, and a multi-billion-dollar industry of compliance products, experts, trainings, and technologies that are to ensure compliance with these proliferating regulations, has been repeatedly designated as failing, but simultaneously deemed as the only winning strategy. With the war in Ukraine, this widely remarked upon failure has been strategically recast as success, as can be exemplified in the same *Dekleptification Guide* by USAID,

> The window of opportunity that opened with Ukraine's 2014 Revolution of Dignity is the clearest model of inclusive institutions developing into a virtuous circle. Eight years later, Ukrainian

dekleptification has been effective and popular. It continues to not only help repel kleptocracy and strategic corruption, but also help equip and motivate Ukrainians to defend their sovereignty with historic valor on the battlefield.[30] ...

Dekleptification is not for the faint hearted. The world's most powerful kleptocrats and oligarchs fight back as if their lives and fortunes are on the line. Combatting kleptocracy requires monumental support before and during a historic window of opportunity, unprecedented reforms that show the world what responsive governance can look like, a vigilant network of partners monitoring day-to-day implementation, and concerted diplomatic pressure as corrupt elements endlessly try to thwart reforms. American leadership might even have to culminate in rallying the free world to stand by the country when it faces existential threats meant to forcefully restore the corrupt system. But if done well, dekleptification is not only the way to reclaim sovereignty and pursue an independent destiny. It also builds a great power that soon grows fierce enough to stand its ground on the battlefield against a larger neighboring kleptocracy.[31]

At the same time, media supplied a steady stream of corruption scandals in Ukraine, and we could read headlines such as 'Ukraine Confronts Two Enemies: Russia and Corruption' (Shankar & Savage, 2023); we could also read of the Ukraine's clampdown on corruption coming under scrutiny, a 'diplomatically sensitive' issue, 'since critics are wary of playing into a Russian narrative that Ukraine is endemically corrupt, or suggesting that anti-corruption institutions, which western allies and Ukrainian civil society played a large part in establishing, have gone off the rails' (Wintour, 2023).

The anti-corruption apparatus is itself deemed as potentially corrupt (but also pointing to a struggle over the very definition of 'corruption'). One could ask whether there is another industry in the world that spends so much while failing so greatly in its core objective? There is hardly any book or article on the fight against corruption that does not open with its *failure*. And so, we too begin with this failure, arguing that it is generative and productive of a vast global industry of regulators, monitoring and standard-setting bodies, audit companies, compliance and financial crime experts, tech companies, and the intelligence industry – as well as various self-declared crime fighters, populist politicians, activists and others proclaiming to act in the name of the good and to purge all evil; and that there is enjoyment attached to this repeated failure, as well as dangerous and criminogenic forms of emptiness in the solutions that it offers. While it may fail in delivering a world free of corruption, it indeed does succeed in spreading the underlying visions of neoliberal market society, and reforms aligned with American foreign policy interests. The readers are referred to and can indulge on this point in the 13-step Ukrainian model of dekleptification developed by USAID.[32]

In the next chapter, we turn to Russian kleptocrat luxury, the figure of Aleksei Naval'nyi, Russia's foremost dissident and likely the world's most famous anti-corruption activist, and to the 'anti-policy syndrome' (Kuldova, 2022a) that his anti-corruption campaign is a paradigmatic example of. We argue that twin images of the dirty, corrupt Other and its nemesis, the clean, morally pure dissident (anti-corruption activist), contribute to reviving the moral superstructure of capitalism and show how luxury plays a central role in this. In other words, in the context of crisis for the liberal or 'rules-based' world order, Russia – a monster with three heads: corruption, authoritarianism, and expansionism – has returned to become the West's constituting Other. The persecuted anti-corruption activist, on the other hand, represents a positive rallying point devoid of any content except being the opposite of evil.

Russian Kleptocrat Luxury, Naval'nyi's Exposés, and the Global Anti-Policy Syndrome

At a no-sailing zone of the Black Sea coast, with 7,000 hectares of Federal'naia Sluzhba Bezopasnosti (FSB)-owned land around it and a no-flying zone above it, lies a 17,691 m² Italianate palace containing, among many other things, a doctor's surgery, Turkish bath, massage room, spa zone, hair dressing salon, beauty salon, cinema (100 m²), swimming pool, aquadisco, wine cellar, wine tasting room, separate kitchen departments for fish and meat, desserts, eggs, and vegetables, respectively; a fully equipped gym (with chandeliers), gaming room, casino, indoor theatre including a foyer, hookah salon with a dancing pole; bar, office (with adjoining 'negotiations room'), billiard hall, a 260 m² bedroom for the host, and of course a panoply of guest rooms. The furniture and decorations belong to the most exclusive and expensive category. For instance, the 47 couches cost up to €25,000 each, whereas the most expensive table costs €50,000. On the surrounding property, there is a church, helipad, full-sized underground hockey rink, a 2,500 m² restaurant complex, an 80 m long bridge to a 'tea house', one tunnel to the beach and another to a wine tasting cabin overlooking the ocean, and a classical amphitheater; 40 gardeners attend to the greenery. In the vicinity, there are vineyards and an enormous wine factory under construction, to employ hundreds of people. Here, one of the bathrooms has a toilet brush at the price of €700 and a toilet paper holder at €1038.[1]

What dream is Putin realizing? For what did he arrange all this? 20 years in power, repressive laws, a people who is robbed and poor, complete destruction of politics, rewritten Constitution, people in prison? We will now see the answer. For gold and marble, for sofas and couches in the style of Louis XIV, for mosaics, frescoes, stained glass windows, a home theatre, and even an aquadisco.[2]

This was posted on Aleksei Naval'nyi's YouTube channel and a dedicated website on 19 January 2021, while Naval'nyi was under arrest upon his return from Germany, where he had been recovering from severe illness after the FSB had tried to kill him with a nerve agent. Instead of backing out, Naval'nyi had decided to double down and confront Vladimir Putin head-on, instead of by proxy, by attacking his cronies.

One year later, with the full-scale and brutal invasion of Ukraine, Russia returned with vengeance to occupy a prominent, if not the first place among the contenders to the status of the West's mortal enemy and constituting Other, which it had all but lost with the fall of communism and the dissolution of the Soviet empire. Wartime alliance and periods of détente notwithstanding – during the communist period, in Western official parlance, the Soviet Union represented the negation of the West: it was anti-democratic and anti-capitalist – and thus the main enemy of the West's 'way of life'. Today, anti-democratic and corrupt Putinist Russia is seen as an equally existential threat to the so-called 'rules-based order' that remains essential to the West's self-perception. In this narrative, as in Naval'nyi's campaign, *corruption* is an important cause of Russia's descent into dictatorship and expansionism. The luxury with which the members of the Russian elite surround themselves is a symptom of their immorality, not because it is luxury, but because it is acquired by illegal, corrupt means. It is dirty luxury, as opposed to the 'clean' luxury of 'proper' capitalists (T. Kuldova, 2020).

In this chapter, we turn to the figure of Aleksei Naval'nyi, Russia's foremost dissident and likely the world's most famous anti-corruption activist. We outline, in the context of continuing global crisis, what function the image of the corrupt Other and the figure of the dissident and his individual sacrifice serve in the West's self-perception. We argue that the twin image of the dirty, corrupt Other and its nemesis, the clean, morally pure dissident (anti-corruption activist), contributes to reviving the moral superstructure of capitalism, much like communism and the image of the post-Stalin dissidents (human right activists) did with capitalism during the post-Watergate crisis in the West. The Western image of Soviet dissidents fits the neoliberal agenda perfectly. Similarly, the Western image of Aleksei Naval'nyi fits very well the agenda of 'regulatory capitalism' (Levi-Faur, 2017; Kuldova, 2022a), with its fetishization of data, transparency, and integrity.

The functions of Aleksei Naval'nyi and Russian corruption

Given the complete global agreement that corruption is *evil*, it is surprising that with the exception of the valuable historical and analytical overview in a recent book (Dollbaum et al, 2021), there has, to our knowledge, been no academic study of the Naval'nyi phenomenon analysing in a consistent way by far the most important topic on his agenda, namely *corruption*. Previous research has focused on arguably more or less peripheral subjects, such as Naval'nyi's nationalistic views (Laruelle, 2014; Moen-Larsen, 2014), views on foreign policy (Patalakh, 2018), social media-based populism (Glazunova, 2020), Russian media's coverage of him (Kazun, 2019), his networked issue agenda (Kazun & Semykina, 2020), his 2018 presidential campaign (Dollbaum et al, 2018), the dynamics of framing and mobilization (Fomin & Nadskakuła-Kaczmarczyk, 2022), and a comparative study of American and Russian TV channels' coverage of Navaln'yi (Oates & Rostova, 2023). Researchers have also analysed his digital supporter base (Dollbaum & Semenov, 2021). Recognizing the value of and building on this research, our approach in this chapter is somewhat different.

Our point is not that members of the Russian regime and indeed much of the political elite do not live ostentatiously beyond their legitimate incomes, or that Russia does not use illicit financial means actively in order to further its aims abroad. To the contrary – both of these are well documented. Nor do we argue that Aleksei Naval'nyi is wrong to address these problems. His civic courage and personal sacrifice are highly admirable, and his present existence in the dismal conditions of Corrective Colony no. 2 in the town of Pokrov stand in the starkest of contrasts to the luxurious lives of Putin and his entourage. However, in this chapter, we situate Naval'nyi's anti-corruption activism in a broader context and analyse it from a different perspective. We start out from the crucial insight that corruption is an *essentially ideological concept* (Kajsiu, 2021). The very metaphor 'corruption is cancer' has become so widespread and aggressive (pun intended) that it has become one of the metaphors global society lives by (Lakoff & Johnson, 2003) – one takes it for granted without questioning or even noticing it. Corruption is equally repetitively referred to as the 'scourge', suggesting that it is imagined as the *cause* of great suffering – even there where it is simultaneously deemed a symptom (as paradigmatic example, see for instance: McCarthy, 2014; Hoffman, 2021). This ideological fantasy of the cancerous scourge imagines that if only we surgically remove this pathological growth, that is – the corrupt *individuals* – we shall be miraculously left with a healthy system, a world without corruption where the majority of our problems will be solved, where the benefits of good governance would finally materialize, a world of efficient and just markets. However, as we explain later, such an understanding of corruption is short-sighted, both temporally (as the concept of corruption has changed in the course of history) as well as culturally (as even today, different societies have different understandings of corruption, despite the global proliferation of the Western narrative). Therefore, we argue that corruption can only be understood in relation to a certain perceived ideal, as an aberration or degradation from that ideal. Elimination of corruption is thus just a means to an end – a means to implement an order. Hence, we must ask two questions: 1. What political, economic, and social ideal will be realized through the elimination of corruption? 2. To what extent does the anti-corruption strategy obscure or spell out the political, economic, and social ideal that it purports to implement (Kajsiu, 2021)?

With the case of Russia and Aleksei Naval'nyi's anti-corruption exposés, we argue that today's corruption essentially serves the same function as Soviet Communism did during the Cold War. Corruption is the main reference point in opposition to which the West constitutes itself, and without which the Western political model would be thrown into ontological insecurity. 'The West', after all, is what the psychoanalyst Jacques Lacan (1993) would describe as a 'master signifier': a powerful organizing abstraction with which subjects identify and which subsequently structures the subject's understanding of the wider symbolic order. But it is also a signifier that refers only to itself. It has no foundation, no positive and definitive content, and any attempt to define it always comes up short and fails to capture the *essence* of the master signifier. Other master signifiers might be things like 'cool' or 'Britishness'. We may identify with these master signifiers, and they may structure our understanding of the symbolic order and our place within it; but they are nevertheless somewhat ethereal, defying definition.

In order to have any meaning, such master signifiers require what Lacan describes as a 'quilting point' which can anchor the master signifier, provide it with some stability and halt its slippage of meaning. Often, such quilting points are negatives. They define the master signifier and help us to identify what the master signifier *is* by identifying *what it is not*. The classic example is the master signifier of 'German' under Nazism, whose quilting point was the figure of the Jew (McGowan, 2013). To be 'German', and to know that one was being 'German', was simply to know that one was not a Jew. Similarly in the US in the Cold War, 'communism' operated as a quilting point for the master signifier, 'American'. Today, particularly in the contemporary context with the Russian invasion of Ukraine and the sanctions against various Russian oligarchs and officials, 'corruption' operates as the quilting point for 'the West', much in the same way that the fundamentalist terrorist has since the attacks of 11 September. All identity is organized around an exclusion, and in the current moment, 'Russia' – and specifically Russia as the corrupt Other – operates as the exclusion that constitutes 'Western' identity.

While being despised, this excluded and constituting Other is also, crucially, *enjoyed*. We are not saying that the collective despising of Russia as the corrupt Other is unjustified. We are merely observing that such collective despising – and by extension excluding – is the means through which we can experience and enjoy our collective identity. Consequently, there is a certain attachment to this excluded Other, such that we are tempted to say that if the corrupt Other did not exist, it would have to be invented, and that without the invention of corruption and the corrupt Other as the enemy, the Western model as we know it would be in crisis. Military defeat of Russia, the elimination of the corrupt Other, and their inclusion and incorporation into the global anti-corruption landscape – while temporarily satisfying – would actually be experienced as a loss, for it would entail the destruction of the very basis for collective identity. Corruption, autocracy, and human rights violations form a three-headed monster against which what we call the global anti-policy syndrome is constructed. Like in the case of communism, the idealized figure of the dissident plays an important part in the reinvigoration and perpetuation of capitalism in the wake of deep and systemic crisis. However, the two varieties of capitalism reinforced by the communist threat in the past and the corruption threat in the present, respectively, differ. The communist threat, and – paradoxically – the ultimate fall of communism, contributed to justify neoliberal deregulation globally. The corruption threat, on the other hand, is, in the context of the war starting in 2022 and the American securitization of anti-corruption evident in 2021, serving to imbue *regulatory capitalism*. Corruption is thus not only being ascribed to the corrupt Other, as a form of external threat, but is also increasingly conceived as a matter of the corrupt Other *within ourselves*, that is: as an 'internal enemy' and an internal (security) threat. The blurb on the book cover of Ceva and Ferretti's *Political Corruption: The Internal Enemy of Public Institutions* sums up this view succinctly:

> political corruption is the Trojan horse that undermines public institutions from within via an interrelated action of officeholders. Even well-designed and legitimate institutions can veer off track if the officeholders fail through their conduct to uphold a public ethics of office accountability. … From this perspective, political corruption is an internal enemy of public institutions that can only be opposed by mobilizing officeholders to engage in answerability practices. (Ceva & Ferretti, 2021)

Both the external and internal threats of corruption demand regulation, accounting and accountability procedures, or else: they demand a system of purging and purification in order to restore the health of organizations, nations and of the global (financial) system itself.

The 2020s as the new 1980s

Although the strong support for Ukraine is likely to cede in some countries as the economic consequences will be aggravated and heavier weaponry is sent, it is safe to say that the full-scale invasion of Ukraine bolstered the unity of Western countries to a level that only months earlier were unthinkable. The

West is unanimous in its condemnation of Russia. Kyiv gets massive political support, Russia is heavily sanctioned, and Sweden and Finland, two countries with long traditions of neutrality in their security policy (and, in the case of Sweden, with a national identity partly founded on neutrality), quickly started the process of joining NATO. Authoritarian Türkiye's foot-dragging on this issue, especially with regard to Sweden, has only emphasized this, as the former is largely perceived as an outlier in NATO and even more so in 'the West'. The Western disunity from the days of the war in Iraq is long gone. Although with a somewhat stumbling American president, and despite increasing friction created by problems such as the European energy crisis, the broader West appears to be back on track, displaying self-confidence in international relations. As G. John Ikenberry, a leading international relations theorist, remarked, 'Europe has found a new calling, in many ways. The EU has charisma. Who could have imagined that? ... Nato has a purpose again. The Atlantic alliance, I think, has reaffirmed its fundamental importance. The US has found its voice again.'[3]

Considerable economic hardship notwithstanding, the socioeconomic model in itself is not questioned in any substantial way – in the mainstream at least. Since the Russian regime, as the invader, beyond doubt carries the moral responsibility for the war, trouble in the West aggravated by the war is scarcely explained by pointing to inner weaknesses and flaws in the system. Instead, focus is directed at measures intended to increase the resilience of the system that currently exists – measures that seek to combat and eliminate both external and internal enemies (or else, *enablers* and gatekeepers)[4] that are seen as undermining this system and as the very cause of its failures.

US President Trump's alleged coup attempt in 2020 is taken very seriously, but it has nevertheless acquired the status of a *scandal* – a despicable aberration from the normal, harmonious state of affairs that is *external* to the present system, rather than a symptom of something seriously wrong that is *internal* to the system itself. In this sense, the suffix '-gate' is appropriate (to be discussed later). The newly gained self-confidence and unity comes after a decade that contained a financial crisis originating in the US, the Arab Spring – initially celebrated by the West as progress for democracy but ending up as a disaster for most countries, the annexation of Crimea (and the weak Western response), democratic backlash and growth of right-wing populism in several Western countries and elsewhere, Russian meddling in American elections, and, finally, a global pandemic with disputed handling in the West, but with dictatorial China as the perceived star – to mention but a few of the major issues and crises. We should also add the humiliating Western withdrawal from Afghanistan – after more than two decades of warfare, counterinsurgency, and efforts to democratize the country.

In this sense, the 'long 2010s' (starting with the financial crisis in 2008 and ending with the full-scale invasion of Ukraine in late February 2022) are similar to the 1970s. Both were decades of crisis, disunity, and insecurity. In the same vein as the West managed to come to terms with itself after the turbulent 1970s, it appears to have done so again, after the unsettled 2010s. For the West, the 1970s were a decade of trouble and instability. The Soviet Union had recently crushed the Prague Spring, and in 1974, 77 countries of the Third World sought a New International Economic Order (NIEO), demanding self-determination, sovereignty, control over natural resources, and the right to nationalization. Further, oil crisis, disaster and defeat in Vietnam, social unrest and atomization, recession, the Watergate scandal, and a perception of American military weakness vis-à-vis the Soviet Union (Simes, 1978: 47) – all contributed to Western introspection, loss of self-confidence, and moral doubts (Barthel, 2022). Could it be, after all, that the Western political-economic model was neither superior, moral, nor universal?

Nevertheless, by the early 1980s, this self-doubt was all but gone in the Western mainstream (Barthel, 2022). In our perspective, the most important factor was that the West, at least in its own eyes, was able to claim the moral high ground. It did so not so much by changing its basic thrust in international policies as by *reframing* them to emphasize particular moral aspects and the struggle against evil, making the West emerge as the unquestionably good. Until the 1970s, Communism was mainly a geopolitical adversary. Democratic slogans were actively used internationally, but loyalty and usefulness in the geopolitical game against the Soviet Union were of overriding importance (Pee & Schmidli, 2018: 4). For instance, American foreign policy giant and Secretary of State 1973–77, Henry Kissinger, was (and remains, 100 years old, at the time of writing) a hardcore realist, seeing human rights as a domestic concern first and foremost. Ronald Reagan, by contrast, was firmly convinced that the Soviet Union was the Evil Empire, in the literal, biblical sense (Boyer, 1992: 162). His administration integrated democracy promotion at 'the level of strategy, organization, and tactics' (Pee & Schmidli, 2018: 4). The twin concepts of Western-defined democracy and human rights were framed as universally and unassailably good. Internationally until the 1970s, human rights were less strictly defined and delimited, and were used in post- and anti-colonial struggles. For instance, the aforementioned Group of 77 used the language of human rights when challenging international economic power relations, to much distress in Western capitals (Simpson, 2013: 252).

However, as several newly independent developing countries descended into brutal dictatorships, the West discovered that human rights could – according to the US Ambassador to the UN, Patrick Moynihan – be their 'secret weapon' (Sargent, 2014: 139). After this rediscovery, the US and the West were able to hijack the concept of human rights (Slaughter, 2018), depoliticizing it and making it 'neutral', as it focused on the rights and freedoms of the individual to the detriment of states' right to economic self-determination and sovereign equality (Whyte, 2019: 438–44).

> [The] belief in the complementarity of interests and values, free markets and human rights, was central to neoliberal attempts to develop a universal morality to support the global extension of a competitive market. For the neoliberals, unless individuals are free to pursue their own interests on the market, all talk of human rights is meaningless. (Whyte, 2019: 444)

This hijacking of human rights and dignity became the moral bedrock of the Structural Adjustment Programs, or else, neoliberal reforms, imposed by Western-dominated structures such as the IMF, the World Bank, and the US Treasury (Slaughter, 2018: 757). As Harvey pointed out, the growing importance of human rights issues in this sense corresponds exactly with the surge of neoliberalization (Harvey, 2005: 176). In this perspective, American post-Cold War promotion of a 'low-intensity democracy' became 'a structural feature of the new world order: it is a global political system corresponding to a global economy under the hegemony of a transnational elite which is the agent of transnational capital' (Robinson, 1996: 4). Anti-corruption was instrumental in these processes, evolving not only to promote neoliberal reforms (Katzarova, 2019), but also to be subsumed under and key to the human rights agenda – human rights even becoming the *tool* for anti-corruption (Pearson, 2001; Bacio-Terracino, 2010). Or, as Pearson argued for this position,

> Taking a human rights approach to corruption ... acknowledges that corruption is a global problem, requiring global action and solutions. Giving corruption a 'human face' may lead to increased efficiency of anti-corruption efforts through better awareness of the effects of corrupt behaviour, increased calls for improved accountability and transparency in governments, and increased varieties of strategies that are available to combat corruption. (Pearson, 2001: 59)

Today, *individual* anti-corruption activists, sacrificing their lives, careers and more at the altar of the noble fight against corruption, have become and are celebrated as human rights defenders[5] – enlisted in a global economic and moral project. The anti-corruption activist of today, in particular the one located in countries deemed systemically corrupt (unlike the developed nations, where corruption is per definition an aberration, one to be blamed on the few bad apples) – such as Alexei Naval'nyi, bears a striking resemblance to the Soviet dissident. That is, particularly in the way he or she is being framed, perceived and instrumentalized by the West.

The Soviet dissidents as the West's *Ich-Ideal*

Apart from being the West's constituting Other, the Soviet Union was also home to a number of dissidents, who came to be much more known and revered in the West than in their home country, where they were persecuted and marginalized by the regime and to a great extent ignored by the atomized population. The prominence the post-Stalin dissidents enjoyed in the West was naturally built on a negative principle, namely their staunch opposition to the evil Soviet regime, and the personal sacrifice of their careers, freedom, health, and sometimes their lives. The dissidents were simply seen as the West's allies in the struggle against evil.

As it emerged under and in the aftermath of the Khrushchev 'Thaw' from the mid-1950s, the dissident movement was non-political and deeply moral in its underpinnings. The dissidents saw themselves as fighting for the state's observance of its own laws. They were simply acting on their own conscience by speaking out, rather than simply abide. According to the legendary dissident Vladimir Bukovskii, '[i]t wasn't a political struggle, but a struggle between the living and the dead, the natural and the artificial' (Bukovsky, 1988: 546–7). Their writings, both in clandestinely circulated editions (so-called *samizdat* – self-publications) and in their open letters to the Soviet authorities, belonged to a socialist-legalistic discourse: the Soviet regime should simply observe its own laws.

From the mid-1970s, however, the dissidents started using international media, addressing their open letters to Western countries. The language of socialist legality was replaced by the trope of universal threat (Oushakine, 2001). This was very well received in the West, in fact so much so that armed with little more than pens and their moral conviction, a rather small circle of soft-spoken and often bespectacled intellectuals was able to dominate Western perceptions of the Soviet Union (Horvath, 2005). Not only their moral orientation but also the new trope of the universal threat fit the Western *Zeitgeist* perfectly. During a crisis for the Western model, these intellectuals presented themselves to the Western audience, ready to die for their ideals. The Western public was particularly susceptible to the idea of *individual* sacrifice. In the mid-1970s, there were estimated to be about 10,000 political and religious prisoners held in heinous conditions in the Soviet Union (Service, 2009: 891), in addition to thousands locked up in psychiatric institutions, but much of the West's attention was directed towards a few iconic individuals that acquired global fame. It can be argued that for the Westerners, the dissidents functioned as their Ego-Ideal (*Ich-Ideal*), that is how the West would like to see itself. The dissident discourse was perceived in the West as representing freshness and novelty, materializing in the perceivedly child-like, naïve eyes with which the Soviet intellectuals admired Western democracy: 'It is as if the Eastern gaze is still able to perceive in Western societies its own *agalma*, the treasure that causes democratic enthusiasm and that the West has long ago lost the taste of' (Žižek, 1993: 200).

Of course, this fascination was very much ideological and therefore resistant to the realities that ran counter to it. To begin with, prominent 'dissidents' such as Andrei Sakharov and Aleksandr Solzhenitsyn were very dissatisfied with being labelled as such (Nathans, 2015: 581). Western journalists considered the term a label of honour, but the Soviet regime used it as a stigma. Further, according to Nathans (Nathans, 2021), Soviet dissidents should not be seen as avatars for Western liberalism, but as heretics of the Soviet orthodoxy. Being critical of the Soviet regime did by no means translate into support of liberal democracy or market economy. In the more mature dissident movement (in the widest sense), radically different ideological strands had crystallized, such as revisionist socialists, human rights activists, national liberation movements, Russian nationalists, and various religious movements (Alexeeva, 1985). Not only the democrats, but also the early post-Soviet foes of Russian democracy had a dissident lineage (Horvath, 2005).

Weaponized corruption as 'autocracy promotion'

For the West, during the Cold War, the threat, reference point, and hence the constituting Other, was the Soviet Union. Communism and its planned economy represented another socioeconomic model, another political and legal system, another ideology. From the liberal democratic West's perspective, it was both inefficient and immoral. But despite its inherent weaknesses, degeneration, inflexibility, cruelty, and manifest failures, Communism represented, for a time, a real, complete, political alternative. It was well understood what it meant, both in theory and in practice. The disagreements about what it was were most often between those who stood on theoretical ground (how it should be) and those who stressed the failings, or stemmed from disagreements as to what was perceived as important (for instance, personal freedom versus economic equality). In addition, the Soviet Union also actively promoted its ideology internationally, not least in the newly independent states of the Third World. From the perspective of the West, Communism was an alternative; it was just a very bad alternative.

For the contemporary West, Putin's Russia represents autocracy and corruption first and foremost. There is a considerable academic literature on the nature of the country's political system, with scholars launching new concepts and applying old ones to characterize the mode of governance and/or illuminate certain of its aspects (Lipman & McFaul, 2001; Krastev, 2006; Averre, 2007; Okara, 2007; Sakwa, 2010, 2015, 2021; Dawisha, 2011, 2015; Krastev & Holmes, 2012; Gel'man, 2015). There is also a debate whether the label 'fascist' can be meaningfully applied to Putinite Russia

(Motyl, 2012, 2016; Laruelle, 2021, 2022; Snyder, 2022b). However, there is consensus that late Putinist Russia is anti-liberal and anti-democratic. Furthermore, several politicians, commentators, and even academics have deemed Putin to be bent on promoting autocracy for its own sake, much like the West has been doing with democracy (Burnell, 2010; Melnykovska et al, 2012; Yakouchyk, 2016). This literature has been criticized (Tansey, 2016; Way, 2016), to the extent that the academic consensus appeared to be that autocracy is *not* a goal in itself (Yakouchyk, 2019). Russia has in fact been manifestly inconsistent in this respect – it has been supporting greater pluralism in countries where such a strategy has been deemed to serve Russian interests (Way, 2016). Nevertheless, in public discourse, the invasion of Ukraine reinvigorated the dichotomy, seeing the war not as an invaded nation's fight for its freedom, sovereignty, and territorial integrity, but as a Manichean struggle of epic proportions, the outcome of which might tip the scales of history. Indeed, much Western government rhetoric, as well as the arguably most influential strand of commentators, portray the war in Ukraine as a, if not *the*, decisive global battle between democracy and autocracy. For instance, David Kramer of the George Bush Institute has stated that securing a Ukrainian victory is 'vital to the future of democracy' globally (Kramer, 2022), whereas political scientists Kacper Szulecki and Tore Wig claim that the war 'is all about democracy vs dictatorship' (Szulecki & Wig, 2022). Perhaps the most forceful declaration came from Yale history professor Timothy Snyder. In a *Foreign Affairs* article, he stated that the Ukrainians were reinvigorating democratic ideals:

> At a time when democracy is in decline around the world and threatened in the United States, Ukrainian resistance to Russian aggression provides a surprising (to many) affirmation of faith in democracy's principles and its future. In this sense, Ukraine is a challenge to those in the West who have forgotten the ethical basis of democracy and thereby, wittingly or unwittingly, ceded the field to oligarchy and empire at home and abroad. (Snyder, 2022a)

Likewise, US President Joe Biden has stated that '[t]he democracies of the world are revitalized with purpose and unity found in months that we'd once taken years to accomplish' and has vowed to 'save democracy' by supporting Ukraine.[6]

Saying that the planned economy was the Soviet alternative to the capitalist market economy is stating the obvious. Everybody knew the basic tenets of this system, which, despite considerable variations within the bloc, was fundamentally different from the West's. Although its deficiencies were obvious to Western observers – and, by the 1980s, increasingly also to a growing strand of Soviet reformers (Sutela, 1991; Mau, 1996), the model and the accompanying offer of Soviet support had considerable appeal for Third World countries, given their experience with colonial oppression (Westad, 2007). The case with Putinite Russia's economic 'alternative' is more complicated. Russia cannot plausibly be regarded as anti-capitalist, but its economic system can be described as an 'adjective capitalism', with various qualifiers indicating in what way Russia's capitalism has been 'improper' in a given period, for instance 'gangster capitalism' (Klebnikov, 2000), or first crony capitalism and later state capitalism (Djankov, 2015), or somehow the other way round; first state capitalism and then crony capitalism (Åslund, 2019), 'predatory capitalism' (Hedlund, 2002), 'oligarchic capitalism' (Baumol et al, 2007) or 'selective capitalism' (Kimmage, 2009). All of these monikers arguably imply that Russia's capitalism is seriously *ill*. The unanimous diagnosis is that it suffers from *corruption*. Corruption is understood as a serious and contagious disease of which Russia is the most important host. But this disease is also, allegedly, used strategically and against other countries – a biological weapon of sorts. In fact, as such, it is framed as an even greater threat than Communism. During the Cold War, Western countries had their share of Soviet influence operations and political warfare (Rid, 2020), but the real battles happened in what were then the geopolitical margins, such as Asia, South America, and Africa.

Russia's 'strategic' or 'weaponized' corruption is routinely referred to in Western commentary, think tank reports, and strategic documents (Bellows, 2020; Zelikow et al, 2020; The White House, 2021a, 2021b, 2022). Weaponized corruption is characterized as a 'preferred instrument of Kremlin statecraft' (Owen, 2021), and, the narrative goes, much more than simply the exploitation of global financial markets to gain piecemeal advantages. The 'Kremlin is driven to legitimize ... state-sponsored oligarchy at home by exporting and embedding it abroad as an alternative to democracy' (Murray et al, 2021), 'taking advantage of globalization to export its own version of crony capitalism to many countries in the OSCE region' (Massaro, 2017). In this narrative, the trope of 'taking advantage' is crucial, along with related concepts, such as 'loopholes' that need to be closed, which indicates that with more regulations, capitalist economy can be made resistant against the alien and dangerous virus of corruption. These regulations typically aim to close these gaps by increasing transparency, which is, as Bono put it during the Forbes Philanthropy Summit in 2014, seen as *the* 'vaccine against corruption',[7] promising to immunize the body politic. But the corrupt one is, in this ideological imaginary, always the Other (in the West we at best find enablers and corruptible bad apples lacking in integrity). Corruption appears to emanate from the inside of the Other, independently of external factors. When foreign corrupt actors influence politics in the West, the sources are to be found in the other country. It is never the other way round. For instance, corruption involving Russian money and Russian actors in the West is treated as a problem stemming solely from Russia (Wedel, 2014).

Since corruption's rise to the top of the global agenda in the 1990s, it has often been understood in sexualized terms. Words such as 'impotence' and 'potency', 'penetration' and 'transparency', 'seduction' and 'resistance', 'incest' and 'unbridled passion' are frequent in the anti-corruption literature of the World Bank, Transparency International, and at academic gatherings such as the Anti-Corruption Conferences (Miller, 2008). In the discourse of 'weaponized corruption', the metaphor of *rape* is implicit: the dirty and sinful Other, perhaps with help from a few mischievous accomplices inside the court, penetrates into the clean and chaste virgin, contaminating her with sin and infectious disease. Such a perspective ignores how, if one were to elaborate on the same metaphor, all the palace's doors and windows were open to those who would kindly wash the blood from their hands in the fountain outside and put on a perfumed wig and an expensive Baroque suit before entering. More to the point, not only does the ironclad 'loophole logic' make systemic criticism impossible; it is also a prime example of what psychoanalysts would call the yearning for 'the lost object'. Despite the failure of this or that regulation to close the loophole that was deemed to be the most important one, and/or to solve the problem, the attention is quickly turned to a new, shiny, cure-all regulation or transparency measure that captures the desire. Like in consumerism, it is always the object that we do not have (yet) that is most important (McGowan, 2016). Hence, regardless of repeated failures to reach lasting satisfaction, we are perpetually driven to chase after more of the same.

Corruption as the cause and consequence of authoritarianism

In US President Biden's 2021 *Interim Security Strategy*, a direct line is drawn between corruption and authoritarianism (White House, 2021a). In the rhetoric of Western leaders, corruption has become the missing link constructing a socioeconomic as well as political alternative and threat: vowing to 'defend' and 'revitalize' democracy globally, the US 'will take special aim at confronting corruption, which rots democracy from the inside and is increasingly weaponized by authoritarian states to undermine democratic institutions' (White House, 2021a: 19–20). This is seamlessly integrated with the human rights agenda – the very next sentence reads: 'We will defend and protect human rights and address discrimination, inequity, and marginalization in all its forms' (White House, 2021a: 20). In this perspective, corruption is seen not as stemming from capitalism, but from autocracy. The securitization of anti-corruption was reiterated in an ensuing memorandum explicitly 'establishing the fight against corruption as a core United States national security interest'.[8] The subsequent *National Security Strategy* codified corruption as a 'unique threat' to US national security, vowing to treat 'the fight against corruption as the core national security interest it is, countering transnational repression, and standing with people around the world on the front lines of the fight for dignity, equality and justice' (White House, 2022: 18, 36). In this way, corruption has been established as 'the new Communism' (Whitmore, 2016), and framed as an equally or even more dangerous threat, and as such it may therefore be an equally unifying force. For instance, the constructed binary opposition between liberal capitalist democracies and corrupt autocracies is succinctly summarized by former general and CIA director David Petraeus and Democrat senator Sheldon Whitehouse:

> Thirty years after the end of the Cold War, the world is once again polarized between two competing visions for how to organize society. On one side are countries such as the United States, which are founded on respect for the inviolable rights of the individual and governed by rule of law. On the other side are countries where state power is concentrated in the hands of a single person or clique, accountable only to itself and oiled by corruption. (Petraeus & Whitehouse, 2019)

This rhetoric became sharpened after Russia's full-scale invasion of Ukraine. According to Huss and Pozsgai-Alvarez, Russia's 'weaponization of corruption against other states in pursuit of national goals ... must be identified as among the biggest threats to international and human security' (Huss & Pozsgai-Alvarez, 2022). By the same token, in a *Foreign Policy* op-ed, Loiseau and Meijer state that 'Russian corruption is an urgent security threat', proposing a set of measures to 'defend the democratic world against the Kremlin and other authoritarian regimes reliant on using weaponized corruption in their foreign policies' (Loiseau & Meijer, 2022).

While corruption and communism serve(d) the same function in hyperreality, they are very disparate phenomena. Most importantly, communism was a philosophically grounded ideology and an alternative sociopolitical model. During the Cold War, the struggle for global hegemony between capitalism and communism (the respective adherents of which both saw themselves as the true democrats), political/ideological differences were acknowledged, despite both parties' claim that exactly *their* ideology was the moral one. The triumphalist Western-proclaimed 'end of history' trumpeted in the early 1990s (Fukuyama, [1992] 2006) also implied an end of ideology and politics, with morality and economy now coming to run the show. In the hegemonic global discourse, either one is in favour of neoliberal reforms, anti-corruption, and 'democracy', assessed according to standardized criteria of 'good governance' (purportedly leading to economic development), or one is in favour of corruption and authoritarianism (and hence also against economic development). Corruption is merely an empty signifier. It exists only as an aberration from something, and there is absolutely no consensus about what it actually is, only that it is bad and must be combatted. This is *anti-policy* part and parcel (Walters, 2008b).

Anti-corruption: from taboo to tabernacle

While 'everybody' at present agrees that corruption is an evil, there is, paradoxically, no consensus as to how it is to be defined. Hence, people and policy makers across the world are programmatically and emphatically against corruption, although they do not know precisely what it is. Since the mid-1990s, the most common definition of corruption has been the following: 'the abuse of public office for private gain'. This definition is both very narrow and very wide. On the one hand, it excludes operations and practices within the private sector. It also focuses on individual transgressions. On the other, endless and very different phenomena can be put under this definition (Kajsiu, 2016: 28). And what is 'public office' in a world where the traditional divide between public and private has been blurred by decades of outsourcing, public-private partnerships, and 'revolving doors' between official bodies and private enterprises? In a partial recognition of this, the current most popular definition by Transparency International has replaced 'public office' with 'entrusted power', defining corruption as 'the abuse of entrusted power for private gain',[9] thus also encompassing the private sector – but with it also further expanding the playing field of this empty signifier. It says a lot that in 2012, Transparency International stopped defining corruption altogether for its much-cited Corruption Perception Index (Holmes, 2015: 49) – and the index still focuses on the *perceptions* of public sector corruption. A World Bank policy paper even refers to the 'elephant test', also known as the 'pornography test': it is difficult to define or quantify, but 'you know it when you see it' (Wei, 1999: 4).

Anti-corruption is a relative latecomer to the global 'anti-policy complex' (Kuldova, 2022a), but has increasingly come to dominate over democracy and human rights, since corruption is now viewed as the main impediment to both. Many practices that today are collected under the umbrella term of 'corruption' have existed since time immemorial, and have, varying with time and place, been seen as everything from signs of individual moral bankruptcy to simply acceptable ways of getting things done. As late as half a century ago, there was no consensus as to whether corruption was good or bad. Many scholars perceived it as a simple fact of life in developing countries and employed a functionalist perspective rather than a moralistic one. Pointedly, in a much-cited article from 1966, Bayley stated that 'it is surprising that so little attention has been given to its [corruption's] role and effects within the developing political situation', and that 'most Western observers have manfully striven to avoid assuming a moralistic posture' (Bayley, 1966: 719). Hence, in the 1960s and until the 1980s, several American and British scholars argued that corruption could, in some cases, be beneficial for the development of a country, since it could help get things done even if the state was weak and ineffectual (Leff, 1964; Bayley, 1966; Holmes, 2015: 120–1). As late as 1987, Samuel Huntington held that corruption was an inevitable part of economic and political modernization (Huntington, [1987] 2002). At that time, academics could present a cost-benefit analysis of corruption in relation to development, or discuss when corruption is harmful and when it is not (Heidenheimer & Johnston, 2002). Moreover, in corporate life, bribery of foreign officials was often seen as an expected cost of doing business abroad, a way of fighting protectionism, even a means to increase the marketization, as a corrupt bureaucracy allegedly functioned more like a market than the ideal-typical modern, rational one (Tilman, 1968). In fact, in a much-cited article, Leff even went so far as to see bribery as a morally legitimate 'safeguard against the full losses of bad economic policy' (Leff, 1964: 11). In several developed countries, overseas bribes were tax deductible, in some major economies until the late 1990s (Pacini et al, 2002).

During the Cold War, many military coups and communist takeovers were sought legitimated as anti-corruption measures, to the extent that scholars saw anti-corruption rhetoric as a 'cover for communist revolutionary rhetoric' (Krastev, 2004: loc. 362). Analogically to the case with human rights, in the early 1970s, the Group of 77, led by Allende's Chile, was the proponent of a leftist understanding of corruption – as corporate influence over politics. Multinational corporations' chase for profit was seen as detrimental to democracy, and G77 made the case for international regulation (Katzarova, 2019: 77–82). Allende's drive was likely motivated by his personal conflict with American telecom company ITT, which had tried to block his election, for instance by offering financial support to CIA in the order of more than a million USD (Katzarova, 2019: 80, 107; National Security Archive, 2020).[10] Before long, this was turned on its head, and anti-corruption slogans became a powerful vehicle for the institution of a neoliberal order in developing and former Communist countries, presented euphemistically as 'structural adjustment' (Brown & Cloke, 2004; Krastev, 2004; Hadiz, 2006; Swain, 2006; Swain et al, 2010; Kajsiu, 2016; Katzarova, 2019). This is of course the diametric opposite of the G77 demands. The failures of structural adjustment reforms to achieve their goals, despite even outstanding, to-the-letter implementation, have often been explained away as stemming from corruption (Krastev, 2004), resulting in glaring paradoxes such as the example of Albania, which was lauded for its exemplary anti-corruption programmes and *simultaneously* criticized for increased corruption (Kajsiu, 2016: 1). Nevertheless, this circular argument is still stock of the trade, with anti-corruption advocates promoting further reform and promoting regulations along the same lines (Swain et al, 2008: 4).

The origins of the hegemonic (neoliberal) concept of corruption, as we know it today, can in part be found in the American legitimacy crisis and introspection in the 1970s. The congressional hearings after the Watergate scandal had revealed that American corporations had made illegal payments to domestic and foreign political parties and officials using numerous slush funds. A voluntary disclosure program resulted in 400 American corporations admitting that they had made such payments, often falsifying or manipulating company records in order to hide them from their own directors, not to mention auditors and stockholders (Hutchison, 1980). Suddenly, the public understood that corruption was not delimited to developing countries, but had a crucial impact on domestic political and economic life. The remedy was the Foreign Corrupt Practices Act, adopted in 1977, which criminalized what was popularly known as bribery of foreign officials (Koehler, 2012). This led to complaints about the competitive disadvantage for American companies vis-à-vis foreign companies that were allowed to pay bribes. The US started pressing for other nations to adopt similar laws, but the potential losses involved also contributed to sparse enforcement of the Act (Perlman & Sykes, 2017). While still far from reaching any impressive numbers, the FCPA enforcement actions have increased since around the financial crisis of 2008, the period after seeing a visible spike in actions by the DOJ and the SEC.[11]

Several factors contributed to the meteoric surge of corruption on the global agenda from the 1990s on. This process is inseparable from globalization and the end of communism (Kajsiu, 2016; Katzarova, 2019). As Krastev argues, the very transition from socialist planned economies created an enormous space for corruption (Krastev, 2004). Huge state enterprises were privatized, and the socialist economy of favours increasingly gave way to outright and monetary bribery. With the globalization process, Western businesspeople were increasingly exposed to, and had to struggle with, unfamiliar business cultures abroad. The spread of democracy led to increased public scrutiny, and investigative journalism and new media contributed to increased visibility. As ideologies were pronounced dead, political discourse became centered on the *individual*, *personal*, and *moral* qualities of the leaders, whose reputation could be damaged by evidence or even rumours of corruption – to the advantage of their political rivals. Until the 1990s, pheonomena such as bribery, cameradery, and economies of favour were studied by anthropologists, sociologists, and political scientists, in local contexts and often treated with a certain cultural relativism (Krastev, 2004). This stands in a stark contrast to the standardized, decontextualized, and technical approach to corruption we see today, which is in large part the consequence of economists' dominance of the study of corruption from the mid-1990s. An important role in this decontextualization of corruption was played by Transparency International and its Corruption Perception Index, first published in 1994, creating an illusion that corruption could be easily quantified and thus measured (Katzarova, 2019), and aligning with larger trends of governance through metrics and indicators (Merry, 2011, 2016; Supiot, 2017). Econometrists eagerly seized the opportunity and produced various quantitative studies based on the Index, giving further validation to this approach (Krastev, 2004), regardless of the evident reification of 'data' that had been produced with a highly questionable method.

The World Bank and the International Monetary Fund were Cold War institutions established to prevent the spread of Communism to Third World countries. Analogically to how human rights until the 1970s were seen as too political an issue in the context of the Cold War bipolar geopolitical confrontation (mentioned earlier), corruption was largely out of bounds for the World Bank until the mid-1990s. With Communism out of the way and complaints about the World Bank itself being the source of corruption, the Bank launched a new strategy, where the battle against corruption was central (Krastev, 2004: loc. 311–30). Corruption was proclaimed to be a policy problem of central importance to the globalized order (Katzarova, 2019). Similarly to the case with human rights and democracy, corruption was crucial in the creation of the image of a corrupt developing world, contrasted with a clean developed world, a bipolar picture explaining, sustaining, and legitimizing the asymmetrical power relationship between the First and the Third World (Kajsiu, 2016: 40–1).

The reduction of a complex phenomenon to a ranking list has been a necessary precondition for the emerging hegemony of the standardized package ostensibly bringing development, democracy, and combatting corruption – a package 'offered' by global structures such as the World Bank and the International Monetary Fund as conditional loans. Director of the latter from 1987 to 2000, Michel Camdessus, formulated this global hegemonic moral consensus rather precisely:

> Structural adjustment is adaptation to a new world. You cannot denounce structural adjustment and be – as the Christians are – against the structures of sin, to take the words of the Holy Father. If you are against the structures of sin that plague our world – corruption, nepotism, collusion, protectionism, rigidities of that kind – you must go for structural adjustment, like it or not. If you want to fight poverty, you must go for structural adjustment, like it or not. (Camdessus & Naím, 2000)

Hence, morality – even quasi-religion – have, surprisingly, returned to the foreground in the anti-corruption discourse. Through the quantification of corruption, the 'economification' of the study of it, and its reduction to a technical problem, the struggle against corruption has, paradoxically, become a moral one, with an even stronger urgency – up to the point of Manicheism. The prominence of this global anti-corruption drive is such that what would earlier be seen as *political* struggles are often framed as struggles between the corrupt and the non-corrupt. With this depoliticization, and with structural adaptation measures being uncontestable, popular anger against the spectacular inequality brought about by these very prescriptions (such as deregulation, privatization, and reduction of welfare) often takes the form of anti-corruption struggle (Krastev, 2004). In the post-Soviet space, the notion of corruption has even been used as a discursive weapon to align leftist concerns about marketization, inequality, and poverty with Western geopolitical and economic interests (Swain et al, 2008: 22). The promotion of the now-hegemonic notion of corruption has been 'one of the most powerful mechanisms underpinning attempts to realize neoliberalism in post-Soviet Eastern Europe' (Swain et al, 2010: 113).

The depoliticization and 'moralization' of anti-corruption should not deceive us, however. Although presented as a moral choice between, on the one hand, technical, scientifically proven methods to achieve the goals of democratization and prosperity, and on the other, elite kleptocracy and poverty for the masses, the consequences of anti-corruption policies are deeply political: '[T]he war against corruption can easily serve to divert attention from the evaluation of the justice, legitimacy and the functioning of a given political order' (Kajsiu, 2021: 46). Regardless of the strong global hegemonic pressure of specific, neoliberal anti-corruption policies, there are alternative approaches. Choices have to be made. For instance, the former Ecuadorian president, Raphael Correa, saw the private sector as the principal location of corruption, and envisaged an increased role for the state, that is, a solution diametrically opposed to the global-hegemonic one (Kajsiu, 2021). Within certain national contexts, corruption has even functioned as a 'floating signifier' (Kupka & Naxera, 2023), that is, a signifier to which political actors may seek to attach a certain signified. For instance, in early post-Communist Albania, the ruling Democratic Party articulated corruption as a communist degradation, which was unsurprising since the main opposition, the Socialist Party, was the successor of Enver Hoxha's Labour Party, in power during the entire communist period. The Socialist Party, by contrast, framed corruption as the abuse of power for private ends (Kajsiu, 2016). Nevertheless, these approaches are marginal. The standardized package of solutions of the Washington consensus dominates almost completely, first in the guise of neoliberal deregulation and now increasingly as regulatory capitalism (Levi-Faur, 2017), shaped by 'the compliance-industrial complex' (Kuldova, 2022a).

Aleksei Naval'nyi: the anti-policy messiah

In a world divided between 'clean' developed countries and 'dirty' authoritarian states (albeit, as the narrative goes, with the clean world heroically striving to close the loopholes to the dirt constantly penetrating from the outside), contemporary dissidents fill an analogous function to that of their Communist bloc predecessors. The often brutal persecution they face at home serves as a powerful *pars pro toto* narrative of the continuous battle between good and evil. Their personal sacrifice, regardless of their own motives, is, with few exceptions, interpreted in the light of and taken into the matrices of the very specific anti-corruption agenda prescribed by international financial institutions and, increasingly – the compliance-industrial complex, which has become indistinguishable from the former (Kuldova, 2022a).

Russia, the global hub of expansionist corrupt authoritarianism, if one is to believe the dominant Western narrative, is also home to Aleksei Naval'nyi, perhaps the world's most known and iconic anti-corruption activist, politician, and new media personality. Through years of hard work and trial-and-error, Naval'nyi worked his way up to become the most prominent leader of the Russian opposition, focused almost exclusively on corruption. Ultimately, he evidently was so successful that the regime ordered his assassination. Always a staunch liberal, albeit paradoxically (and unsuccessfully) dabbling for a while in nationalist activism, he made his name as a social media-savvy anti-corruption activist with a strong political ambition. His organizational structures and activities combined features from investigative online journalism, grassroots activism and social movements, NGO work, crowdsourcing, and more traditional party politics. Naval'nyi's way of doing politics was shaped by his team's remarkable creativity in the Putin-era context of increasing political repression, tight state control of broadcast media combined with relative (though fast-shrinking in later years) internet freedom, and relatively easy access to tax declarations and real estate registers, as well as accessible new technologies, such as drones. Unabashedly populist though still idea driven, his team has tried to win the people's support by repeatedly pointing out, in grotesque detail, the extreme level of corruption-induced inequality, and (to a far lesser extent) promising fast and easy solutions.

All of the Naval'nyi team's communication and activities are permeated by anti-corruption fervour. Their struggle for power is simply inseparable from their struggle against corruption. On the most basic level, the anti-corruption message has been an attempt to unite the conflict-ridden Russian opposition and an effort to harness widespread but directionless discontent among the population. Anti-corruption is both the end and the means, both the core and the frame of Naval'nyi's ideology, activities, and political programme. Etkind has claimed that Naval'nyi is a single-issue politician (and journalist) (Etkind, 2022). This is to a certain extent true – Naval'nyi has, most likely for both pragmatic and strongly ideational reasons, a mono-focus on corruption. But as explained previously, anti-corruption is not an issue among other issues. Certainly, in Naval'nyi's argumentation, anti-corruption is not just the most important issue. Judging by his own presentations, it is a super-issue both encompassing and permeating all other issues. Corruption is Naval'nyi's answer to everything that is wrong, it is the cause of all of Russia's ills. This is of course reflected in the name of their organizational umbrella, namely the Anti-Corruption Foundation (*Fond bor'by s korruptsiei*, hereafter FBK). Registered in 2011 and launched the year after, it has retained its name and brand, despite being formally disbanded in 2020 and established as a new legal entity, and despite being outlawed as 'extremist' in 2021 and 'undesirable' in 2023. By contrast, Naval'nyi's political party, in large part due to problems getting it registered and spoiler efforts from the regime, such as the creation of a namesake party, changed its name several times. Corruption investigations and their publication have been timed and targeted, forming the basis of Naval'nyi's political campaigns, for instance when he was running for president in the 2018 elections or during the subsequent 'smart voting' offensive for voting against United Russia lawmaker candidates.

Western (and Russian liberal) commentary has, especially after the assassination attempt and his imprisonment under harsh conditions, portrayed Naval'nyi as Russia's foremost dissident of today. The blatant repression of his organizations and the violations of his basic human rights are beyond dispute. The Russian regime has punished Naval'nyi's relentless struggle with, among other things, numerous cases of harassment and physical attacks, constant smear campaigns, several administrative arrests, various administrative impediments for his organization, including the official labels of 'foreign agent' and, ultimately, 'extremist', a lengthy prison sentence for his brother Oleg, and an attempt on Aleksei's life by poisoning. Upon his return to Russia after treatment in Germany, Naval'nyi was sentenced to unconditional prison for, among other things, having violated the probation terms (while being in coma and subsequently receiving medical treatment). On top of it, he is regularly put in solitary confinement, denied medical help, possibly slowly poisoned (Sauer, 2023), and otherwise severely harassed in labour camp. In January 2022, while still under investigation for 'extremism', Naval'nyi was, together with his close collaborators, himself added to the Federal Financial Monitoring Service's list of persons involved in 'extremist activities' and terrorism.[12] In March 2022, 9 more years were added to his sentence, this time for fraud and contempt of court. In August 2023, his sentence was increased by 19 more years.

In 2021, Amnesty International, despite controversy related to some 'discriminatory statements' from 2007 to 2008, designated him 'Prisoner of Conscience'.[13] The European Court of Human Rights has demanded his release for reasons of his personal safety,[14] and has previously judged in his favour in a number of cases, including his sentence to conditional imprisonment in the so-called Yves Rocher case. In Western and Russian independent press, parallels to lionized Communist bloc dissidents, such as Lech Wałęsa, Václav Havel, Andrei Sakharov, and Natan Sharansky abound (Stephens, 2021). In 2021, several Russian academics as well as Lech Wałęsa[15] and a few Norwegian parliamentarians[16] nominated Naval'nyi for the Nobel Peace Prize. The only taints on Naval'nyi's image are his nationalistic statements and activities in the past, such as when he, in a rather clumsy video from 2007, introduced himself as a 'certified nationalist', posed as a dentist prescribing the deportation of 'what troubles us', and compared Central Asians to caries and Nazis(!).[17] Predictably exploited by his Kremlin enemies at various points in time and sowing division among Russian liberals, this has been played down by most Western observers. For instance, an opinion piece in the influential *Foreign Policy Magazine* online compared him to two of the most celebrated dissidents of the 20th century, namely Aleksandr Solzhenitsyn and Nelson Mandela (Antonova, 2021). The author pointed out that the former's non-democratic views became increasingly salient during his last years, whereas the latter, in a distant past, had advocated for organized political violence. Masha Gessen argues that Naval'nyi's views, while strict on immigration, have evolved considerably (Gessen, 2021). In any case, Natalia Antonova holds, one does not need to be a saint to be a dissident and a prisoner of conscience (Antonova, 2021).

However, even before the drastic increase in political repression following the Russian invasion of Ukraine in February 2022, Naval'nyi was not the only contemporary Russian politician or activist being subject to persecution for his political views and activism. The renowned but now prohibited NGO Memorial's updated list of people it defined as political prisoners, contained, in April 2022, more than 400 names. There were several leftists and nationalists, but the majority were Muslims who were persecuted for their religious views and activities.[18] Nor are liberals the only ones to struggle for democracy and freedom of expression in Russia. Even many radical nationalists have at least presented themselves as defenders of freedom of speech (Verkhovsky, 2016: 90), and leading intellectual nationalists have framed themselves as democrats (Kolstø, 2014). Leftist activist Sergei Udal'tsov has, short of (publicly known) assassination attempts, suffered persecution similar to that of Naval'nyi, including harassment, smear campaigns, administrative arrests, and finally 4.5 years of imprisonment. As a matter of fact, Udal'tsov was also recognized a 'Prisoner of Conscience' by Amnesty International,[19] and went through a lengthy hunger strike, protesting against his treatment in prison.[20] In its assessment, the European Court of Human Rights ruled in favour of Udal'tsov on a range of counts.[21]

Nevertheless, he has not been given anywhere near the same attention in the West as Naval'nyi.

What makes Naval'nyi stand out from others to become the West's Russian dissident of choice, is undoubtedly his stance against Russian corruption. Whereas there are several other Russian investigative outlets focusing on corruption (Smith, 2021), Naval'nyi's ability to communicate online and to use this anti-corruption message to generate public outrage is unparalleled. More to the point, he puts the blame for Russian corruption exclusively on the *individual* members of the incumbent authoritarian regime. His views on corruption are in harmony with Western-dominated global structures such the World Bank and the International Monetary Fund, and thus also the consensus of Western mainstream politics, if there ever was one. This way of attacking corruption also appears to liberate him, in the eyes of many Russian liberals and most Western observers, from charges of xenophobia and nationalism. For instance, when discussing Naval'nyi's disturbing statements one-and-a-half decades back, prominent Russian cultural historian Alexander Etkind argued that Naval'nyi deserved the Nobel Peace Prize for his anti-corruption struggle, stating that 'Russia and the entire world know Navalny as someone who fights against corruption. And corruption is the leading threat to the global world' (quoted by Gessen, 2021).

While Naval'nyi was not awarded the 2021 Nobel Prize, for which he was nominated, the European Parliament selected him for its Sakharov Prize for Freedom of Thought for, according to Parliament President David Sassoli, having 'campaigned consistently against the corruption of Vladimir Putin's regime'.[22] Not only is the Sakharov Prize an official recognition of Naval'nyi as the heir of the West's favourite Soviet dissidents; the statement also places Naval'nyi firmly in the contemporary anti-policy discourse. In fact, his position in the West is in some ways even stronger than that of his Soviet predecessors. In contrast to the Soviet dissident movement, which ran into the thousands and consisted of several well-known figures such as Aleksandr Solzhenitsyn, Andrei Sakharov, and Natan Sharanskii, Naval'nyi is arguably the only contemporary Russian dissident to be widely known abroad – even more known than Nobel Peace Prize laureate Dmitrii Muratov. Some Soviet dissidents were assassinated in a spectacular manner, such as Ukrainian nationalist Stepan Bandera and of course Lev Trotskii, and some were sought assassinated but survived, like Aleksandr Solzhenitsyn (Orr, 2020). However, the botched assault on Naval'nyi could, thanks to social media, be followed almost in real time. His courage and determination, but also his suffering and personal sacrifice – he willingly returned to Russia to be arrested – makes him the Messiah of the secular religion of anti-corruption. For instance, major American TV channels have presented him as Russia's 'democratic savior' (Oates & Rostova, 2023). In this way, sacrifice is outsourced to Naval'nyi – the courageous individual.

Regenerative scandals versus disruptive scandals

For Baudrillard (Baudrillard, 1994: 14–15), Watergate, arguably the gold standard of all subsequent political scandals,[23] 'succeeded' in actually being perceived as a scandal, which, according to Baudrillard, it was not. Through the very outrage, indignation, and denunciation the revelations generated, they served to conceal capital's 'instantaneous cruelty', 'incomprehensible ferocity', and 'fundamental immorality', all of which should have been seen as the real scandal, as per leftist thought's axiom of moral and economic equivalence. By directing the public anger at Watergate and not the system as such, the *Washington Post* journalists, paradoxically, revived the moral superstructure of capitalism. Most simply put, the very framing of Watergate as a *scandal* hid the fact that such amoral practices constitute not the exception, but the norm. In this sense, Watergate was 'a simulation of scandal for regenerative ends' (Baudrillard, 1994: 16).

The Russian regime stages its own corruption scandals following the Watergate logic. For the elite, corruption is the go-to pretext to put away one's internal and external enemies. In 2012, the Minister of Defence, Anatolii Serdiukov, had to resign following the arrest of his lover on embezzlement charges. In 2017, after a spectacular sting operation involving Igor' Sechin, CEO of Rosneft, the incumbent minister of economic development, Aleksei Uliukaev, was sentenced to 8 years in prison for bribery (and was released in May 2022). It is of course ironic that Naval'nyi himself is serving prison time in part for what can be presented as corruption. Persecuting corrupt individuals is also a way for the regime to 'address' (explain away) political and even strategic failures. For instance, the Kremlin appears to have based its initial plan for the 2022 invasion of Ukraine on erroneous assessments of, among other things, the country's military strength, political resilience, and public opinion about Russia. When this became clear to the Kremlin, Sergei Beseda, head of the FSB's Fifth Service, responsible for intelligence collection as well as subversive activities in Ukraine, was reportedly arrested and charged with embezzlement.[24]

In such cases, whether or not the suspect has committed grave crimes is less important. Selective law enforcement is a key feature of Russian political life (Bækken, 2018). Indeed, Russian politics, society, and economy is pervaded by a culture of informality – Russia is over-regulated, but the regulations are under-enforced. To navigate in the political and economic spheres, one has to abide by the unwritten rules, which may be in conflict with written laws and regulations. This combination of over-regulation and under-enforcement makes a majority of Russians willing or unwilling violators of at least some laws. Anybody can easily be framed as a criminal. In effect, this threat functions as a suspended punishment (Ledeneva, 2006, 2013). It is illustrative that Uliukaev, while not confessing to the specific crime he was set up for (he claimed that Sechin had told him that the bag that was revealed to contain the alleged bribe of $2 million contained wine to go with the home-made sausages Sechin often gave to his associates), declared: 'I am guilty of compromising and picking the easy way out too often. I preferred my career and well-being instead of insisting on principles. I was part of a bureaucratic carousel, received some presents and gave some myself, I tried to build relations, put on a front.'[25] For this, he asked the Russian people for forgiveness. Though rather euphemistic, this seems to be a surprisingly frank statement by a man who had little to lose,[26] and who more than hinted that bribery, for instance, is widespread.

Nevertheless, and regardless of powerful actors' immediate motivations for singling out individuals such as Serdiukov, Uliukaev, and Beseda – with Baudrillard, we could say that the corrupt regime perpetuates itself through these scandals, similarly to Watergate (Baudrillard, 1994: 18–19). Crucially, they are *simulated* scandals. Of course, the alleged crimes may well be real, and in any case, the scandals all have material, serious consequences for those involved. But the moral shock that make the scandals is simulated, and the public denunciations by members of the elite (who likely are just as corrupt themselves) are purely performative. It is widely acknowledged, not least among the Russian public, that the members of the Russian regime are spectacularly corrupt. In a 2019 survey, for instance, 77 per cent of the respondents believed that the country's top politicians and officials were hiding *most* of their assets from the compulsory income and asset declarations (40 per cent answered that they thought the elites were declaring a very small part (*men'shaia chast'*), while 37 per cent said that they thought they were declaring only a fraction (*nichtozhno malaia chast'*).[27] Corruption in the Russian elite is also well documented in detailed and even monumental scholarly (Dawisha, 2015) and journalistic (Belton, 2020) English-language accounts, as well as in Russian independent investigatory outlets. Scholars have argued that informal practices, including corruption, are central to how Russia 'really works' (Ledeneva, 2006, 2013; Hale, 2015; Marten, 2015b). Crucially, allowing officials to profit from corrupt practices is one way of securing loyalty (Dollbaum et al, 2021: 34). Even Dmitrii Medvedev, as president, stated that according to conservative estimates, one fifth of the funds allocated for state orders, that is, one eighth of the state budget, is siphoned off (*spilivaetsia*).[28] And if Transparency International's ratings are of any use, they at least show that Russia is *perceived* as extremely corrupt – the country was ranked in 126th place on the 2021 CPI.

The Naval'nyi team has built its campaign precisely on scandals. Using their YouTube channel, they expose instances of grand corruption, mostly targeting politicians and high officials and their luxurious lifestyles. They do so to generate outrage in order to mobilize people to support Naval'nyi. The simple message is that those in power do not live as they preach. Members of the regime may talk at length about patriotism, Russian spiritual-moral values, and the decadent West, but at the same time they relish in luxury, not least real estate in the West, and often, their families reside there, or at least did so before the sanctions – now many having moved to Dubai, their 'wartime harbor' (Smith, 2021). The exposé videos also substantiate how these riches almost certainly have been acquired by illegal means. The paradox is that although the videos follow the logic of the scandal as far as moral outrage goes, they lack the element of surprise, because the essence (if not the details) of what they 'reveal' is already well known.

The media is the message: the importance of the exposé videos

Naval'nyi's organizations, and the FBK in particular, have a heavy internet footprint. The strict management of what political content could appear on federal television combined with the more long-lived internet freedom and drastically improved internet access in the 2010s laid the conditions for Naval'nyi's rise to prominence. State-controlled media often describe him derogatorily as an '(unemployed) blogger', in order to make him look politically insignificant. But the new media channels became his most important weapon, to the extent that it became inseparable from his politics. Starting out on LiveJournal in 2006, he and his team have, regardless of his numerous arrests and now incarceration, maintained a blog with regular postings. He also established the YouTube channel @navalny, initially as a sideshow, consisting mostly of short videos with low production values and a few thousands views. The first large-scale exposé of an individual took place only in 2013, after the team had run the names of all State Duma deputies through a Miami real estate register. Although dozens of them were found to own properties there, the exposé was concentrated on one individual – Vladimir Pekhtin. The investigation, posted on the blog, made a splash and resulted in Pekhtin's resignation.[29] Subsequent investigations were publicized on the blog. In August 2020, just before the assassination attempt on Naval'nyi, the FBK stated that its central staff (that is, not counting those of the regional staffs), starting with the case of Vladimir Pekhtin in 2013, had conducted 79 investigations.[30]

The real breakthrough for these investigations came when they were filmed and posted on YouTube: in late 2015, the 43-minute investigation of Prosecutor General Yurii Chaika and his businessman sons gained millions of views. In a Levada Center survey, 38 per cent of the respondents said that they had heard about the investigation.[31] A new genre was born: the FBK YouTube corruption investigation, or else, exposé. The blog was still cultivated rigorously, and many investigations were also publicized as long-reads, or even as separate websites, with access to the documentation.

Naval'nyi Live, a livestream channel with daily shows, was launched in 2016. The year after, as part of his subsequent presidential campaign, Naval'nyi started hosting a daily show where he commented on events, answered questions from the viewers, and explained his political strategy, with each show gaining 400,000 views on average that year (Dollbaum et al, 2021: 46). However, the well-produced and by now refined investigation videos exposing grand corruption in the ruling elite, posted on @navalny, became Naval'nyi's and FBK's trademark and most important information channel, topping out with the 'Putin's palace' video in 2021 that has gained more than 127 million views.

In early 2022, that is, after one year with its master in prison, @navalny still featured in the top-100 of Russia's most popular YouTube channels, at 6.45 million subscribers, more than twice as many as the YouTube channel of TV Dozhd', a round-the-clock liberal, online TV channel, and with a comparable amount of total views.[32] According to the FBK's report for 2020 and the first half of 2021, Naval'nyi Live gained nearly the same amount of total views as @navalny (430 million, as compared to 433.8 million), but spread over 590 videos, as compared to 41 videos in the case of @navalny. In addition, the most viewed videos on the latter channel are typically those of the exposé variety. It is therefore safe to assume that the impact of each video on @navalny is much higher than the ones on Naval'nyi Live, many of which also refer to the exposés. For this reason, and for the sake of delimitation, it is the material available on @navalny which has formed the main empirical basis for our analysis.

'Here, truth is spoken': uncovering the 'truth out there'

The exposé videos are of varying length and also, to an extent, composition. However, they typically consist of two basic elements: identification and documentation of corruption schemes, and naming and shaming of the perpetrators and their lavish lifestyles. The genre is driven by the logic of revelation, of uncovering the truth that is hidden or at least hidden in plain sight. Telling the truth at all times is a tall order for any politician, but Naval'nyi has made it into his trademark. As a rule, the videos on his YouTube channel end with the urge 'subscribe to our channel – here truth [*pravda*] is spoken'. In videos published after his detention in January 2021, 'free Aleksei Naval'nyi' has been added – making an even stronger connection between Naval'nyi and truth. The implicit presumption is of course that official media are lying, and that the regime tries to hide the truth at all costs. The biblical notion that 'the truth will set you free' (John 8:32) looms even stronger with the truth-teller (Naval'nyi) in prison. Moreover, in a world of increasing disinformation and information overload, and in a country with a rich tradition for conspiracy theories, with the incumbent political elite as an active disseminator and Naval'nyi as a 'hero' in some of these narratives (Yablokov, 2018), the Naval'nyi team is very concerned, even obsessed, with evidence and raw data. According to their own statements, in some cases they have refrained from publishing material for years, even if they were convinced that they were right, due to the lack of conclusive evidence: 'for us, it is important to keep the standard of evidence high. You trust us because we never lie, and our evidence is always 100 per cent'.[33] Their adversaries, on the other hand, are presented as liars, capable only of countering with contentions that are not backed up by any evidence.[34] For several of the investigations, the FBK makes the evidence available to the general public. There is, for instance, an entire website with the details and documents of the Medvedev exposé and a separate one for 'Putin's palace'.

In this perspective, the team prefers to present their message as a scientifically, or even mathematically proven truth. For instance, elections fraud is not only sought proven by showing footage of ballot stuffing, but also by using statistical methods: 'There is a lot of scientifically proven, mathematical [emphatically] calculations [showing photos of graphs] showing how elections are falsified.'[35] Another example: 'let me prove to you right now through mathematics and documents'.[36] There is a preference for conclusive evidence that can be found in a single document, the '100 per cent documentary proof'.[37] Hence, in an exposé about deputy prime minister Aleksandr Khloponin, the presenter stated that his house in Italy was sold to the oligarch Mikhail Prokhorov, at three times its estimated market price, triumphantly showing the two contracts: one from 2008, when Khloponin bought it for €11 million, and one from 2017, according to which the oligarch bought it for more than three times more. According to the presenter, this was perhaps 'the most clear-cut, conclusive and indisputable proof of corruption that we have ever uncovered. There is no more need for speculations, assessments, comparisons and presumptions'.[38] At its extreme, this logic even betrays what we might term a mathematical positivism or even mathematical fetishism (Mácha & Zouhar, 2020). In one video, after revealing a complex scheme, the presenter stated:

> I'm looking at all of this, and I'm filled with joy, really, like a mathematics student who has just proven a complex theorem. It's really beautiful. They used a cover-up Russian company, a Cyprus offshore company, an offshore on the British Virgin Isles, and a passport for another name, but still we caught them![39]

Much of the success of the exposé videos likely stems from the cleverly produced visualization giving the impression of self-evident truth. Sales contracts with inflated prices and print-outs of real estate registers are presented as speaking for themselves. The often very complex ownership structures, on the other hand, are demonstrated with diagrams and charts which give detail to what most Russians seem to already have known, but in generic terms only: that their elite is thoroughly corrupt. This indeed mirrors the fetishization of data as well as investigations and 'intelligence' gathering, typically open source intelligence (OSINT), in Western anti-corruption activism, data-driven anti-corruption journalism, as well as in technocratic governance by numbers and the compliance industry, where the regulatory capitalism goes very much hand in hand with 'surveillance capitalism' (Supiot, 2017; Zuboff, 2019; Kuldova, 2022a, 2022b). However, what really sets the FBK's videos apart from other media is the visualization of the elite's *luxury*, namely footage of their real estate and their luxury consumption. For instance, when the investigation of Prime Minister Mishustin was posted, other media had already written about his dacha, but FBK was the first to show photos of it.[40] The photos, whether they were originally posted by relatives on social media, leaked by construction workers, or simply taken by journalists, add concrete details to the abstract numbers in the documentary evidence. Often, they need triangulation in order to verify the ownership, but this also plays into the narrative logic of revealing 'the truth out there'. The FBK team is well versed in OSINT, and, for instance, often compares geolocated social media postings to the positions of planes on FlightRadar or yachts on MarineTraffic, and to the official schedules of politicians. Until they were forced into exile, the team also operated their own drone, offering impressive overviews of the palaces of the elite.

In 'Putin's palace', the need for visualizing the truth went into overdrive. In line with the genre, an important part of the video was to show the immense luxury of the place. The drone footage showed a lavish estate with multiple buildings and facilities, such as, among other things, an indoor hockey rink, a winery, and what was presumed to be an orangery but was later revealed to be a restaurant. The problem was that when the YouTube video was being produced, the main building was empty, since a serious mould problem had necessitated a capital renovation. The team's solution was to have the interiors reconstructed digitally, in part from photos that workers had posted online years earlier, a leaked floor plan, and consulting architecture and interior experts. In this way, they had a three-dimensional visualization made.[41] They did so openly, but the problem with this was that they crossed a boundary. Until then, Naval'nyi's team had been preoccupied with revealing the things as they actually were, with multiple, triangulated sources. Now, they presented a blend of the luxury that *had been* (based on photos that were taken before the renovation) with the one that *was going to be*, in the future (based on the leaked floor plan), and also with their own imagination about how it *should have looked* (where there were no photos available). Unsurprisingly, this was immediately seized upon by the state's propagandists, who stated that the videos were fake, airing a tour of what was essentially a construction site, while not mentioning that it had been decorated in the past. However, this is less important. What Naval'nyi's montage does reveal, apart from the huge attention paid to visualization, is the team's commitment to the truth, which is so strong that it sometimes *overtakes* the available evidence. A year later, Naval'nyi's team could triumphantly show newly leaked photos, which revealed that they had been more or less correct in their guesswork:

> Everything we showed you a year ago is completely true (sootvetstvuet deistvitel'nosti). And sometimes reality is much worse. This will be the case with all of Naval'nyi's investigations. This time, a year has passed, and we have received irrefutable evidence that we were right. ... The obvious truth (*pravda*), the truth that is impossible to dispute, we will find it, no matter what.[42]

They had been *intuitively* right, in their opinion.

The quest for the objective and untainted truth is indeed a central notion in all of Naval'nyi's activities. As we have seen, his method is geared towards cutting through all layers of opacity, disinformation and misinformation, but also of culture. The complex informal dealings of the elite, ripe with meanings and codes of the hybrid culture of nascent private business, the secret services, and organized crime that emerged from Russia's chaotic attempts to transition from a planned economy to a market one, are dissected, visualized, and duly ridiculed. The historical and cultural context is stripped away, but also power – the regime's power to define the truth. What remains is 'pure' (mathematical truth) – and morality. In Naval'nyi's final words in court in February 2021, when he was being sentenced to prison camp, he paid considerable attention to the human quest for truth. Here, he quoted Danila Bagrov, the hero of *Brother 2*, the Russian cult movie from 2000, who states that 'power resides in the truth' (*sila v pravde*). Declaring himself a Christian believer, Naval'nyi linked this popular quote to the Bible, citing Matthew 5:6: 'Blessed are those who hunger and thirst for righteousness, for they will be filled', which he took 'more or less as a call for action'.[43] Thus, in his final words before his imprisonment under strict conditions made it very hard to communicate, Naval'nyi chose to make his moral purpose explicit.

Entertainment and simulacra

Equally important as the truth-telling is the entertainment element. Journalist Mikhail Loginov has commented that 'Navalny is something of a science populariser for whom the audience is just as important as the science' (Loginov, 2011). For Naval'nyi, it has been a conscious strategy from the beginning to make the fight against corruption entertaining. In a 2010 interview, he explained: 'I'm trying to do this in an entertaining format. I'm trying to prove to everyone that the fight against the regime is fun'.[44] It evidently became a goal in itself for the videos to have many views[45] and subscribers (in one video, Naval'nyi proudly 'unboxed' the congratulatory plaquet from YouTube for one million subscribers).[46] To reach this goal, a high degree of attention is paid to the production of the videos. For instance, preparing for the 50-minutes exposé of the Prime Minister Dmitrii Medvedev, 'Don't Call Him Dimon' (2017), the creator of the introduction sequence, Georgii Alburov, is said to have studied 200 title sequences to various TV series over a few days. Especially the longer videos are composed in such a way as to build up dramatic momentum. The luxury real estate and luxury objects are not merely listed, but introduced one at the time, with a rising degree of ostentatiousness, obviously for dramatic effect. They are presented using humouristic visual montages and jingles reminiscent of glamourous celebrity documentaries, showing the vices and opulent luxuries of the super-rich.

In general, the most viewed among Naval'nyi's videos are those featuring visible and well-known personalities, such as political leaders (Putin and Medvedev), high officials such as Dmitrii Peskov, the President's press secretary, and popular TV hosts Vladimir Solov'ev and Elena Malysheva, with their spectacular luxuries. The few more 'dry' videos that focus on the corruption schemes and do not feature luxury exposés are typically less viewed.[47] Such a historic moment as Naval'nyi's speech at his nomination event for the 2018 presidential elections received only slightly more than 1 million views (as of early 2022).[48] Even the video of his arrest in late January 2018 got only 1.37 million views.[49] When the 2018 hugely unpopular pension reform was launched, Vladimir Milov, a highly competent economist and former deputy minister, hosted a few videos to explain it, only to discover that these videos received comparably few views.[50] Furthermore, according to Naval'nyi himself, many viewers criticized and even ridiculed the team for focusing too much on the pension reform (at the expense of corruption), in fact to such an extent that he made a dedicated video to explain why criticizing the reform was important, stating that 'the most important videos about corruption are exactly those that concern the elevation of the retirement age'.[51] Alas, that video was viewed by less than 1.7 million.

The exposé videos are replete with visual and verbal jokes, often accompanied by short sequences and references to Russian and American popular culture, typically films and TV programmes, and internet memes. These are most often used in order to ridicule the Russian elite for their incompetence, avarice, pomposity, servility, or double standards. Other features of entertainment shows have also been tried and tested. For one of the most-viewed videos, 'He is not Dimon to you', about Dmitrii Medvedev, they even made a 21-minute 'behind the scenes film'[52] where some of the public's questions and reactions were addressed (or joked away), but where there also were shown several 'bloopers' – short sequences of failed takes sometimes shown after the end of film comedies.

On a few occasions, Naval'nyi has made use of gaming elements, announcing competitions in order to generate interest for his activities. In the aftermath of the Medvedev exposé, FBK even announced a competition for the best poster at the following demonstrations, where the prize would be a pair of shoes identical to those of Medvedev's that gave the investigators the clue about his corruption scheme.[53] For the participants of another demonstration, he would award a camera to the author of the best selfie from the event.[54] On the occasion of his birthday in 2017, he announced an award of half a million rubles to the best political video blogs (500,000 to the winner), stating: 'Don't be afraid. Have a try, and maybe you will be a YouTube star tomorrow, and Dmitrii Kiselev and Vladimir Solov'ev [the regime's foremost TV propagandists] will cry like little girls, envying you for [the size of] your audience.'[55]

Indeed, Naval'nyi and his team has used popular culture not only for illustration and ridicule, but also as a source of inspiration. In fact, on such a serious occasion as his final words in court in February 2021, he quoted the nihilist cartoon character Rick Sanchez of his favourite TV programme, 'Rick and Morty'.[56] Popular culture is even the source of some of Naval'nyi's ideas for political work. In an interview, Naval'nyi stated that his mayoral campaign was inspired by the American series *The Wire*, with certain elements picked from *Homeland* and even *House of Cards*.[57]

More to the point, in his videos, even the most serious of issues are treated with humour and sarcasm. Most tellingly, on several occasions, he has been able to put a spin on the attacks against him, the idea clearly being to show that he would never lose his cool.[58] In 2017, when he went for a few days to France with his wife, the tabloid LifeNews announced a reward of 100,000 rubles for holiday videos of him. His wife made a deliberately poor-quality and supremely uninteresting video of Naval'nyi strolling the streets of Rouen, and LifeNews paid a reward to the individual who had forwarded the video, Naval'nyi could triumphantly announce.[59] When he was attacked by a hooligan throwing green liquid in his face, Naval'nyi had to undergo surgery for chemical burns to his eye.[60] However, soon afterwards, he posted photos of his green face on his blog, stating that this would not stop him, to the contrary, the bright colour made campaigning 'a hundred times cooler'.[61] Further, in 2018, after a YouTube exposé of a corruption scheme in the domestic security force, the National Guard, its commander, long-time renowned 'violence specialist' General Viktor Zolotov, posted his own video where he challenged him to a duel, threatening to make a 'juicy bottom round' out of Naval'nyi. The latter responded with yet another video, mocking the general even more and inviting him to a debate instead (Østbø, 2020).

Back in 2011, Naval'nyi was criticized by Ivan Begtin, a much more low-profile anti-corruption activist, for creating 'a show instead of working systematically with the problems at hand. ... It is as if you promise to release a new season of [the reality TV show] Dom-2 if the viewers transfer a given amount [by their mobile phones]. ... Instead of doing something useful, Naval'nyi makes a circus'.[62] Unperturbed, Naval'nyi went even further, taking the logic of entertainment to its utter extreme. Shortly after his recovery from the assassination attempt and having identified the team behind the operation, he called each of them on the phone, posing as an official of the Russian Security Council. The one team member who was willing to talk to him was asked about minute details, even chastised for the botched operation. The recorded conversation, where Naval'nyi's helpers from Bellingcat can barely control their laughter as the operative describes in detail how the poison was applied to the seams of Naval'nyi's underwear and tries to explain the failure, was subsequently published on YouTube.[63] The way the attempted assassination was turned into a show is perhaps the clearest illustration of how Naval'nyi's political campaigning has become inseparable from entertainment. Everything must be visualized and put in a theatrical yet ironic and halfway cynical context. The Naval'nyi team has not merely made anti-corruption work entertaining. Following the logic of YouTube, they have taken entertainment as the template of anti-corruption work.

The corrupting state versus idealized business and Big Tech utopia

Naval'nyi's discourse is a textbook example of the hegemonic view of corruption – the state as the source of corruption, as opposed to capital. In his exposés, Naval'nyi focuses on holders of political office and high-ranking public servants. By extension, he also focuses on the state's cronies – businesspeople whose success is deemed to stem not from their innovations, genius, or hard work, but from their connections to the regime and its rigged tenders for state orders. Hence, in this corrupt universe, the state occupies the central position. Corrupt people have captured the state: 'We have reached the point where it is no longer a group of people who rob the state, but the state itself has become an instrument of theft'.[64] The idea of the importance of having a strong state, very much in vogue in Putin-era Russia, is mocked in several videos, with reference to the luxury with which officials and their families surround themselves. Dmitrii Rogozin, head of the state's space agency and 'life-long official' is ridiculed in a video showing his son's (also a state official) car – at 8 million rubles with panorama roof and massage seats, with the voiceover 'a true state administrator, look at him' (07:35).[65] Likewise, a Novosibirsk City Duma Deputy's ideological image and constant repetitions about the importance of state-oriented thinking (*gosudarstvennoe myshlenie*) are derided, precisely with reference to the luxury with which his family surrounds itself (29:00). Three of his wristwatches are identified and priced in the range between 1 and 2 million rubles each, and his 600 m² house with a private pool is also exposed, as is his daughter's luxurious lifestyle in Dubai and his son's Porsche.[66] In another video, Naval'nyi shows the estate of Sergei Chemezov (CEO of Rostec, the state's defence technology mammoth), commenting 'sculptures of naked women ... fountains, and here, the main fountain with columns and a lion. It's obvious at once: a man of the state [*gosudarstvennyi chelovek*]'.[67]

Naval'nyi even descends into describing representatives of this elite as parasites, in the almost literal sense, cross-clipping their images with vivid pictures of parasites such as worms in the human digestive system. Explaining the corruption scheme of state propagandists Tigran Keosaian and Margarita Simonian and exposing their luxuries, Naval'nyi adds: 'if we don't fight the parasites, they will not stop, and they will not be satisfied until they kill the body. And we have only one country'.[68] Aram Gabrelianov, owner of tabloid news website LifeNews, which is rumoured to be close to the security services, is characterized as 'an animal' and a 'journalistic prostitute'. This is illustrated by a photo montage of Gabrelianov's head on the body of a stereotypical street prostitute.[69]

It is important not to underestimate the vital ideological function that anti-corruption, the corrupt (Russian) Other, and Naval'nyi all collectively play for capitalism. It is useful here to briefly refer to McGowan's (McGowan, 2019) pseudo-Hegelian theory of ideology, its function, and how it operates. McGowan's argument is that ideology is simply a narrative that provides a justification or a cause of our lack. As numerous continental philosophers and psychoanalytic theorists have established, we are all lacking beings. Lack is an unavoidable feature of the human condition that actually constitutes human subjectivity and allows it to come into being. So for McGowan, ideology simply provides a narrative explanation or purpose for our lack, and also provides a fantasy that allows the subject of ideology to envision some point in the future where they can overcome and resolve their lack.

Within Christianity, for example, lack is explained through the notion of original sin. After the Fall of Adam, human beings are inherently tainted with and participate in sin, and this sin is the cause of our lack, which can only be resolved or overcome through eternal salvation in the afterlife. For social justice, various intersecting inequalities and prejudices are the cause of our lack, and this lack can be resolved through dogged political action and progressive policies which redistribute wealth, challenge prejudice, and increase representation. Capitalism's explanation for lack, McGowan argues, is organized around the idea of merit. Our lack is not because of structural inequalities, but because we are not meritorious or deserving. We have not studied hard enough or achieved well enough during our education, made ourselves more 'employable', or been sufficiently creative or competitive in the marketplace. This lack is resolved through the fantasy that if one works hard and engages in hard-but-fair competition, then one will ultimately succeed and be prosperous. Coincidentally, this fantasy is known throughout the capitalist world as the 'American *Dream*' – the term 'dream' perhaps being an unconscious acknowledgment of its phantasmic nature.

However, every system has certain internal contradictions, and the second thing that ideology does, according to McGowan, is to transform these internal contradictions into *external oppositions* that can ultimately be resolved or overcome. This transformation of an internal contradiction into an opposition external to the system is arguably the precise role that the corrupt Other, anti-corruptionism, and Naval'nyi's own brand of politics play within capitalism's ideological universe. Corruption, while not unique to capitalism, is nevertheless arguably inherent to it. It is an internal contradiction. In the same way, capitalism's narrative explanation for lack is organized around the idea of merit, and the solution to this lack is hard work, industriousness and, above all else, *competition*. A pseudo-pacified competitive individualism is the predominant characteristic of capitalist subjectivity; a fundamental pre-requisite for survival in the market (Hall, 2014). Through ruthlessly competing in the market – and winning – one can ultimately overcome one's lack, and also benefit the collective as well. This is the basic promise offered to us by capitalism (McGowan, 2016). However, capitalism's encouragement of this kind of competitive individualism, its emphasis on winning, and its emphasis on wealth and luxury goods as the measures of one's success also has the tendency to cultivate 'criminal undertakers' – figures who 'get things done' by invoking a *special liberty* to do what is necessary to win and achieve an advantage (Hall, 2012). This tendency leads to the emergence of criminality and corruption which, by definition, is the antithesis of meritoriousness. The criminal or corrupt actor has not achieved their wealth meritoriously but has bent or broken the rules of the game. But while such actors may have transgressed norms, they have not necessarily transgressed *values* (Hall et al, 2008). At the level of values, such actors are arguably *hyper-conformists*.

This is a basic contradiction *internal* to capitalism. It is an ideological system which places meritoriousness as the narrative explanation and solution for our lack while being an economic system based upon intense and ruthless competition in which one must do whatever it takes to win in order to resolve that sense of lack. Organized crime figures, corrupt corporations engaged in bribery and bid-rigging, and Russian oligarchs alike are all manifestations or symptoms of this internal contradiction. As McGowan (McGowan, 2019: 13) writes, 'those we imagine as enemies most often turn out to be versions of ourselves'. As he is quick to point out, this doesn't change the need to fight such ills, it merely changes the way in which one fights. One fights by fully confronting the internal contradiction. However, rather than identify, accept, and confront this internal contradiction, anti-corruptionism and activists such as Naval'nyi turn their gaze away from it, and instead transform these manifestations of capitalism's internal contradictions into corrupt 'Others' that are in opposition to capitalism, an externality or aberration that can ultimately be resolved or overcome. This is a critique that is arguably applicable to all business ethics. As Bloom has argued, capitalism as a whole – but neoliberalism in particular – has always relied on non-market ethical principles and values to sustain and 'perfect' capitalism; a project that is never realized and incessantly pursued. As he writes, 'In terms of capitalism, the market is portrayed as a necessary but commonly flawed mechanism for achieving individual and collective progress. Its dominant framing, then, was as a perfectible system that, although overall beneficial, required ongoing improvement' (Bloom, 2017: 33).

The very idea of a perfectible system involves rejecting its internal contradictions, and instead transforming them into external – and ultimately resolvable – oppositions. The perfect example of this can be found in the following excerpt from a Naval'nyi video, where the ills of post-Soviet Russian economy are blamed not on the market reforms or capitalism, but for not being properly capitalist:

'I am not against capitalism. I just don't think that what we see around us is capitalism, and I don't regard [Alisher] Usmanov or other natural resource oligarchs as businessmen at all [photos of Abramovich and Deripaska are shown]. These people have not created anything, they didn't invent anything, they are just parasiting (*nazhivaiut*) on old Soviet enterprises and the sales of natural resources that belong to me and you and everyone else. It's a monstrous, distorted and unjust system. Let them go to hell with such capitalism, where all the national wealth belongs to a couple of dozen people, Putin's friends. There is no such thing in any other capitalist country, neither in Europe, nor in America'. (04:00)[70]

For Naval'nyi, the likes of Usmanov, Abramovich, or Deripaska are not true capitalists. There is no merit to their wealth, no creativity, no ingenuity. What lies behind their vast riches is merely an original act of seizure that occurred in the chaos of Post-Soviet privatization and market reforms (Logvinenko, 2021). This, of course, is a basic disavowal of the fact that capitalism itself was, and continues to be, based on original acts of primitive accumulation and dispossession (Harvey, 2003). Naval'nyi goes on to state that these people should be heavily taxed, and to lament that 17 oligarchs do not pay taxes to Russia, claiming that this constitutes 'the real war against our country' (05:00). This betrays, at best, poor knowledge of the world's ultra-rich, where, for instance, the richest Americans pay only miniscule taxes (Eisinger et al, 2021). There are enough leaks, and scandals surrounding tax evasion in the West, and, as *Chicago Policy Review* puts it: 'It is no secret that the rich hate paying taxes. ... The Department of Treasury estimates that in 2019, the amount of tax that should have been collected, but was not, amounted to $600 billion. ... the top 1% is responsible for 36% of all unpaid individual income taxes annually' (Lipman, 2021).

The same way nobody is really surprised by the revelations of corruption in Russia, nobody is really surprised by the revelations of tax evasion by the ultra-rich in the West. It is safe to say that Naval'nyi's ideal capitalism does not exist anywhere in the world. In the US, for example, what once perhaps resembled a competitive, free market has long been supplanted by an oligopolistic system, where the state instead of securing free competition 'through regulatory capture has created rules that limit competition' (Tepper & Hearn, 2019: xviii).

In Naval'nyi's anti-corruption discourse, market and business principles are mapped onto politics (as it should be). This is, of course, a hallmark of neoliberalism: Adam Smith's *classic* liberalism was concerned with *creating* a free market within a pre-existing political entity, such as the nation state. In neoliberal discourse, this is turned on its head – the free market becomes 'an organizing and regulating principle of the state, from the start of its existence up to the last form of its interventions. In other words: a state under the supervision of the market rather than a market supervised by the state' (Foucault, 2008: 116).

This is reflected in how Naval'nyi built up his organization. The Anti-Corruption Foundation (*Fond po bor'be s korruptsiei*, FBK) consisted of local chapters of dedicated activists as well as fundraisers. However, it was not a traditional grassroots movement. Unlike typical social movements or even democratic political parties, it did not have an institutionalized bottom-up channel for rank-and-file activists to influence the policies or decisions made at the top, nor could they elect new leaders. In this sense, FBK was more like a business structure, a 'vertically organized commercial campaign with a team mentality than a political organization open to public discussion of its decisions and interaction with other political forces' (Budraitskis, 2022: 183).

The professionalization had started early on: in early 2012, Naval'nyi published a vacancy for the position of press secretary, demanding 'red diploma' from the university and the highest professionalism, leaving the selection to HR experts.[71] When it was banned as 'extremist' in 2021, the FBK had 40 employees, many of them highly competent professionals. Considering the personal risk these people were taking, working for Naval'nyi was of course much more than a job, and we can safely assume that most of them could have found safer and/or better paid jobs elsewhere.

Nevertheless, even during the 2018 presidential campaign, hiring procedures resembled less those of a social movement than those of a commercial firm. The 2018 campaign had 230 salaried employees who coordinated the activities of 130,000 volunteers. According to Naval'nyi, his organization went through more than 6,000 resumes to select the hired staff.[72] The selection followed clear criteria. The procedure was presented as the very opposite of the informal, opaque practices and patron–client relations that are associated with Putinist politics (Hale, 2015). The meritocratic principles and the professionalized recruitment process were justified both on utilitarian and ideational grounds: In order to conduct a successful campaign, the organization needed competent people, but it was also a clear aim to use the recruitment and the organization work to give a foretaste of the 'wonderful Russia of the future', as one of the main slogans went (Dollbaum et al, 2021: 122–3). In this sense, Naval'nyi's future Russia was to be run more like a private business, where managerial skills would trump political positions. This was evident in the campaign's choice of co-ordinator in Krasnodar, where the controversial (at least for mainstream liberals) nationalist, paganist, and businessman Miroslav Val'kovich was selected. But Naval'nyi's close collaborator, Leonid Volkov, praised the open and competitive process that first and foremost had assessed the candidates' professional and organizational experience.[73] Volkov explained how the leadership required weekly activity reports, and emphasized that while 'very idea driven', the organization used 'business solutions' to pursue their goals.[74]

The long-time executive director of FBK, Vladimir Ashurkov, has a solid background from the finance sector. Trained at Wharton Business School, he worked as director of group portfolio management in the oligarch Mikhail Fridman's Alfa Group until early 2012, when he was forced to choose between his job and activism in support of Naval'nyi.[75] In May 2012, Naval'nyi posted his list of '16 brave ones' who had agreed to be donors in public. The list contained two famous writers, one journalist, and two high-profile economists, but the rest were investors, businesspeople, and managers.[76] In a late 2012 op-ed, Ashurkov, seemingly without irony, even made the case for investing in the opposition to be regarded not only as an idealistic act, but also as a 'business project' with a potential return far surpassing that seen in conventional business.[77]

In Naval'nyi's videos, the private tech industry is idealized, whereas the state-owned hydrocarbon exporting industry occupies the other extreme of the spectrum, representing the worst of today's Russia. For instance, he compares Apple with Gazprom and Rosneft, where the former is praised for its profitability and moderate CEO salary (8.7 million USD for the preceding year), as opposed to the latter, where the opposite is the case (Gazprom's CEO earned 17.7 million that year), although these state companies are 'managed very poorly' and 'headed by unprofessional and incompetent men'.[78] The state's initiatives to stimulate high technology, such as Rusnano and Skolkovo, are thoroughly (and correctly) ridiculed as corrupt, inefficient, and essentially futile. For instance, one video was modelled on the popular YouTube genre of 'unboxing' tech gadgets, presenting a Popslate, an iPhone cover with an additional (malfunctioning, as it turned out) screen on the back, a prototype given to him by then Rusnano CEO Anatolii Chubais. Naval'nyi sarcastically presented it as 'the quintessence of all the super-inventions of Putin's Russia; this is cutting-edge stuff, the representation of what Putin and his team have achieved in the sphere of high technologies', adding that Rusnano had invested 10 billion rubles in PlasticLogic, the company developing it.[79] The obvious failure of this project or the very poor results of the state's investments in Rusnano and Skolkovo are of less importance here than the ideal alternative presented by Naval'nyi: Silicon Valley functions as a utopia, conveying technological development, prosperity, transparency, and, above all, independence from the state. In one of his last videos before he was poisoned, Naval'nyi described Novosibirsk, which is known for its multitude of educational and research institutions and its concentration of highly educated people, as 'the city of the failed Russian dream. Everything is there for it to prosper. If history went a little differently, it would be our Silicon Valley. ... This [Akademgorodok] looks very much like Stanford or Palo Alto. ... But while Silicon Valley grew around Stanford, that didn't happen with Akademgorodok'.[80]

The blame was put on the local United Russia elite, who had oligopolized the construction market, erecting huge panel ghettos of poor-quality buildings with deficient infrastructure, while they themselves resided in secluded palaces, surrounded by luxury. Once this elite had been removed, for instance through 'smart voting', the city would usher in a high-tech utopian future: 'This could be one of the most successful cities in the world but instead became a Russian panel ghetto. ... Our task is to free the capital of Siberia from the invaders'.[81]

By the same token, Naval'nyi has glorified the exiled tech billionaire, Pavel Durov, founder of the social network VKontakte and the messaging app Telegram, which had been blocked in Russia:

> A Russian citizen, he has created a wonderful international business ... here we have our billionaire who has made his fortune not on oil, gas or raw materials, but on the Internet. Let's invite him here and help him. He should be doing everything in Russia. He will be earning money for us, paying salaries and taxes here. He will be making us richer. That's great! Thank you, Pasha!'[82]

It is not clear how Russia as a country would benefit from a messaging app company that has little more than two dozen employees globally (Hebel et al, 2021), whose logo refers to the founder's throwing 5000-ruble bills folded as planes out of the window, and which, in order to avoid taxes, is registered in the UAE, where Durov also 'resides' (known to roam the world, he is also a citizen of the tax haven St Kitts and Nevis, as well as France, after having fled Russia for fear of persecution) for the same reason.[83] More to the point, the juxtaposition between 'clean business' on the one hand and the authoritarian regime and its cronies on the other does not hold water. Two years after the statement by Naval'nyi, Telegram was unblocked in Russia. Surprisingly, Durov and the Kremlin had reached a pragmatic working relationship, with Putin later holding up Telegram as an example of 'normal' interaction between the authorities and social networks.[84] Some sources claimed that the state-owned VneshTorgBank was involved in the preceding negotiations, and that it helped Telegram reaching out to investors, of which it was in dire need (Loucaides, 2023). Three weeks after the unblocking, Telegram's vice president appeared at a conference that was dedicated to development of the IT industry and arranged by the Russian government, complaining about Apple's commission on apps, which he compared to the taxes imposed on Russians by the Golden Hordes during the Mongol yoke.[85] For its part, the Russian media regulator praised the company publicly for its readiness 'to combat terrorism and extremism'.[86] In this connection it must be noted that in addition to their more narrow usage, the terms *terrorism* and *extremism* are actively used, legally and rhetorically, by the regime to stigmatize and persecute any kind of political opposition. Furthermore, Russian opposition activists have described experiences indicating that Telegram now complies with the Kremlin's legal requests to give access to their user accounts, making it easy to track down and detain them (Loucaides, 2023).

Depoliticization and the consumerist utopia of pure morality

At various times, there have been numerous attempts to characterize Naval'nyi's ideology, as center-right, centrist, or even center-left, according to the eyes of the beholder (Light & Sauer, 2021). It has often been pointed out that his views have evolved considerably over the years, from youthful market fundamentalism, according to his own retrospective assessment (Voronkov, 2011), via a more moderate liberalism, then a brief flirt with opportunistic nationalism, before incorporating moderate social demands. Hence, his 2018 presidential campaign programme (he ran as an unregistered and therefore 'prohibited' candidate due to technicalities) proposed several social measures, for instance increasing the minimum wage, abolishing military draft, cutting taxes for small businesses, increasing the expenditure on the health service and education, and, perhaps most controversially, guaranteeing an interest rate of only 2 per cent on mortgages. The 1990s privatization was not to be revised, though a small 'fee' or tax was to be imposed on those who had profited illegitimately. Naval'nyi promised drastic cuts in the bureaucracy and law enforcement, and, crucially, a reduction of the state's intervention in economic life. He would save 750 billion rubles by economizing on bureaucrats and law enforcement, and save 2 trillion rubles on state subsidies to state companies on big projects.[87] As for the military, the budget would stay the same, but much more would go to salaries of professional soldiers. State media would be the subject of drastic cuts (0.02 trillion instead of 0.12 trillion). Observers noted that the programme was short on concrete details, sometimes self-contradictory, and that the economical part lacked a sound basis.[88]

The main source of extra revenue was to come from the combatting of corruption. More to the point, both in the public's reception, and, arguably, in his own communication – during the campaign as well as at other times – budgetary details were completely overshadowed by the issue of corruption. Naval'nyi has actively framed his political campaign as a clear-cut battle between the corrupt and the pure. As for the former, he claimed that the traditional division within the regime between *siloviki* and 'systemic liberals' was nonsense. As evidence, he pointed to how, for instance, Finance Minister Anton Siluanov and First Deputy Minister of Defence Ruslan Tsalikov had very similar – and adjacent – dachas:

> There are no towers or wings in the Kremlin, no siloviki, no liberals – that's all a play for the public! There is just one completely monolithic group that is called 'crooks and thieves from Putin's government'. People who use Russia and its people for personal enrichment. ... Our silovik and our liberal live together in perfect harmony, only separated by a tiny fence.[89]

Promoting himself, he declared: 'I am the only presidential candidate who not only speaks openly about corruption, but also fights it. So therefore you can agree with me about some things and disagree with me about other things, but if you are fed up with the authorities' stealing, then support me.'[90] As for the opposition, he has, at this stage, tried to rally everyone against corruption rather than for anything at all: 'Whether you are leftist or rightist, it doesn't matter. Whether you are liberal or conservative, Westernizer or conservative. Let's all go out to the streets against the corruption that has devoured the entire state machinery and prohibits any development at all.'[91] Many of his followers seem to have followed his appeal: acknowledging his real charisma and personal popularity, many regional staffers in his organization have described their alliance with him as temporary. Though they disagreed considerably with him on different issues, they let such 'political and even ideological disagreements [take] the back seat' (Dollbaum et al, 2021: 132).

Worldwide, popular outrage following corruption scandals have led to impeachments, resignations, or ousting of presidents and governments. It must also be pointed out that many citizens seem willing to tolerate corrupt governments if they are able to deliver tangible benefits (Manzetti & Wilson, 2007), or those that are successful precisely *because* of being corrupt (Michelutti, 2010; Vaishnav, 2017), but in conditions of colossal and growing inequality and poverty, popular discontent often takes the shape of anti-corruption protest. Where there is perceived to be no alternative to market and democracy, anti-corruption discourse is the 'most popular discourse to criticize market and democracy' (Krastev, 2004: loc. 800). Naval'nyi's exposé videos are geared towards generating maximum outrage. Increasingly, alongside the documentation of the corruption schemes and the luxury revelations, they have also been explicitly contrasted with footage of social problems in Russia (Sakhnin, 2021). Naval'nyi has been making comparisons of how state budget funds are spent unevenly – for instance, he contrasted the salaries of employees of state-controlled propaganda television channel RT to those of ordinary state employees, teachers, submarine sailors, and cosmonauts[92]; and pointed out that the state contracts of Putin crony Arkadii Rotenberg's company Stroigazmontazh (1 trillion rubles) was three times the size of Russia's health budget and twice the size of the education budget.[93] Another example is how the opulent luxuries of VneshTorgBank CEO Andrei Kostin and his young girlfriend were contrasted with desperate parents asking for donations for their sick children.[94] Hence, poverty is directly linked to corruption, in the sense of state servants or businessmen close to the state devouring state funds. According to Naval'nyi, 'the principal reason for our poverty is corruption and abominable state management over the last two decades'.[95] This is depoliticization in practice. As Krastev states, '[c]orruption-centered politics in a way is the end of politics. It moralizes the policy choices to the extent that politics is reduced to the choice between corrupt government and clean opposition. Corruption-centered politics is one of the explanations for the transformation of East European democracy into protest vote democracies' (Krastev, 2004: loc. 827).

To an extent, early Putinism (2000–11) functioned according to the logics of consumer capitalism, that is on the basis of the promise of a satisfaction, in the shape of more and more consumerist goods getting affordable to more and more people. McGowan has emphasized the importance of the *promise* as the guiding principle of the basic rules of capitalism (McGowan, 2016), but in what was still seen as a transition period, the promise is even more central. A transition society is on its way to something better, never to something worse. As long as one accepts the logics of transition, there is almost no limit to what failings can be explained away by pointing to the future – all bad things are either residues from the past or can be explained (away) by the past, whereas the best things are to come in the future.

By 2012, it had become apparent that the regime was unable to continue fulfilling the promise. The economic growth curve flattened, and the leaders were unwilling and/or unable to conduct what leading economists prescribed in order to continue the growth despite the lower oil price. No radical choice was taken, either in the direction of market reform or more firm state leadership. Faced with mass demonstrations, Putinism changed in the course of a few months, turning instead to the *threat*. The trope of the threat did not come out of the blue. In the 1990s, president Boris Yeltsin pointed to the threat of the return of repressive communism and consumer goods shortage. Putin, though personally installed by Yeltsin, presented himself as his predecessor's antipode, implicitly and sometimes also explicitly pointing to the threat of a return to the chaos of the 1990s, and increasingly drawing on anti-Western sentiment. But from 2012 on, the threat of deprivation took center stage. Following the new narrative, the West was bent on weakening Russia's newly regained power and economic strength, and even more importantly, its age-old values and national identity. Only the people's rallying around the flag, and, above all, the regime, could prevent the deprivation. With the full-scale war in Ukraine, the logic of the threat came to dominate completely, and in September 2022, the regime went to the unprecedented step of 'partial' mobilization. The proverbial unwritten social contract between the regime and the people – increased or at least not drastically diminished living standards in exchange for passive support or at least passivity – was torn apart.

Naval'nyi's communication, by contrast, has all along been strongly influenced by consumerist culture. Most glaringly, in one blog post, he evaluates the Russian constitution as if it were a new iPhone:

> Let's just take apart the first 16 articles of the Constitution (they describe 'the fundamentals of the constitutional order') the way it is done in online overviews of phones and other gadgets. Let us throw away political preferences and establish objectively if there is such a function in our device [*ustroistvo*] or not. As if it would be a 10 megapixels camera or a complete charger. Let's insert YES or NO under each of the described functions.[96]

More to the point, Naval'nyi's highly populist discourse, by contrast, is permeated by a *promise* reminiscent of consumerism – the promise that satisfaction is 'just around the corner' (McGowan, 2016: 11). Despite numerous obstacles, he has repeatedly communicated an extreme optimism about what can be achieved even in the short term, arguably superseding even many of the most populist of politicians worldwide. For instance, on the eve of the 2019 regional elections (and State Duma by-elections), his team stated that 'even a single really independent deputy will immediately destroy this entire corrupt scheme and send it to hell at the very first session of the new Duma. One deputy can ask a question, file a complaint or make a speech on TV ... and that will be the end of it all!'[97] Or, a more succinct slogan from a video that was recorded just before he was poisoned, and published while he was still in coma: 'A normal life is closer than you think. Do something to bring it even closer.'[98] As part of the investigation of 'Putin's palace', Naval'nyi stated:

> If everybody who reads this investigation, spreads it, we will tear the censorship to pieces. If 10 per cent of the discontented goes out in the streets, they will not dare to falsify the elections. If every one of us will register and take part in the 'Smart Voting', then United Russia, Putin's party of theft and degradation, will lose the elections, there will be political competition, and the quality of politics and bureaucrats will begin to improve. There will be honest courts. Normal prosecutors. It will be impossible to steal in such amounts as now. And step after step, we will be richer and live better.[99]

Despite the consumerist form of much of Naval'nyi's communication, satisfaction is ultimately not to be reached by obtaining the newest commodity, but in the uncovered truth and pure morality. Or rather, in truth as a (promised) commodity. Nowhere else is this as evident as in his last words in court before his sentence, where he kept repeating 'sila v pravde' (power resides in the truth).

> To all people: it is important to not be afraid of these people, to not be afraid of those who are searching (dobivaetsia) for the truth. Because many are afraid: oh God, what will be, there will be revolution, there will be nightmares and upheavals. But think for yourselves, how good life would be without constant lying.[100]

The apparent paradox is that Naval'nyi himself through his exposés had, again and again, 'uncovered' this truth. But this is part and parcel of the fundamental dynamics of capitalism, according to McGowan (McGowan, 2016). Once we acquire what seemed the object of our complete satisfaction, it is quickly revealed that it was not the case, and our attention turns to the future – again.

The repeated exposés of corruption schemes and luxury, perhaps particularly real estate abroad, all come down to showing the double standards of the elite, whose propaganda increasingly, particularly during the war against Ukraine, relies on patriotism, anti-Westernism, and 'spiritual-moral values' (Østbø, 2017). This is particularly visible in one video where Naval'nyi first shows a speech by Putin where the latter talked about Russian 'spiritual bonds' (*dukhovnye skrepy*) and then immediately turns to Naval'nyi himself, who states: 'Putin's regime is shameless and degradant. Every one of us must make at least a little effort in the struggle against it.'[101] Later, he continues:

> Under the pretext of some kind of encroachment on our spiritual bonds, an external threat, [Putin] turned Russia into an impoverished rogue state, a state that for some reason is forever in the trench and is at war with everyone. Tons of lies about family, love, loyalty, and patriotism pour out on us, but all this is hypocrisy. Their real life is second families, yachts, airplanes and palaces. A royal, glamorous life at the expense of oligarchs. This is Putin's ideology.[102]

For years, Naval'nyi's blog has been headlined 'The final battle between the good and neutrality.' In April 2021, at the time of his hunger strike in prison, his team called for demonstrations in his support under the slogan 'The final battle between normal people and the absolute evil'.[103] Although it is hard to disagree with the Naval'nyi team's moral condemnation of the Russian regime, the exposé discourse simplifies corruption in a manner that supports the global anti-corruption hegemony. The complex phenomenon of corruption is stripped of structural, legal, and transnational aspects, taken out of its context, and for all practical purposes reduced to a moral feature of the individuals comprising the regime. In a sense, Naval'nyi draws a picture of the Russian regime as the *immoral Other* of idealized business, with corruption as the standard cause of economic and developmental failure. This resembles the Western discourse on the Third World, with ex-colonial powers or global structures dominating them, earlier as exploitative colonial powers, but later as exploitative in another way, by dictating structural adjustment (Felices-Luna, 2016: 130–2).

Reversing the reverse cargo cult

Russian political scientist and commentator Ekaterina Schulmann has coined the term 'reversed cargo cult' to describe a particular form of whataboutist mentality that not only is prevalent in the Russian political elite and the population at large, but which also is weaponized in state-controlled media's propaganda and in foreign policy. For Westerners, this logic is particularly visible in the news coverage of the international, multilingual TV channel RT, which is controlled by the Russian state. The underlying premise is that everyone understands that Russia has numerous political and social problems. Most significantly perhaps, liberal values are enshrined in the Constitution, and Russia formally is a democracy, but as far as important and strategic decisions go, its political institutions are in many ways a mere decoration. Real power resides in informal networks (Ledeneva, 2006, 2013; Minchenko Consulting, 2019; Belton, 2020). Hence, the political elite cannot convince either its own electorate or the international society that Russia has free elections and a competitive economy. The solution is to present Western democratic institutions as even more of a sham; it is just that Westerners allegedly are much better at pretending:

> Cargo cult is the belief that models of airplanes made of manure and straw will attract real ones that will bring a lot of canned beef. Reverse cargo cult is typical for developing countries, and their political elites are particularly fond of it. They preach that in the First World, the planes are also made of straw and manure, and there is no canned beef. They are just better at pretending and hiding this fact. When you are being told about the vanity of bourgeois elections, the comedy of parliamentarism, and police violence, remember: airplanes exist, and they transport people. Economic competition, free elections, and independent courts are also real.[104]

Perhaps most of all a sarcastic remark, this nevertheless points to the importance of *imitation* when it comes to Russia's relations with the West. More to the point, according to Krastev and Holmes (2017), Russia has gone from a *sincere* imitation of Western models to a *cynical* one. In the Soviet period, the capitalist West was the Other, but with the fall of Communism, almost overnight Russia was required to *become* the Western Other, the antithesis of Sovietness, in order to achieve a 'normal, civilized life' (Fitzpatrick, 2005: 304). Under Putin, by contrast, an important part of Russian foreign policy is to imitate, not the prescribed Western ideal of liberal democracy, but what the Russian elite regards as the 'real West', which is hypocritical, sanctimonious, and cloaks geopolitical interests in talk about allegedly universal values. This is 'aggressive mimicry', in the sense that they imitate what they deem to be the worst aspects of American foreign policy; not only to get away with geopolitical dominance, breach of other countries' sovereignty, and meddling in their internal affairs, but also as a way of discrediting the Western model as such (Krastev & Holmes, 2017). Most Western commentators rightly characterize whataboutist arguments, or else, *tu quoque* arguments – as a logical fallacy. However, this is beside the point. In his speech marking the 'accession' of Crimea and Sevastopol to the Russian Federation, Putin (2014) referred explicitly to the precedent of Kosova, and took passages of the Kosovan declaration of independence almost verbatim (Light & Sauer, 2021).

More importantly, the concept of reverse cargo cult highlights the emptiness, in the sense of 'a breakdown between the signifier and the signified ... when the image ... fails to correspond with the thing it purports to represent' (Stakun, 2017: 7). As Stakun (2017) points out, this 'breakdown in the signifying chain' (Jameson, 1984: 71–2) corresponds to Baudrillard's concept of the simulacrum (Baudrillard, 1994). Russia has experienced this numerous times through history. From the adoption of Christianity in 988, through Peter the Great, the Bolshevik revolution, and post-Soviet political and economic reforms, ideas have been imposed from above, producing reality instead of reflecting it. Signs of a new reality, such as Stalin's giant hydroelectric plant on the Dnipro river, or Brezhnev's numerous autobiographies, should demonstrate the superiority of ideas over simple facts (Epstein, 1993). At the time of writing, the latest important addition to the huge Russian catalogue of such breakdowns is of course the quintessentially postmodern complex of often mutually contradictory ideologemes spewed out in the Putin regime's propaganda about its war in Ukraine. While there is not room here to go into detail, we can mention a few examples of the signifiers that have partly or completely lost their connection to the signifieds in the course of the war that started in 2014 and was escalated in 2022: 'Nazism', 'attack', 'special operation', 'genocide', 'foreign agent'. We could even speculate that instead of the oft-repeated characterization of Putin's decision to launch the 'special operation' in January 2022 as a massive intelligence failure (Miller & Belton, 2022), it is better interpreted as a result of the regime's self-inflicted breakdown in the signifying chain – or else, Baudrillardean simulation.

However, it would be a mistake to look at Russia in isolation. Surely, Russia at war in 2022 exhibits a rather extreme case of simulation. But it is easy to find examples of empty signifiers among the crucial concepts in global hegemonic discourse. On a generic level, it is quite plausible to at least in part explain anti-elite sentiment, the rise of the far right, and the loss of faith in democratic institutions to a breakdown in the signification chain. More specifically, to mention but a few examples, apart from 'corruption', 'sustainability' (Brown, 2016), 'megatrends' (Von Groddeck & Schwarz, 2013), 'the people' (Laclau, 2005), 'governance' (Offe, 2009), 'rule of law' (May, 2011), and 'climate protection' (Methmann, 2010) have all been analysed as such. Moreover, even staunch libertarians may argue that monopolization has made capitalism a myth (Tepper & Hearn, 2019). The increasing power of a few corporate global elites, what Tombs and Whyte (2015: 11) call 'oligopolistic capitalism', is a far cry from 'dominant representations of what capitalism is supposed to look like and how it is claimed to work'.

Naval'nyi, by contrast, not only sincerely believes in democracy, rule of law, anti-corruption, and capitalism, but has sacrificed his own freedom and health, and narrowly escaped death for these ideas. As Masha Gessen argues, he has been acting as if Russia were a 'normal country' – as if the authorities actually were following their own laws, and he conducted and presented the corruption investigations '*as if* the corruption they uncover were not hopelessly self-evident' (Gessen, 2016). This gave his campaigning a 'spiritual core' of sorts (Gessen, 2016). The legalistic discourse is of course one of the things he has in common with the early post-Stalin dissidents. More to the point, from the Western perspective, his very sacrifice, honesty, and fervour appear to fill the empty signifiers 'democracy', 'rule of law', and 'capitalism' with content. In this sense, Naval'nyi is working to reverse the reverse cargo cult – despite his nationalist leanings on some issues, he is an adherent of a return to the sincere imitation of the West. This image of 'the West', however, is an empty 'master signifier', as it is composed of the aforementioned empty signifiers. Hence, the content Naval'nyi provides is not substantial and political, as Naval'nyi is firmly embedded in the anti-policy discourse, but fundamentally *moral* – it serves to reinvigorate and perpetuate the West.

There is this striking contrast between the political emptiness and the moral urgency that Naval'nyi attaches to his message. As mentioned, the headline of Naval'nyi's blog still is 'the final battle between good and neutrality' – but now it could have been changed into 'the battle between good and evil'. In the next chapter, we shall transition into the world of art, antiquities and luxury in the West and the proliferating regulations and anti-policies that target it, underpinned by the same logic of the perpetual battle between good and evil – a good that is only defined as the absence of evil. We shall see how the relationship between external and internal threats and enemies comes to be conceived and sought combatted, as we investigate the 'enablers' facilitating the 'penetration of the evil into Western jurisdictions' and the fantasies of closing loopholes and gaps in regulation. Returning to some of our opening remarks, we will dig a bit deeper into the dynamics that reproduce and sustain neoliberal financial capitalism, challenging the premises of the hegemonic anti-corruption consensus.

3

Compliance, Defiance, and the Fight against Crime through the Markets in Art, Antiquities, and Luxury

'Luxury is not a proxy for the general economy', the CFO of LVMH Jean-Jacques Guiony remarked in October 2022 as 'the bling behemoth reported a 19% increase in sales' (Felsted, 2022). Another headline read: 'The Rich Are Spending on Luxury Goods Like It's 1999' (Rascouet, 2022). Reporting on Christie's record-breaking $1.5 billion auction sale of The Paul G. Allen Collection,[1] *The Art Newspaper* could further explain 'Why the Global Explosion of Billionaires will Keep auction Houses Afloat – For Now' (Reyburn, 2022). After assuring readers that all proceeds of the sale – barring Christie's cut – went to philanthropy, the article remarked quite appropriately on the multiplication of billionaires and the accumulation of wealth at the stratospheric end of the economy: 'In 1992 there were 275 billionaires in the world; now there are 2,668, according to Forbes. Buoyed by financial deregulation, globalisation and ever more sophisticated strategies of tax minimisation, these billionaires are worth a collective $12.7 trillion' (Reyburn, 2022).

It concluded by asking, also rather appropriately: 'what, exactly is being applauded?' (Reyburn, 2022). Indeed, all these news items come in times of dramatically rising inflation. The renowned economist, Nouriel Roubini, has predicted a 'severe, long, and ugly' (Bove, 2022) recession ahead amidst the war in Ukraine, souring US–China relations, and other geopolitical tensions. Indeed, the luxury economy appears as unique and as detached from reality as the promises of its luxury goods; a world of the superrich playing by its own rules secluded in its securitized protective bubbles, a world apart. After all, we could read similar headlines during the financial crisis of 2008, and we know that the luxury industry was one of very few that did not decline in that period. On the whole, the ongoing crisis has done nothing to alter the trend of wealth accumulation at the very top. Despite all the philanthropic efforts of the likes of Paul Allen and other elites, it is the poor that are getting poorer, the middle class increasingly disappearing and squeezed, while 828 million are facing hunger.[2] As Oxfam put it: 'The "cost of living" crisis is more accurately a "cost of profit" crisis – of rising billionaire wealth and corporate mega-profits – that is driving up poverty, hunger, indebtedness and deprivation around the world.'[3]

None of this comes as a surprise. We all know these truths, even if we often *disavow* their reality. It is this disavowed reality that creates the most favourable conditions for both the luxury, art and antiquities markets on one hand, and for the security, intelligence, and risk management industries on the other, which operate as part of a wider 'compliance–industrial complex' (Kuldova, 2022a). Both of these global multi-billion-dollar markets have grown exponentially over the last decades as wealth at the top accumulates, and as risk and threat scenarios multiply and the need to protect wealth and luxury assets – from criminals and regulators alike – increases. It is not surprising that the art market thrives in times of crisis; the rich consistently turn to 'collectible assets as a safe hedge against inflation' (Graham, 2014: 322). But it is worth reminding ourselves of these fundamental dynamics of contemporary neoliberal financial capitalism. Even more so, as we will, in this chapter, explore *the ideological reproduction of neoliberal governance* that perpetuates, and even exacerbates these dynamics, and we will do so by looking more closely at the fight against crimes – in particular money laundering, corruption and terrorism financing – *through* the markets in art, antiquities and high-end luxury goods. In other words, we will explore the relatively recent introduction of *anti-policies* into these markets which pass as a form of 'market regulation'.

Nouriel Roubini, popularly known as Dr. Doom, famously argued in Davos in 2015 during the World Economic Forum (WEF) meeting that the art market is 'shady' (Cascone, 2015), used for money laundering, tax avoidance and evasion, and more. His recommendations were more 'codes of conduct' and more 'self-regulation' to increase efficiency and price transparency.[4] This remark on the art market, even if repeatedly cited by regulators, compliance market actors and academics alike, is just a footnote to his underlying vision of the world. This is a world subject to extreme 'megathreats', from the debt crisis, the 'demographic time bomb', financial instability, economic depression and financial crisis, the dangers of artificial intelligence, the potential for a new Cold War, an environmental apocalypse, rising income and wealth inequality, cyberwarfare, future pandemics, and so on. Roubini can be seen as the prophet of the rapidly expanding and accelerating risk universe, a dystopian vision of the future shaped by all of these 'megathreats' which come together and amplify one another (Roubini, 2022). While his incremental solutions may differ, it is precisely this vision of interconnected and mutually amplifying 'megathreats' that fuels the compliance, audit and consultancy industries – or 'consultocracy' (Ylönen & Kuusela, 2019) – which increasingly shapes regulation to its own market advantage (Frasen & LeBaron, 2019) and cashes in on dystopian and apocalyptic visions of a world under permanent assault by both minor and major threats.

These megathreats may at first seem unrelated to corruption, crime and money laundering in the art, antiquities, and luxury markets. But the solutions – which we must remind ourselves translate into regulatory, technological, and audit *products*, *commodities*, and *markets* – are the same. The commodification of regulation driven by anti-policies translates into increased security, surveillance, intelligence, crime fighting, transparency, auditing, reporting, and technosolutionism (Morozov, 2013); all of which seek to control and eliminate these (mega)threats. Moreover, these threats are similarly imagined as intersecting and inextricably entangled, making it impossible to think about or tackle one without the other. Consequently, it comes to appear as sensible to use the same comprehensive arsenal of assault weapons to target them; and both soft and hard regulations tend to evolve into forms of purification and the elimination of various gaps in the control architecture.

These regulations then descend into forms of control that are *driven by the negative*: by the quest to combat, fight, and eliminate through empty and procedural technobureaucratic formulas and surveillance, remarkable only by their lack of any positive vision of a world where life is worth living. This absence of a positive vision is rather striking and appears to be the defining feature of this form of regulation and of anti-policies at large, where the elimination of the bad comes to equal the good. We have come to be so used to this way of speaking that we no longer even pause to ask what kind of a world would be left. What would this 'good' look like? Is the driving idea that we would be left with a 'pure', formalized, 'moral', consumerist, efficient, well-regulated market utopia? And what of inequality, poverty, wealth accumulation after this final 'dekleptification' (to use USAID's[5] newspeak)? Would we just be left with power concentrated among the benevolent, moral, and philanthropic multibillionaires of the likes of Bill Gates, backed by the state with its politicians and bureaucrats oozing integrity? While we are being told on the one hand that *zero tolerance* and a 'world free of corruption'[6] is the core vision, few appear to really believe that zero corruption could ever be achieved. The perpetual deferral of the ultimate 'dekleptification' is precisely the point, as is not asking questions about the positive content of these policies.

As we will see in more detail in the following chapter which interrogates the ethics underpinning these various anti-policies, there is certain indifference as to the kind of world that will emerge once the evil is finally eliminated. Tackling the evil is simply a categorical imperative, irrespective of whether it produces positive or even negative outcomes. At best, it is assumed that some vague and nondescript 'good society' will emerge automatically from these processes, although what that is and what it looks like is scarcely discussed. Almost always, it is imagined merely as the world we currently inhabit, minus the evils with which the various anti-policies are preoccupied. It is unsurprising that this preoccupation with fighting against the negative comes to dominate the world of art and antiquities, given that we live in a society where art itself has become reduced to a utilitarian object of financial investment for the few, despite the residual tensions and appeals to its higher functions and the difficulties inherent in attaching a price to the invaluable.

Compliance, defiance, and the quest for purity

Legal scholarship on regulations (Vadi & Schneider, 2014; Wiktor-Mach, 2019; Baranello, 2021), paying little attention to socio-cultural context, has failed to interrogate the compliance industry, the commodification of regulation, or how this commodification shapes post-national and privatized forms of criminal justice (Nieto Martín, 2022). In other words, it has ignored the multi-billion-dollar industry in the business of *translating regulations into commodities* – consultancy services, legal intelligence, background checks, training courses, certifications, authentication, verification, screening services, regulatory technologies (RegTech) – that *promise* to *ensure* legal, regulatory, and ethical compliance, fight crime and 'do good'. Trade in art, antiquities and luxury collectibles is still a recent addition to these portfolios, but we already see compliance actors proliferating, stimulated by the financialization of art and luxury assets (Taylor, 2011), from big players such as Deloitte, LexisNexis Regulatory Compliance, Refinitiv Risk Intelligence, Thompson Reuters CLEAR and Regulation and Compliance Management, to more specialized players, such as FCS Compliance, Arcarta: Art Market Due Diligence Platform, ArtAML, Art World Compliance, Comply Advantage, and others. These actors are central in the mediation and shaping of regulatory compliance. We will get to these in more depth later, for now, let us look at what is at stake here from an ideological point of view.

Markets in art, antiquities, and luxury collectibles are often deemed as the 'last unregulated' markets. They are characterized as opaque, secretive, elusive, and nurturing privacy, personal relations, and informality as well as various cultural codes and cultural capital. As such, they stand in opposition to the technobureaucratic visions of the regulators, crime fighters, and of the compliance industry driven by visions of transparency, accountability, 'good governance', and very specific fantasies of 'purity'. The worlds of luxury defy the logic of compliance, not merely through the possibilities of evasion that these markets offer, but more fundamentally, they are driven by an opposing logic of transgression, excess, pleasure, secrecy and so on. By juxtaposing them, we will be able to understand how the worlds of compliance and defiance depend on each other, how they feed off each other and how they, in tandem, even where in tension, generate misery, pseudo-solutions and more incentives and opportunities for fraud, all the while disavowing and distracting from the real problems at the core. In the same way in which luxury branding promises but repeatedly fails to fill the consumer's real or manufactured lack and make them whole; the regulation – or what could even be called regulatory branding – promises to fill the 'regulatory gaps' or lack in existing regulation, and finally deliver a fully regulated and impenetrable world without (loop)holes.

Both the world of luxury and the world of compliance that seeks to regulate it can be understood as quests for *purity*, albeit in different forms. In the luxury consumer, it is a quest for direct access to pure and unadulterated enjoyment. In the sphere of regulation and compliance, it is a purification of the hidden, opaque, private, obscure, unique, and idiosyncratic. It is an attack on what defies easy categorization and that defies the now hegemonic 'cybernetic imaginary' of governance (Supiot, 2017: 30), that which cannot be assigned a 1 or a 0. Ultimately, it is an attack on culture, informality, and on the messiness of being human. This quest for purity and the fetishization of order and control manifests in the proliferation of technobureaucratic and pseudo-legal *empty ritualism*, a form of governance and regulatory *ritualism* that cultivates 'rituals of verification' that are key to audit culture (Power, 1997). Audit, 'law and ritual resemble one another' having a 'shared tendency to fetishize order' (Just, 2007: 113). As Just further observes, 'it seems possible that as societies increase in scale of size and organizational complexity they tend to rely less on legalizing ritual and more on ritualized law' (Just, 2007: 113). Today, these juridified rituals of verification increasingly coalesce with different forms of investigations and intelligence gathering for the purposes of *authentication*, verification, and the performance of due diligence and compliance. Since ritualism's answer to failure is *more* of the same ritual, these systems have a tendency to grow into monstrous proportions, into apparatuses of control now fuelled by massive amounts of data, including the 'new oil' of 'behavioural surplus' (Zuboff, 2019), resulting in new forms of uncontrollability (Rosa, 2021). Regulatory capitalism merges with surveillance capitalism.

As Mary Douglas observed, the quest for purity – which reveals itself primarily through the negative and the quest to eliminate and do away with the impure – points to how a given society and culture conceives of and reproduces social order (Douglas, 2001). Or, as Moore put it, purity 'is defined in the Hegelian manner by what purity is not, namely, impurity or pollution. Thus a morally pure person is free from moral pollution' (Moore, 2000). It is beyond doubt that *anti-policies* are neoliberal capitalism's purification and sanitization machinery. Anti-corruption measures target what they label as *dirt*, *decay*, *disease*, *cancer*, and *virus*. AML measures, for instance, target *dirty* money, be it those of oligarchs and kleptocrats or the dons of transnational organized crime, while the overlapping measures that go under the name of combatting the financing of terrorism (CFT) try to prevent money falling into the *dirty*, *dangerous*, and *evil* hands of terrorists and their helpers.

The ideological fantasy of the integrity of the financial system

It may be a simple observation that the distinction between *pure* money and *dirty* money (hence the need to *launder* money) is fundamental to our social order. But it is a significant observation and one that is, as a rule, left unquestioned. We hear time and again that corruption and money laundering are undermining the '*integrity*' of financial markets, and we should remind ourselves at this point that the word integrity stems from the Latin *integer*, meaning 'whole', 'complete', or 'untainted'. But when we hear these platitudes, do we really know what they mean? Do we stop and pause to contemplate their meaning? In failing to do so, we fail to question the basic premises of our social order. Douglas remarks that 'to be holy is to be whole, to be one; holiness is unity, integrity, perfection of the individual and of the kind' (Douglas, 2001: 55). Indeed, one could argue that in our society the ideological fantasy that underpins our social order, that needs to be reproduced and which must not be traversed is the fantasy of the *integrity of the financial system*. We may no longer believe in God, but we sure have faith in the global financial system which has come to bear the mark of the sacred (Dupuy, 2013). Whereas 'In God we trust' which is imprinted on all American coins and banknotes, the trust is increasingly to be placed in the very financial system, now worshipped by the globalized secular religion. Or else, that which must not be defiled and must be protected from the *dirty* and *tainted* money and the corruption and immoral contagion it spreads, is the financial system itself (not the citizens, for that matter).

This is also where the crux of our moral order lies: *our financial order is our social order is our moral order*. The fight against dirty money is a fight against moral impurity, which boils down to the pollution and defilement of the sacred financial system, a system that cannot and must not be questioned. Hence the policy fetishization of the (moral) distinctions between clean/dirty money, legitimate/illegitimate, formal/informal, transparent/opaque, where the dirty, the illegitimate, the informal, the opaque, the private, appear as without any redeeming cultural qualities. And how does the dirt enter into the pure system (and infect it)? Through the notorious (loop)holes. As noted in the press release from the White House on the Anti-corruption Strategy that established the fight against corruption as a core U.S. national security interest: 'The Biden-Harris Administration is committed to tackling corruption as an economic and national security priority, and has pledged to lead international efforts to bring transparency to the global financial system and close loopholes that undermine democracy.'[7]

Note that it is the *loopholes* that undermine democracy and that must be closed to once more protect the integrity of the global financial system. This closure, again, has to go with efforts to bring transparency – and what else is this quest for transparency than an act of purification? After all, as judge Louis Brandeis noted in 1914: 'Sunlight is said to be the best of disinfectants; electric light the most efficient policeman'.[8] This quest for purity and the belief that we can achieve it is at the core of the ideological reproduction of the neoliberal social order, sustained by the fantasies of compliance/defiance and purity/ danger on one hand, and the fantasy of wholeness on the other. Enforcement of these ideological fantasies takes the form of an expansive apparatus of regulation that seeks to prevent the by-default sacred, pure, and hence moral financial system from being flooded with dirty money that is compromising its integrity. Alas, as the systems architects and defenders themselves admit, the system is not perfect, but only insofar as it proves time and again to be *leaky* and full of holes through which the evil can easily penetrate. These threats appear to proliferate as the dirty money scours the global economy probing for holes and weak points in the financial system's protective fencing, thereby demanding that ever new areas of social life be securitized. This results in the proliferation of risk and threat intelligence, and surveillance apparatuses directed toward authentication and verification, and the elimination of the corrupt and of imposters, fakes, and fraudsters (T.Ø. Kuldova, 2020).

Furthermore, the neat separations between clean and dirty money have revealed themselves to be illusory at best, and the various frauds and crimes perpetrated by the giants of the financial system have undermined the credibility and explanatory power of those narratives which claim that it is the 'dirty' money *external* to the financial system that is compromising its integrity. Such issues only amplify the need for these apparatuses to balloon in size and scale in order to sustain this fantasy of an otherwise pure financial system besieged by external malevolent forces and kleptocrats. Hence the hyperactive manufacturing of new threats and risks, and the simultaneous discoveries of new or previously unnoticed holes, which are deemed as alluring and inviting for the tricksters, fraudsters, imposters, and the evil. And herein comes the trade in art, antiquities, and luxury.

Financialization and assetization of art, antiquities, and luxury

The financialization of this market has seen art and other cultural artifacts become used as objects of investment, speculation, and tax optimization, with a proliferation of supporting infrastructures such as luxury freeports, security, and financial and asset management consultants (Helgadóttir, 2020; Dörry & Hesse, 2022; Hall et al, 2022). No longer a mere object of 'conspicuous consumption' (Veblen, 1970), blue-chip art, antiquities, and luxury assets, from rare wine, whisky, classic cars, and diamonds, to watches, have become objects of what could be called 'conspicuous investment and speculation', as the wealthy seek to diversify their portfolios (Naylor, 2011). In other words, these luxury objects have become effectively 'assetized' (Birch & Muniesa, 2020), and as we shall see, this was partially enabled precisely by the commodification of the 'data exhaust' from due diligence and compliance processes. The latter were in turn a response to the proliferation of mediated corruption, fraud and crime scandals involving the art and luxury goods markets. While Peter Watson's journalistic revelations have tainted the reputation of Sotheby's and the trade in antiquities (Watson, 1997; Watson & Todeschini, 2006), authorities have uncovered the role of antiquities in terrorism financing, of art in money laundering, corruption, and more.

In light of these scandals, the art and antiquities markets have come to be seen as populated by professional *enablers* of the flow of dirty money into the financial system. This was amplified by the perception of art and antiquities as one of the last 'unregulated' markets mentioned earlier; an elite world of its own that has been largely undisturbed for centuries, operating on its own premises in the most exclusive and mysterious crevices of financial and cultural life that are governed by confidentiality, privacy, custom, and informal networks and relationships. Some have deemed the entire market to be one such dark hole in the financial system, while others insist it is a licit market, just far more susceptible than others to various holes, precisely due to its secretive nature.

Another effect of the financialization of the market in art, antiquities, and luxury collectibles has been its subjection to regulation largely modelled upon banking and financial institutions regulations, prime among these being AML with its imposition of due diligence obligations. The EU's 5th Money Laundering Directive, for example, broadened the scope of the directive to explicitly bring freeport operators and other actors in the art market within its purview. Consequently, freeports – the jurisdictions-in-jurisdictions that effectively amount to intentionally created 'holes' in the system to protect the rich from taxation and regulatory scrutiny – are now to be 'closed' through the imposition of compliance, reporting and transparency obligations. Due diligence here becomes a form of symbolic purification of the holes intentionally created by policy, and a form of *legitimation* rather than regulation (alas one that can be turned into new products, services and even sources of value on the speculative financial markets).

Eliminating dirt: privatizing and pluralizing policing and intelligence

We are, as it turns out, not really discussing the closure of any holes per se, but rather their closure to whatever is deemed as *dirty* money – hence the due diligence on source of funds and beneficial ownership, and the demand to generate 'suspicious activity reports' (SARs) (Amicelle & Iafolla, 2018). The wonderful paradox, of course, is that the very same freeport operators, auction houses, art dealers, and other intermediaries who were perceived as leaky and populated by money laundering enablers, and who therefore needed to be brought within the scope of the EU's money laundering directive, now 'take on the role of AML *gatekeepers* as they will have to report suspicious transactions to the financial intelligence units (FIUs)' (Korver, 2018: 6; emphasis ours). Under the rhetoric of compliance, this 'regulation' enlists freeport operators and art market actors as agents of private policing and intelligence gathering. Through regulation that implements compliance and due diligence, these once risky and suspect actors undergo an alchemical transformation into agents of private policing and intelligence who have to investigate, collect data and information, conduct background checks and risk assessments on their clients, and produce intelligence reports that effectively make decisions on who or what is to be deemed as risky, and thereby reported to the FIU. This is why compliance is best understood within the framework of pluralization of policing and intelligence (Verhage, 2011; Kuldova, 2022a).

The result is a proliferation of agents enlisted to police the purity/integrity of the financial system, actors who are deemed *gatekeepers* and tasked with the closing of the doors, including the doors of the (loop)holes, to those deemed dirty, risky, and threatening to the system (often the usual suspects). It does not matter that these are the same actors who were initially deemed as suspect, as enablers, and that in turn rely on service providers, such as the big audit and consultancy companies, that have been similarly implicated in a great many scandals (Mitchell & Sikka, 2011; Sikka, 2016). What allows this to happen is the cultural perception that despite these occasional failings, scandals, and revelations of fraud and crime, these predominantly Western actors can never really be systemically corrupt (unlike the kleptocratic, authoritarian, and corrupt Others). Rather, they are largely unwitting victims of crime and exploitation, and this status entitles them to be granted the role of aligned crime fighters.

This framework makes it simply unthinkable that there might be a more fundamental issue with the financial system and neoliberal capitalism; the epistemic framework will simply not allow it. Since the problem is posited as one of *nefarious external actors* (from countries pervaded by corruption) exploiting the holes in the otherwise pure and sacred system, in which they prefer to place and enjoy the proceeds of corruption, the solution that will always present itself as the most natural will be the path of control, surveillance, policing, and securitization. Furthermore, since the system is global, immensely complex, and the actual law enforcement units are underfunded, the policing and intelligence powers need to be delegated to ever more 'legitimate' actors and their agents, in both the private and public sectors. Bank employees, insurance agents, and gallerists must double-up as cops of the global economy. Just as teachers and social workers under the UK's Prevent Duty are under both a *legal* and *moral* obligation to report to police those students who they view as 'suspicious subjects' or as displaying 'red flags' of radicalization (Kaleem, 2022), so too, art gallery employees and freeport operators are to come under the dual moral and legal obligation to report the dirty and suspicious and prevent (or at least 'risk manage') their entry into the pure realm. Here, we argue, we are not dealing with any meaningful regulation *of* markets, but rather *the delegation of policing powers* to purify the market of dirty and tainted money, individuals, and now also cultural objects: only the pure are allowed to circulate (at least in the ideological fantasy, if not in reality).

This logic is also manifest in the discussions around the 'regulation' of cryptocurrencies. These markets have been notoriously linked to cybercrime, fraud, abuse, scams, Ponzi schemes, money laundering, organized crime, tax evasion, and more. They have been described as a Wild West of the economy (Mackenzie, 2022), a dirty, dangerous, and disorderly realm outside of the purview of the law, a world where anything goes and which therefore needs to be tamed.[9] Two recent enforcement actions by OFAC and FinCEN against the Virtual Currency Exchange Bittrex Inc. were for the 'apparent violations of multiple sanctions programs and wilful violations of the Bank Secrecy Act's (BSA's) AML and suspicious activity report (SAR) reporting requirements',[10] resulting in settlements of $24 million and $29 million, respectively. These enforcement actions neatly exemplify what the 'taming' of this Wild West really translates into. Namely, the compliance-driven imposition of practices, rituals, and mechanisms of self-purification on these market actors, along with comprehensive training in these compliance rituals such as the data-driven elimination of sanctioned individuals and jurisdictions, and reporting of the suspicious to the authorities. The fine is effectively a fine for the inability to self-purify, for the *failure to eliminate the dirt from within*, for the failure to screen for the sanctioned and risk-assess the potentially criminal and suspicious. This again implies that nothing is problematic with cryptocurrencies *per se*, but that it is the threats associated with nefarious actors that undermine these markets. Bittrex, like others who have been fined for sanctions and AML violations, were fined for:

> deploying inadequate and ineffective transaction monitoring on its platform resulting in significant exposure to illicit finance.

Further, Bittrex's AML program failed to appropriately address the risks associated with the products and services it offered, including anonymity-enhanced cryptocurrencies. Bittrex failed to file any SARs between February 2014 and May 2017, a period of over three years. Bittrex also failed to file SARs on a significant number of transactions involving sanctioned jurisdictions, including transactions that were suspicious above and beyond the fact that they involved a sanctioned jurisdiction.[11]

This is at the core of this form of 'regulation'. The ordinary citizen is easily misled to believe that the word 'regulation' would imply a targeting of the more fundamental problems with cryptocurrency. Alas, this would be incorrect. Instead, the regulation does precisely the opposite. The fines here can be read as a modern form of the Medieval Catholic Church's selling of indulgences, monetary payments which absolve the crypto market operators from their sinful failure to combat the evil. It is worth remembering that in the 16th century, the perception of the selling indulgences as a form of grand corruption under Pope Leo X splintered the Western church and sparked the Protestant Reformation. Nevertheless, the monetary fine, accompanied by the company's promise to '*remediate* any identified compliance *gaps*',[12] thus becomes an agent of purification which restores the integrity of the market. Remediation is a key term that is used in almost all compliance violations enforcement actions, with the remediation also counting as a mitigating factor in the size of the fine. It is a term with etymological roots in *remedie*, a 'means of counteracting sin or evil of any kind; cure for a vice or temptation',[13] one that implies the removal of something unwanted and the restoration into a proper state, herein the state of integrity, purity, wholeness, and thus health of the market.

Purging the impure and reproducing the neoliberal sacred

These fantasy systems of control fail in their stated goals, as has been shown time and again for a wide range of reasons. What comes to mind might be that delegating policing powers to those you wish to police may not be the best way to go about control. Moreover, solving the problems of market capitalism cannot be done by generating *further markets* in control and compliance and subsequently reducing these problems to the issue of corrupt, criminal, and suspect Others. The repetitive failure legitimizes their further proliferation. These architectures do succeed in the sense of being material infrastructures that reinforce this ideology and its fantasies, facilitating the systemic disavowal of the fundamental problems of capitalism and the consolidation of the hegemonic narrative. Here we see the contours of how the dynamics of compliance and defiance serve the ideological reproduction of neoliberalism. But more needs to be said. For this quest for purity is *not* benign, which is something we shall turn to later in this chapter. As Mary Douglas rightly observed:

> The quest for purity is pursued by rejection. It follows that when purity is not a symbol but something lived, it must be poor and barren. It is part of our condition that the purity for which we strive and sacrifice so much turns out to be hard and dead as a stone when we get it. It is all very well for the poet to praise winter as the:

> > 'Paragon of art,
> > That kills all forms of life and feeling
> > Save what is pure and will survive.'
> >
> > (Roy Campbell)

> … Whenever a strict pattern of purity is imposed on our lives it is either highly uncomfortable or it leads into contradiction if closely followed leads to hypocrisy. That which is negated is not thereby removed. The rest of life, which does not tidily fit the accepted categories, is still there and demands attention. (Douglas, 2001: 162–5)

The quest for moral purity has been linked to violent persecutions, such as in the Inquisition, the French Revolution, the Nazi concentration camps, or Stalinist purges (Moore, 2000). As Moore shows, in the case of the French Revolution, 'the radical impulse destroyed itself because it had no goal except moral purity and no way of getting there except the guillotine' (Moore, 2000: 76), or to quote his point at length:

> In the case of the French revolutionary radicals there is, in reaction against the prevailing aristocratic culture, more stress on an antiseptic moral purity and its allegedly innocent contentment. For Robespierre, then, purity and vertu represent both proper revolutionary behavior and the kind of society expected to result from the Revolution. Their opposites constitute the obstacles to revolutionary objectives. Here purity becomes the more significant notion. Purity is a separating idea that implies the existence of impurity. Impurity takes the form, among others, of corruption, and corruption is a favorite negative term in Robespierre's vocabulary. What is impure is also repulsive and to be avoided. One should not have anything to do with an individual whose revolutionary purity is suspect. *Indeed corruption and other forms of impurity, like rotten timbers in a ship, should be cut out and destroyed to preserve the sound parts of the structure.* This destruction, actually of human

lives, not mere wood, amounts to the ultimate separation of pure from impure. With appalling consistency, Robespierre the Incorruptible pursued this logic of moral purity to its only possible end: his own destruction and that of the revolution he led. (Moore, 2000: 77–8)

As Moore argued, the ideology of moral purity is an invention of monotheism, one that we could argue in the light of our discussion, has clearly not vanished with secularization. The progressive secularization and moral fragmentation of society thus appears to have accelerated in parallel with the neoliberal *sacralization* of finance and with the offloading of the *sacred*, the *pure* and the *moral* onto the market. We are not the first to note the neoliberal sacralization of the market (Mavelli, 2020). But what has been typically overlooked are precisely the forms of *the purging of the impure on which the reproduction of this neoliberal sacred depends* and which are key to neoliberal regulation and governance *as* 'securitized and criminalized compliance' (Kuldova, 2022a). Alas, where the ideal of moral purity was once pursued through violent purges, we encounter it now more often in its 'pseudo-pacified' (Hall & Wilson, 2014) form, precisely in the shape of the regulatory, technobureaucratic, and policing architectures and products built to protect the integrity of the financial system and purge it of the dirty. Pseudo-pacification works to transform actual violence into its symbolic and systemic form, while ensuring that it shall remain economically functional, and keep on stimulating sociosymbolic competition (Horsley et al, 2015; Kotzé & Lloyd, 2022). At the same time, this pseudo-pacification of moral purging through the compliance-industrial complex not only exerts new forms violence, but can be simultaneously interpreted as a response to the progressive breakdown of the pseudo-pacification process, which 'creates a latently criminogenic climate in which some individuals are willing to inflict harm on others in the process of furthering their own self-interests' (Kotzé & Lloyd, 2022: 39). As this dynamic escalates, manifesting itself in the proliferation of risks, threats, criminal scenarios and so on, the pseudo-pacified control and regulatory structures which are aimed at the elimination of impurities from the markets also become more vigorous. In a dialectical fashion, compliance and defiance become generative of the very criminogenic forces upon which the reproduction of the ideological fantasy of the neoliberal system rests. As Kotzé and Lloyd write in their exposition of ultra-realist criminological theory,

The common mistake is to view these breaches, or what Hall (2014) refers to as 'spillage', as erupting against a backdrop of civility and peacefulness, a kind of non-violent zero level (Žižek, 2009). The reality, of course, is that they erupt against a backdrop of intense objective violence inherent in the 'normal', smooth functioning of global capitalism … objective violence is hardwired into the capitalist system and manifests in ruthlessly aggressive, but often rule-bound, sociosymbolic competition. As over-stimulated drives and desires crystallise in an ultra-competitive world, we now find ourselves inhabiting a social terrain occupied by a society of enemies (Hall, 2012b). In this socially atomised environment, everyone is considered a threat and every social encounter is potentially risky business as we attempt to successfully navigate our way through permanent social competition. (Kotzé & Lloyd, 2022: 38)

The question is, what kind of a world is this quest to eliminate the impure and the filthy, as it is defined by the anti-policies, actually creating? What characterizes the apparatuses used to enforce this order and what logics underpin them? It is precisely here, following this introductory exposition, that we must turn to the market in art, antiquities, and luxury collectibles. These markets are pervaded by tensions between the logic of art and the logic of commerce and money. The tension between the sacred and the profane; the qualitative and the quantitative; and the inalienable, priceless, and immeasurable against the logic of commodification, marketization, and the expression of value in monetary terms. These are tensions which are often resolved through symbolic, narrative, and cultural means that mediate between these logics, translating one realm into the other (Velthuis, 2005).

Moreover, if we instead accept the thesis that the financial system has become our sacred that relies on the dynamics of purification, we could rather argue that art, luxury, and antiquities cultivate an opposing conception of the sacred. Namely, that of the 'filthy sacred' (Pfaller, 2008), one that is capable of *sublimating* the dangerous, the dirty, the polluting, and turning it into something sacred and beautiful. It is this filthy sacred, and the cultural capacity for sublimation, that finds itself under double assault in this realm. First from commodification and financialization, and secondly from the technobureaucratic apparatuses of the compliance-industrial complex where, as we shall see, the vision of purity is a total vision of socio-technical engineering (Frischmann & Selinger, 2018), of being and acting like a machine, a vision of an impoverished life as survival, a life dehumanized (Kuldova, 2022b). What is at stake if we allow the logic of the pure sacred, translated into the technobureaucratic and totalitarian apparatuses of compliance, reign supreme and unfold into excess? Our contention would be that it is our humanity, freedom, and creativity, that is at stake. What is being undermined is our quest for a positive vision of society in which we can live lives that are meaningful, beautiful, and good. Worse, it is that such quests are deemed as hopelessly naïve, romantic, unrealistic, and dangerous.

The 'filthy' markets in art, antiquities, and luxury collectibles

As mentioned earlier, the art, antiquities, and luxury markets are popularly seen as sites of fraud and illicit dealings, and as markets flooded by forgeries, scams, counterfeits, and looted antiquities. Their air of elitism inspires cynicism from onlookers, viewing them as a facilitator of tax evasion, naked speculation, and dirty dealings, as evidenced by the popularity of YouTube videos such as 'The Art Market is a Scam (And Rich People Run It)',[14] which has been viewed 1.8 million times, or 'Fine Art Isn't About Art. It's About Evading Taxes' viewed over 600,000 times.[15] Only a few outsiders to the market appear to sympathize with the 'non-ideal victims' of art fraud: the greedy, naïve, and easy to fool rich in search of status, distinction, and the burning of their excessive funds (Mazurek, 2019). On the contrary, there is pleasure, *Schadenfreude*, when a rich man is fooled by the forger, with the added pleasure of realizing that the emperor is naked. Indeed, 'the perception that participation in legal sales in the art market is inherently foolish because of its astronomical prices' (Mazurek, 2019: 425) is also often shared by law enforcement agencies, who Mazurek (2019) argues do not take these crimes seriously, often lacking dedicated police forces – with the well-known exceptions of the Italian Carabinieri Art Squad, and similar but still fairly small units in France, the US, the UK, the Netherlands, and elsewhere. In most countries such specialized forces are kept small and underfunded, permanently threatened by budgetary cuts and dissolution, with the police in need to prioritize other crimes that are more important to the public at large (Kerr, 2016). If art crime is prioritized at all, attention of law enforcement agencies tends to be drawn towards the issues of the day and political import, such as protection of (national) cultural heritage, looted antiquities, and terrorism financing, or other cases valuable for the purposes of cultural diplomacy. Art fraud *within* these elitist markets, not to mention the frauds *of* the elites, often goes under the radar. These crimes are also underreported, part of the 'dark figure' of crime that escapes official statistics, and cases are resolved more often than not through private investigations and settlements, or by means that avoid legal proceedings altogether (Kerr, 2016; Chappell & Polk, 2019; Mazurek, 2019).

Despite the general lack of enforcement, in recent decades the markets in art, antiquities, and luxury collectibles have been increasingly associated with different forms of crime. The ethics and 'lawful but awful' practices of museums, collectors, art dealers, and auction houses have been called into question just as much as illegal activity, such as in the case of the Panama Papers, revelations about the art market's offshore 'secrets' (Ruiz, 2016). While these 'secrets' did not come as a surprise and merely confirmed what was already suspected, they nevertheless stimulated popular calls for art and luxury market transparency and accountability, as well as the progressive transformation of voluntary standards and soft forms of self-regulation into harder forms of regulation. Moreover, private actors providing services within security, investigations, intelligence, legal, and insurance services found new markets and created new products commodifying these regulations (Pryor, 2016).

At the same time, large market actors have made great efforts to improve their image. Through different forms of self-regulation, voluntary standards, and due diligence practices, they have endeavoured to distance themselves from 'tainted' market actors as well as 'tainted' artworks, antiquities, and luxury objects. They have also lobbied to become subject to the regulatory gaze of the state. As Pryor argued, 'key art market players and trade bodies have played an influential role in the progression of specialist legislation and advocating for greater law enforcement resources' (Pryor, 2016: 157). The realities of 'nodal', 'networked', or otherwise 'blurred' forms of governance mean not only that distinctions between the private and public are increasingly hard to draw, but it becomes increasingly difficult to distinguish between the governing and the governed.

The state as a purifying machine

Nevertheless, it can still be argued that the state is necessary in that it acts as a *superior* purifying machine, an arbiter of that which shall be deemed il/licit and bad/good. If there is something that business desires from the state, that which it wishes to possess, it is precisely this quality and authority that underpins the state's legitimate use of force, which has been culturally associated with the state since its very emergence. Within this cultural imaginary, the market is deemed filthy by default and as such depends for its purification on the state, which is imagined as pure by default. Just think of how the corruption discourse reproduces this imaginary. While the public sector is often positioned as a prime locale at risk of corruption, the demands and expectations of the integrity of public officials are far higher, and it is these individuals who can *be corrupted* by the offerings and temptations of the private sector (suggesting their purity as a default). The private has for a long time been cast as dirty in relation to the public. And while there have been similarly powerful competing notions of the inherent morality of the market, the private is revealed time and again as dependent on the sanctification from the state in order to appear as clean and legitimate.

This sanctification takes the shape of regulation. This is becoming even more important now as the thesis of the inherent morality of the markets is becoming difficult to sustain. The market, in order to reproduce its claims to morality and 'integrity', thus depends on the manufacturing of external 'bad actors' and internal 'bad apples', both of which 'pervert' and 'undermine' the otherwise moral and good system. The manufacturing of criminal and security risks and threats, the manufacturing of morality (that depends on the figure of the criminal Other), serves the same function. This is indeed not to say that there is no crime, or no corruption, but that the crime and corruption as they are framed and sought combatted serve profound ideological functions.

As Laporte opens his *History of Shit*: 'without a master, one cannot be cleaned. Purification, whether by fire or by the word, by baptism or by death, requires submission to the law' (Laporte, 2000: 2). Despite often giving the impression of resisting regulation, market actors often lobby for, demand, and desire their own subjection to the law (especially if on their terms). While we often hear complaints about and resistance to new regulation from industry, there are parallel and more interesting complaints about the *lack* of interest from the police and politicians to police and regulate the markets, or else about the disinterest of the state to 'co-produce' the policing of the market jointly with its actors (see for instance the positions discussed in Kerr, 2016). Regulation translates for the market actors into being seen by the state, police, and the law; and into acquiring and strengthening their appearance of legitimacy and licitness. The state also delegates policing and intelligence gathering powers to market actors – through AML, sanctions, anti-corruption, and related due diligence obligations – allowing them to fashion themselves as legitimate and licit actors fighting bad and illicit actors, and as partners to the state in its crime-fighting mission.

Regulation enables the market actors to police the critical boundary between the licit and the illicit in their own interest, hence the largely discretionary determinations of what and who counts as risk and risky, as a threat, or as illicit and illegitimate. The state, through its regulatory and policing powers, acts as a purifying agent (Laporte, 2000), whose symbolic power does not diminish but rather increases as it simultaneously co-opts and lets itself be co-opted by networked governance and the dispositifs of criminalized and securitized compliance (Haugh, 2017; Kuldova, 2022a). This serves the economic interests of capital first and foremost, and keeps making the rich richer and the poor poorer, while distributing policing powers and delivering moral absolutions.

The expansive universe of risks and regulations

Let us now look more closely at the actual crime scenarios that shape the 'risk universe', as compliance professionals like to call it, when it comes to art, antiquities, and luxury collectibles. The following account will be sweeping, crafted to bombard the reader with all possible crime scenarios, thereby simulating the experience of *being overwhelmed* by the proliferating threats and regulatory risks such as fines for compliance failures. Professionals in private security, compliance, intelligence, and due diligence are similarly both bombarded by and bombarding their (potential) clients with updates on crimes, fines, enforcement actions, regulatory changes, and latest policy discussions. Regular exposure to training on new and emerging risk, crime, and threat scenarios, including those stemming from new regulations, is at the heart of compliance training, certifications, webinars, and conferences. Of course, all of these events typically conclude with a sales pitch for products supposed to mitigate these risks and alleviate this sense of being overwhelmed. What follows, therefore, are selected iconic examples that are used time and again in these settings to expand the imaginary of risk, to generate a sense of permanent threat, and finally, to sell surveillance, compliance, security, intelligence, and other products to address these risks and pre-empt crimes and security threats, as well as problematic and potentially unethical actions that could result in reputational damage.

The expansion of the 'compliance-industrial complex' into the art and antiquities markets is still rather recent. Compliance – modelled on the banking sector and financial industry – expands progressively into new domains, which is a further indicator of its true status as a market-making apparatus rather than a purely 'ethical' one. Its expansion into the art and antiquities market makes is both revealing and interesting because the practices, procedures and habits of thinking associated with the logic of compliance have not yet been fully embraced by actors in these markets. The growth of the compliance market in this sector is a direct response to the incorporation of art market participants under *EU's Fifth Money Laundering Directive (EU) 2015/849*, the inclusion of dealers in antiquities in the US via the *Anti-Money Laundering Act 2020* under the *Bank Secrecy Act (BSA)*, the current *EU Commission's proposal for a Directive on Corporate Sustainability Due Diligence, Regulation (EU) 2019/880* of the European Parliament to the *Responsible Art Market Initiative (RAM) guidelines, OECD Due Diligence Guidance for Responsible Business Conduct*, ISO compliance management and anti-corruption standards and to corporate ethical guidelines, codes of conduct, best practices and zero tolerance strategies, which come atop anti-corruption legislation, the *1970 UNESCO Convention*, the *1995 UNIDROIT Convention on Stolen or Illegally Exported Cultural Objects*, and more.

With the war in Ukraine and the concerns about the ill-begotten luxury assets of the kleptocrats, we also see more calls for the targeting of 'tainted' objects coming from the anti-corruption organizations. Transparency International (TI), summarizing its International Anti-Corruption Day 2022, demanded again more transparency and the closure of loopholes, but also argued that it is 'high time to get serious about creating unified asset registries to record the real owners of properties, luxury goods and other high-value assets – and build the path towards a global asset register'.

Continuing its commentary, TI argued that 'The REPO task force should expand current coordination efforts to trace assets of other kleptocrats and individuals involved in grand corruption, making the multilateral task force a permanent body.'[16] The creation of databases and registers and the tracking of 'tainted objects', be these associated with corruption and kleptocrats, or be they illicitly excavated, exported, stolen, fake, and so on, is a key part of the expanding security and governance agendas. These efforts are also a result of the compliance and audit lobby for more regulation (which translates into more markets) on the terms of these 'regulatory intermediaries' – this often means soft and symbolic regulation, generative of endless and inconsequential paper trail (Frasen & LeBaron, 2019). But let us now turn to the 'risk universe' that both feeds and perpetually evades these regulatory efforts.

Art thefts and looting: from 'tainted objects' to the compliance industry

The *thefts* of art, antiquities, and luxury goods are viewed as a growing threat – hence the need for high-tech security, storage systems, freeports, and privacy. Widely shared threat scenarios by the compliance and security industry are often narratively prefaced by iconic thefts, suggestive both of continuity and expansion of this threat universe. There is the theft of Mona Lisa in 1911 by the Louvre employee Vincenzo Perrugia; the theft of Francisco de Goya's portrait of the Duke of Wellington by John Bunton in 1961, who wished to draw attention to the plight of pensioners and oppressive TV licensing fees and led to the Theft Act of 1968. The theft of works by Edgar Degas, Rembrandt and Vermeer from the Isabella Stewart Gardner Museum in 1990 are often mentioned as well, with the museum still offering a $10 million reward for information leading to their recovery[17] (Boser, 2010). The theft of paintings by J.M.W. Turner from Tate Britain while on loan at the Schirn Kunsthalle in Frankfurt in 1994, and the theft of The Scream by Edvard Munch in 1994 from the National Gallery in Oslo are also noteworthy cases, and we could list more (Fletcher, 2016). From these iconic thefts we move to the more recent ones where private collectors are targeted and often go unreported; this adds to the ominous sense of threat and risk. One can just consult headlines such as 'The 25 Greatest Art Heists of All Times'[18] or watch some of the popular documentaries on art thefts, with the iconic unsolved thefts standing out in the popular imagination, to get a sense of this discourse (Olivieri, 2019). Art thefts of course take different forms and shapes, with different motivations and threat actors lurking behind them. This lends itself to analysis and categorization (see for instance Chappell & Polk, 2019), something which is also prevalent in the context of risk training and threat assessments.

Art thefts feature prominently in the imaginary of the art market, firmly establishing the fundamental links between art and crime. Art thefts are also important in so far as the discussions around the dark figure of this crime and the ever-present risks of art theft fuel the growth of high-end security industry, art insurance industry, and markets for private investigations, or else, 'cultural security' (Nemeth, 2007). These market providers entrench the vision of security and surveillance measures, of gating and *hiding* of art and antiquities in secure and private locations as the *ultimate* solution, that is in locations such as freeports, yachts, or art storage warehouses. These industries, themselves often associated with corruption and at times considered as enablers, are legitimized through their services mitigating the risk of theft. Private collectors, hotels, and auction houses are being promised 'museum-grade security' vis-à-vis the threats posed by art theft, and reminded that only 3–4 per cent of stolen art is recovered.[19]

The focus on anti-theft measures and, by extension, crime fighting also enables these actors to take centre stage in what is deemed the 'co-production' and 'nodal governance' of policing of art theft, a framework that 'allows the public police to use other nodes to do much of the policing for them, but, crucially, still be involved when it is appropriate even if other public or private nodes are producing, directing, or executing certain aspects of the securitization and policing' (Kerr, 2016: 151).

This is of importance in so far as the services of the private security and intelligence industries are increasingly indispensable to the compliance sector. While anti-theft measures may appear as straightforward and indeed reasonable, be it the use of security guards, security systems, protective glass and so on, even here we see a move from reactive and passive to pre-emptive and proactive forms of security, including pre-emptive risk profiling of visitors, the use of 'intelligent' cameras, and so on. Overall, it is a move away from the logic of protection of property to the more proactive measures to *prevent* potential security threats before they have a chance to occur (McCulloch & Wilson, 2016). The same logic is replicated across all levels of crime fighting that can be linked to these markets.

The related looting of art and antiquities is another major preoccupation. From the figure of the art thief – who can even appear glamorous in cinema – we move to figures of evil: Nazis looting art, ISIS looting antiquities in Iraq and Syria[20] to fund its terrorist actions while also destroying historical sites, and other transnational organized crime groups that have been proven to be involved in the illicit antiquities markets, from drug lords in Latin America to warlords in Somalia or Afghanistan (Hardy, 2020). Colonial era looting and historical and contemporary cultural thefts also increasingly capture the imagination of the larger public. These historical legacies and past crimes merge in the discourse with contemporary looting of antiquities by terrorists, criminals, and others supplying the elitist collector markets.

While we see an intensified public discussion and mediatization surrounding these crimes, they are not new to experts and in academia. Nearly half a century ago in 1975, Bonnie Burnham was already writing of an art market in crisis, plagued by thefts, forgeries, smuggling, destruction, and looting, as much as by greed, cynical materialism, and the reduction of art to investment and its consequent degradation. As she put it, 'this malaise' (the crimes in the art world), is 'the result of the current confusion between the material and the spiritual value of artworks, [and] can easily be recognized as the force behind the illicit market and the destruction it causes' (Burnham, 1975: 240). She observed then that

> At a time when museums were condemned for buying Haçilar ware, Sotheby's was selling it openly, illustrated in its sales catalogue. Similarly, smuggled Cypriot figurines, Hellenistic jewellery, Russian icons, Japanese idols, and Benin bronzes (and fakes of all of these) come up so frequently that art price publications have become a standard looter's index to what kind of objects he commissions to be looted. The auction house has no interest in the moral implications of such a practice, and provides, in its unbiased system, a framework for selling anything to which the owner has convincing local title. In assuming such a role, the auction also offers a respectable locality where no one would hesitate to buy. The buyer can legitimately say that anything he bought in London comes from a 'European collection'. Generally he does not know otherwise. (Burnham, 1975: 205–6)

What *is* new, then? Arguably, it is the larger awareness about these issues, the proliferation of (self)regulation to remedy these issues, the increased moralization of this subject, and the creation of dedicated markets for combatting these crimes that are deemed to 'undermine the integrity of the market'. More than anything, what is new is the hyper-active manufacturing of various means to cover and coat these matters in layers of ethical and due diligence procedures, standards, and best practices. It is the enlistment of market actors in crime fighting and purifying the market in which they operate; the very same market actors who constructed the economic means for this 'malaise' to grow by transforming our cultural relationship to art into an economic one, reducing art to an investment asset and chopping up pieces of art to facilitate fractional art investing in the same way a corporation is divided up into shares. What is also rather new is the larger public debate about prominent cases of 'problematic' and 'unethical' provenance, calls for decolonizing the museums (Lee, 2022), as well as mediated legal battles over repatriation which increasingly shape museum politics in the West. This has resulted in museums having to develop and embrace new ethical codes of conduct and audit procedures.

But these issues also increasingly capture popular imagination. In an October 2022 episode of the popular television show *Last Week Tonight*, the British-American political satirist John Oliver took on Western museums and auction houses, looted antiquities, and their more than questionable practices.[21] The 2022 Bollywood movie *Ram Setu*, opened with the destruction of the Buddhas of Bamiyan in 2001 on the order of Taliban and evolved into an epic on the importance of protection of cultural heritage. A better-known Hollywood equivalent to *Ram Setu* might be the 2014 movie, *The Monuments Men*. Directed by George Clooney and featuring an illustrious cast of the likes of Matt Damon, Bill Murray, John Goodman, Cate Blanchett, and Hugh Bonneville, the film is loosely based on the activities of the Monuments, Fine Arts, and Archives Program (MFAA) in World War II which sought to address Nazi looting during the war and invokes similar themes and messages on the sacred nature and importance of art and cultural heritage. In Russia, one could follow a 2002 TV series called *Special Department*, about the heroic FSB officers working to prevent the smuggling of antiquities, Russian art, and other national treasures out of the country, promising elegant investigations of elegantly conceived scams.[22] Concerns about crime in the art world and looted heritage are becoming mainstream, utilized not only in both in identity politics and ultra-nationalist agendas, but also fuelling the global business nexus of surveillance, compliance, and audit that shapes, both covertly and overtly, much of the present regulation.

Interestingly, while Burnham correctly locates the causes for this 'malaise' and corruption of the art world, she ends on a pessimistic note that rather precisely prefigures these developments. After remarking that 'today we could not, even if we wanted to, return to former conditions in which art was not popular enough to draw the attention of speculators and thieves', she recommends 'some constructive actions in which all of us might engage to reduce the present crisis' (Burnham, 1975: 242). What she goes on to propose are various modes of regulation and crime fighting, along with an 'overhaul of the ethics of the art trade' (Burnham, 1975: 242). But there is a seeming breakdown in syllogism here. Initially, Burnham rightly locates the source and genesis of the art world's ethical malaise in the financialization and commodification of art and antiquities. She then goes on to argue that there is no reversing this process irrespective of our desire to do so, and that we must therefore learn to live with it. Finally, she concludes that it is possible to 'overhaul' the ethics of the art trade, despite the fact that there is no obvious syllogism between her major premise that the ethical malaise of the art world is rooted in its financialization, and her minor premise that there is no reversing this process. How can Burnham believe that it is possible to overhaul the ethics of the art world without addressing the economic issues that she conceives as a corrupting force upon the ethics of art itself? What, then, does she mean when she speaks of 'ethics'? How does she understand 'ethics' more generally and what it entails? This is an issue that we will discuss in more depth in the next chapter. Suffice to say for now that, despite appearances, this is not merely a breakdown in syllogism but is in fact reflective of a deeper malaise in how we have conceived of ethics over the past two centuries, whereby despite the quite astounding growth of business ethics (Mees, 2020), there has actually been a divorce between thinking about ethics and thinking about money (MacIntyre, 2016; see also Chapter 4).

This divorce allows for what Burnham ultimately provides us with, which is nothing more than the clearest possible formulation of *capitalist realism* in which capitalism occupies the horizons of the thinkable (Fisher, 2009), including what is thinkable about ethics. Turning back to more innocent days is impossible, and so what we are left with and the only thing we can do is to simply *manage* this malaise. Today, we see this management of malaise on steroids, precisely in the form of the proliferation of experts and markets in the management of this malaise, and megathreats created by the exploitative neoliberal capitalist system. Only audit, compliance, surveillance, crime fighting, securitization of society (Schuilenburg, 2011) and allusions to empty ethics can 'manage' to save us, we are told. In other words – new modes of privatized and pluralized policing and bureaucratic control overlaid by empty 'ethics' and moralizing (rather than morality). Despite the simultaneous talk of total elimination, zero tolerance, and final purification, such a point is never to be reached. The question is, what shall be sacrificed on the altar of this quest and for what vision of a world?

In these discussions, both academic and popular, the 'tainted objects' thus end up in the conflict zones between what are at times aligned and at other times directly opposed discourses. Discourses around the rightful claims on the return of stolen artifacts, fantasies of national purity, and elitist protectionism and other Enlightenment-inspired discourses; discourses around identity politics, cultural diplomacy, and the economic interests of auction houses and collectors, etc. Despite the conflicts between these various positions, the overall message is that of a profound *immorality* penetrating these markets: both as they are exposed to (external) criminals and as they come to perpetuate the (internal) legacies of colonialism. Or, as John Oliver put it when discussing the looting of the Benin Bronzes: 'The British, in effect, stole and scrambled a nation's memories, he said about the looting of the Benin Bronzes. A crime so fucked up that even Black Mirror hasn't thought of it yet.'[23] The looting of the Benin Bronzes is a crime and taint that is just one among many. The explosion of concerns around the possession, acquisition, investments in and display (or hiding) of these variously 'problematic', 'illicit', 'questionable' objects is translated by the compliance, audit, and private security industries into various products that aim to control these 'risks' and 'threats', including (or likely foremost) risks of reputational damage and legal risks of criminal and civil penalties and fines. These products translate into the expansion of the purification apparatuses with all their due diligence procedures and codes of conduct, precisely to remove the taint, improve reputations and continue business as usual. The fact that these initiatives serve market interests and are designed primarily to morally purify the West and improve reputations of Western market players and institutions, becomes apparent when reading the response of the likes of Phillip Ihenacho, the director of the Edo Museum of West African Art in Nigeria, in his piece: 'Benin Bronzes: Whose Restitution is this, Anyway?' in *The Art Newspaper*,

> To date, accounts of cultural restitution have predominantly been a story about Western institutions, told from the West's perspective. The protagonists are benevolent European and North American organisations, whose virtue is manifest in their return of colonial looted objects 'for free'. The focus of Western media on this 'decolonisation' has given rise to a growing set of photo opportunities, accompanied by lengthy interviews with Western curators, followed by a few words of gratitude from 'representatives of Nigeria'. ...
>
> When the same media lens momentarily shifts to Nigeria, it does so only to find inadequacy. 'Chaos' and 'fiasco' are among the milder word choices. To these commentators, it seems fine for the West to take more than a hundred years to begin to act on restitution, but unforgivable that Nigeria does not resolve complex domestic and historical issues instantaneously. (Ihenacho, 2023)

They do little to address the injustice, and much to improve reputations of the perpetrators. What offends the public at the deepest level are the injustices, past and present, the inequalities, and the cynicism of the elites that have profited and continue to do so – as is also the case in the Benin Bronzes. But the solution, the 'best practice', we are told, is to cast the same elite actors who are time and again revealed as either source or intermediaries in many of these crimes into the role of ethical standard setters, law enforcement, and intelligence agents, and to encourage and even demand they police themselves – ethically and actually; and to give them the powers to eliminate those *they* deem unethical, problematic, or illegal and in the process recreate themselves as pure. Compliance, due diligence, ethical codes, provenance investigations, and risk assessments become the go-to solutions to address all these very different issues. Or as Pryor put it,

> If there remains disagreement as to the cause of the art world's problems with criminal activity, there is surprising consensus over one of the proposed solutions: an all-singing, all-dancing stolen art database. The

dream consists of a service that not only collates international records of stolen art onto a publicly accessible, user-friendly platform, but in which known fakes are also recorded. (Pryor, 2016: 149)

The database and the platform feature prominently in the imaginary of this form of crime fighting, and so does the idea of expanding this logic of platform and database to encompass ever more functions. Technosolutionism rules supreme (Morozov, 2013), and regulatory technologies (RegTech) are the latest invention (Barberis et al, 2019), promising to automate compliance and due diligence processes – and ethics itself; platforms and databases are the necessary precondition for these tools. We are promised a technological and even automated solution to injustice, crime, immorality, and ethical breaches – but who decides on the parameters for what the algorithm is to flag as 'risk', 'breach', 'violation', 'deviation', or 'suspicion'? All technology is political, despite what the industry would like to convince us about (Postman, 1993; Benjamin, 2019; Hong, 2020). We thus move from the stolen art databases – such as the private Art Loss Register[24] or the International Claim Database (formerly Art Claim Database)[25] by Art Recovery International, The Watch Register[26] for stolen luxury watches, the public Interpol's ID-Art mobile app[27] or the app iTPC Carabinieri – towards their integration with sanction screening databases, KYC systems, art risk assessment tools, and other art market databases, the latest being blockchain databases (Sousa & Moser, 2020). It is not only the demand for databases and platforms of all sorts that is growing in the light of these revelations. Demand for legal services in these areas is soaring as well.

Legal battles over the restitution of art works looted by the Nazis to their rightful owners and heirs are often protracted (Burris, 2020), especially since the introduction of the Washington Principles on Nazi-Confiscated Art in 1998 and the US Holocaust Expropriated Art Recovery Act of 2016. These legal battles have not only seriously enriched some lawyers, but increased the standards for due diligence pertaining to artworks that may have potentially passed through the hands of the Nazis. One may cynically argue that World War II restitutions has become a multi-million-dollar business in its own right. Georgina Adam of *The Art Newspaper* described this as 'a new breed of Nazi "bounty hunters", lawyers who see potential rich pickings in finding works of art that can then be claimed as war loot' (Adam, 2006). There is much that could be said about the moral and legal elitist battles over luxury goods and their spoils that are fought between museums, collectors, auction houses, and the rightful heirs. For us, it is the potential Nazi-looted provenance that adds another layer of 'taint' and illicitness to the objects that circulate in these markets and to the perceptions of these markets that is of interest. These cases are often complicated, and it is not our aim here to comment on their materiality. But what they reveal rather clearly is that current cultural perspective dictates that it is only through resorting to *legal* and *archival expertise*, through the performance of due diligence (and ideally through the closure of any possible gaps in provenance, through the achievement of 'pristine provenance') that a market actor can cleanse themselves in moral terms. Indeed, as Christopherson remarks,

> due diligence to establish clean provenance has become a requirement of both museums and other potential purchasers, who require assurance against the taint of previous illegal excavation, export, dispossession or sale. Good provenance and the fruits of due diligence have therefore grown to have a direct and significant effect on desirability, saleability and value of the objects concerned. (Christopherson, 2016: 142)

Ethical and moral purification appears to be culturally increasingly linked to legalistic, expert and data-driven procedures which can either guarantee desired purity/authenticity or serve to absolve one of any association with the impure. Ethics, however, is almost entirely eviscerated of substantive content, reduced to compliance with codes, guidelines, and procedural steps despite the repeated insistence on not falling for the 'box-ticking exercise' (an oft-repeated trope, which translates into new markets for 'outside of the box' solutions). While one could argue that for many market actors these procedures in practice boil down to the pragmatic issues of 'good title' and clearing of sound investments, the moral and cultural dimensions of these practices should not be underestimated. They are key to the making of new forms of value and to assetization of luxury collectibles (and other things). The notion of 'good title' can be read as one of the constitutive legal fictions without which capitalism as we know it would not be possible, along with property rights, contract law or corporate law etc. (Pistor, 2019). While it is recognized that the creation of wealth rests upon these legal fictions, and their skilful legal manipulation, regulation still tends to be imagined as a force restricting and putting a break on the excesses of the system. But as we shall see, it is indispensable to the creation of value and new products. Viewing regulation through this common-sense lens would be to completely miss the ways in which *regulatory fictions* have become a new source of revenue, not only for the compliance industry, but also for the regulated. The creation of value and new revenue streams relies precisely on the power to demarcate the line between the licit and the illicit, and to accumulate moral capital and reputation while projecting trustworthiness (increasingly reliant on tech solutions).

The spectre of the Nazi evil haunts the art market, but it also enables it in some ways to insert itself into the distribution of justice and the reparations of historical injustices and crimes against humanity. The taint here is also an opportunity: the fight against this historical taint can transform into a moral legitimatory project and has the potential to recast actors within the market as not only legitimate but also as *good*. Think, for instance, of all the settlements outside of the legal system which cast the market actors as capable of delivering justice based on 'doing the right thing' and displaying care for victims, precisely where the legal system would end up in protracted legal battles.

But it is not only the Nazis haunting these markets. Terrorists and non-state armed groups – particularly in Iraq, Syria, Libya, and Yemen – as well as other organized crime groups, drug traffickers and arms smugglers fuel the 'grey' or 'dirty' economy of the antiquities trade and plunder for profit (for example, Brodie & Tubb, 2002; Mackenzie, 2011; Manacorda & Chappell, 2011; Dietzler, 2013; Hufnagel & Chappell, 2019). Spectacular cases reveal the complicity of antiquities dealers in the looting of antiquities, the laundering of provenance, and the use of freeports to cover up their illicit dealings have heightened and continue to increase the awareness around these issues (Noce, 2022b, 2022c). The well-known 'Medici Conspiracy' is one such case (Watson & Todeschini, 2006), as well as the ongoing global investigation into an international antiquities trafficking ring resulting in indictment of dealers, curators, and collectors in Paris and Germany, and seizures of Egyptian artefacts. The looting of antiquities, smuggling, illicit excavations and export, theft of culture, and so on by ISIS to raise funds for terror activities is by now well documented, from intelligence and other governmental reports[28] to academic writing (Campbell, 2013; Hardy, 2020; Almohamad, 2021). In light of these revelations, FinCEN[29] included those dealing in antiquities under the Bank Secrecy Act (BSA), imposing due diligence and suspicious activity reporting obligations on antiquities dealers pertaining to countering terrorism financing, sanctions, and AML (the same which already applies to precious metals, stones, and jewels[30]). These themes have also been quickly translated into compliance training by major vendors. The Association of Certified Financial Crime Specialists (ACFCS), to give one example, has run training webinars such as *The Art of the Steal – Fincrime Risks in Art and Antiquities*; *Terrorist Finance and Criminal Network Links: Findings on Antiquities Looting from Syria and Iraq*; and *Antiquities Trafficking: The Illicit Trade Fuelling Terrorism and Organized Crime*, which, mirroring the regulatory imperatives and turning these into commercial products, draw the art and antiquities markets into the world of financial and compliance investigations. Here, the art historical notions of provenance smoothly integrate and transform into the logic of financial investigations and intelligence, mirroring detective and intelligence work. Non-profit organizations such as The Antiquities Coalition and the Clooney Foundation for Justice, which has published a report on Conflict Antiquities,[31] have made appearances within these training videos and across platforms. The former has also partnered with Manchester CF, a financial intelligence training firm, to deliver training within the framework of financial crime certification,[32] framing the issue again in terms of market exploitation and the need to fight bad actors. The training session by ACFCS mentioned earlier, *The Art of the Steal*, for instance, opened with the following quote, which is also found on the website of the Antiquities Coalition:

> The U.S. government and private sector must work together to bar criminals from exploiting the $28.3 billion American art market – the largest unregulated market in the world – or risk serious consequence for the country's national security and economic integrity, as well as legitimate collectors, dealers, auction houses, and museums – The Antiquities Coalition Financial Task Force.[33]

This highlights again the framing of this issue in terms of 'national security' and 'economic integrity' being at stake, and posing risks for legitimate actors.

In this and similar training sessions, following short introductions to antiquities looting, terrorism financing, and organized crime groups (OCGs), time is typically spent discussing how terrorists and OCGs whitewash illicit objects through the layering of transactions and the skilful manufacturing of synthetic (fake) documentation: documentation such as certificates of authenticity, import and export licenses, and historical documentation and provenance. Attention is given to the witting and unwitting complicity of certain antiquities dealers and even experts in manufacturing such documents, pointing to the difficulty of distinguishing the fake from the authentic, a problem that is particularly difficult when it comes to objects that have been dug out of the ground and are appearing on the market for the first time. From here, one moves quite quickly into questions of legal and reputational risks to market participants. The focus is shifted to the ways in which one can prevent being exploited by these bad actors and money launderers who take advantage of the 'regulatory gaps' and 'vulnerability' of the market, thus making market participants unwittingly complicit in war crimes and crimes against humanity. The solution presented to address these problems, as readers by now will have predicted, is due diligence, investigation, and more intelligence work.

With the expansion of the AML, CFT, anti-corruption, and sanctions frameworks, this means no longer merely due diligence in the form of provenance research on the object itself. It requires KYC risk intelligence screening, enhanced due diligence, the use of open-source intelligence, and diverse sanctions and PEP (politically exposed persons) screening tools. These tools – such as Sayari,[34] Lexis Nexis Risk Solutions,[35] or World Check by Refinitiv[36] (previously Thompson Reuters) – also include the screening of criminal databases where available, adverse media, social media, and more, able to generate dossiers on both individuals and companies, generating risk flags, and manufacturing suspicion. Such dossiers have been shown to be notoriously flawed, resulting in new forms of harms and injustices, creating suspicious and risky individuals and entities through associations and correlations generated by proprietary and black-boxed algorithms (Pasquale, 2015; Brayne, 2021). This suspicion need not be proven in any way since it is merely a 'suspicion'. But these suspicions can have material consequences; the same tools are used in policing, hiring, insurance, bank loans, and more (for discussion on this see, for example, O'Neil, 2016; Besteman & Gusterson, 2019; Brayne, 2021; Kuldova, 2022a). While these techniques of open-source intelligence and screening may be new to the art and antiquities worlds, they are being smoothly integrated into the pre-existing practices of provenance research, which in itself has become more and more encompassing and reliant on forensics, data, and other evidence-driven practices (Tompkins, 2020).

The logic of private security and intelligence can thus be smoothly integrated into pre-existing practices of pre-acquisition and sales due diligence. The provenance of the object is complemented by the provenance of funds and by more thorough investigations into the client. The various art market guidelines created by the Responsible Art Market Initiative[37] are a good example of this smooth integration of the relatively new practices into the pre-existing logic of art historical provenance research. What is new here, however, is not that these practices are driven by the desire to protect oneself *from* legal risks and *from* fraud in high-value purchases in the spirit of *caveat emptor*, but that they are both legal and moral obligation geared towards the *manufacturing* of suspicion and risk in the name of crime fighting, along with potentially actionable intelligence for law enforcement agencies. It is precisely this perspectival shift that is central to the 'regulation' through anti-policies, where more and more market actors and private and public organizations and institutions are to be enlisted in the manufacturing of intelligence for crime fighting, and encouraged to utilize all possible intelligence gathering possibilities they may have, both through private service providers and by virtue of the information to which they have access or encounter as part of their daily operations.

Social research itself has not been immune to this drive. This goes particularly for research within the field of looted antiquities, where a number of archaeologists-turned-criminologists have increasingly styled themselves along the lines of private sector investigators as researchers-cum-intelligence analysts, delivering actionable insights on criminal trafficking of illicit antiquities for law enforcement and for evidence-based policy. Even the drive towards open access publishing and open data in science has become progressively equated with open-source intelligence analysis, where the researcher becomes an intelligence analyst in service of the crime fighting agenda, rather than a scholar attempting to understand and critically engage with, among other things, the very notion of crime fighting in this area, or the actors involved in these crimes. Instead, one becomes driven by the intelligence quest to identify suspicious actors and supply data to the authorities. To take an example, Samuel Hardy precisely argues for 'innovative assemblages' and the role of private, non-profit, academic, and public actors in crime fighting, and in that effort also moves smoothly from a discussion of 'open science' to 'open-source research', concluding with the following:

> Open-source research may be key in corroborating novel studies that document new evidence for long-disputed phenomena. Thereby, it may change approaches to policing, which, for instance, long denied the possibility of theft-to-order, thus hamstringing investigations into cases of theft-to-order. Critically, then, it may contribute to risk analyses for money laundering and terrorism financing/conflict financing with art and antiquities ... such open-source evidence can identify suspects, routes, and networks, which can then be targeted in law enforcement operations. (Hardy, 2020: 158–9)

This approach is indeed symptomatic of, and underpinned by, the contemporary dominance of evidence-based and data-driven technocratic politics. This technocratic view of politics sees networked and hybrid forms of governance as superior and desirable, and coincidentally both fuels and relies on the practices of 'surveillance capitalism' (Zuboff, 2019) and 'regulatory capitalism' (Levi-Faur, 2017). The convergence of these forms of capitalism, and the commodification of both regulation and intelligence, fuels the growth of the 'compliance-industrial complex' (Kuldova, 2022a) and of the 'consultocracy' (Ylönen & Kuusela, 2019) indispensable to the ideological reproduction of neoliberal governance.

Response to the COVID-19 pandemic was similarly technocratic in nature, and revealed how 'science' could be invoked to support a politically established consensus of how to respond to a public health issue, in ways that perverted the very essence of science and the scientific method (Green & Fazi, 2023). This type of 'research' is predicated upon a similar logic. Both the aims and findings of research are pre-determined by the needs and demands of the compliance-industrial complex and technocratic regulators. Instead of attempting to *understand* and *interpret* social phenomena in all their complexity and cultivate a critical distance towards policy and law enforcement that would leave research open to novel findings, such approaches seek to become *useful* for policy and law enforcement, submitting to pre-set parameters of relevance and 'impact'. This impact lies here first and foremost in the manufacturing of actionable intelligence for both the state and the private actors monetizing this intelligence, that is, it lies in identifying suspects, criminals, dubious and shady antiquities dealers among others. This is the type of research that is cited and amplified in the compliance webinars and trainings. This research prefers not to question whether researchers *should* act as private investigators and intelligence analysts. Under these conditions, the telos of social research – which has traditionally been the pursuit of truth and an accurate understanding of social reality – becomes redefined as intelligence gathering at the behest of particular state and corporate actors and their interests. Advocates of this approach to social research may consider the pursuit of truth and the gathering of intelligence to be one and the same thing. After all, is the gathering of intelligence not an exercise in bringing to light a reality that is otherwise hidden? Indeed, scholarly criminological research data, investigative journalism, and intelligence gathering activities increasingly come to resemble one another, with investigative journalists often appearing superior to academics in their abilities to uncover dirt and gather juicy information (for example, Bullough, 2018, 2022; Blas & Farchy, 2021; Michel, 2021). But we should be cautious here, and consider what is lost, what questions are *not* asked, and what does *not* come under scrutiny when we reduce social research to investigative intelligence gathering.

Such research is a boon for the compliance industry, and tends to contribute to the growth of techno-bureaucratic apparatuses of social control. While they do not succeed in fighting crimes, they do succeed in staging the distinctions between those deemed legitimate and those designated as illegitimate, whitewashing the market and power relations within it. There is research that demonstrates that what is at stake here is the manufacturing and maintaining of the ideological fantasy of the legitimate/illegitimate, clean/dirty distinction (Mackenzie, 2011). It acknowledges that these forms of regulation often translate into 'creative compliance ... where formal responses are likely to ensue which simply use documentation and other routine activities to obscure rather than eliminate wrongdoing' (Mackenzie, 2011: 72). But even here, it ends up arguing for *more* of the same – such as more due diligence – only *this time* done properly or taken more seriously, pointing us again to the horizons of the (legitimately) thinkable. We can thus for instance read that:

> Dealers, (some) museums, collectors, and officials, such as the UK's Department for Culture, Media and Sport, all tend to work on the assumption that the market is composed of 'legitimate' and 'illegitimate' dealers and that therefore if the 'bad apples' can be excised the 'legitimate' market can function without hindrance and will not be in danger of contravening any national criminal laws. This is wrong. The reason the ideology of the legitimate market is wrong is that the antiquities market is best seen as a grey market. (Mackenzie, 2011: 71)

And simultaneously, that for the UK Dealing in Cultural Objects (Offences) Act 2003: 'to be successful in sanitising the market must require of dealers that they take serious steps to investigate the provenance of the objects they routinely purchase from sources they might historically have assumed to be 'trustworthy' (Mackenzie, 2011: 72).

Instead of fully engaging with the interesting finding of the drive to bifurcate the market into the legitimate and illegitimate, the market is slapped with the label of being 'grey' and fundamentally tainted, because, in reality, as we all know, the licit tends to always go hand in hand with the illicit (when first defined along these lines). But this is indeed precisely why all these bureaucratic, technological, regulatory, and ideological tools of purification and sanitization are so desirable. In this sense, the idea of the 'grey market' is not really as opposed to this dichotomy as first suggested. Instead, it depends on it. As such, the grey label does not enable us in any meaningful sense to break with the ideological fantasy and impossible goal of a purified financial system. To the contrary, it is implicated in its reproduction. This is also why no better solution can be proposed apart from implementing *more* due diligence, and preferably more honestly.

What is also often left conveniently unexplored in the discourse on the trafficking of illicit antiquities, are the almost naturalized distinctions between 'source countries' and 'demand countries'. Source countries are positioned as rich in cultural heritage but suffering of conflict, corruption, bad governance, kleptocracy, authoritarianism, lack of law enforcement and even care for their own cultural heritage. 'Demand countries', by contrast, are predictably distinguished by both good governance and wealthy elite consumers. The corrupt Other re-emerges here again, and is sought to be managed precisely through the same logic of anti-policy driven regulatory dispositifs. This corrupt Other is seen as always threatening to pollute the now-virtuous Western markets with 'illicit' and 'tainted' goods of dubious provenance that are associated with crime, war, drugs, terror, corruption, and bad governance, and to use these virtuous pure markets to 'wash' reputations and goods, and abuse them to 'launder' dirty money. But it also sees the 'source country' through the lens of development as weak, as unable to protect its heritage, or even to appreciate its worth, and thus as deserving of help – where this help more often than not translates into forms of control aligned with policy interests of Western actors (for a discussion of the tensions pertaining to the global governance of heritage and development, see Wiktor-Mach, 2019). While global governance and developmental efforts are channelled towards these issues, another notion gains traction. Namely, the notion that while it is difficult to target criminals in these jurisdictions, what we can control is our own market. Herein the anti-policy driven crime fighting progressively transforms into the latest buzzword of supply chain due diligence. From human rights abuses, human trafficking, and smuggling to antiquities looting, corruption, and terrorism financing, there appears to be nothing that could not potentially be solved by the imperatives of risk assessments, reporting, documentation, and enhanced due diligence.[38]

The art and antiquities markets' embracing of their new roles as intelligence suppliers and crime fighters is still a somewhat reluctant one, at least in some quarters, as evidenced by the arguments put forward by the likes of CINOA[39] against urgent and wide-ranging regulatory measures. But as we have demonstrated, there are plenty of researchers in this area who appear both eager and willing to take such tasks upon themselves, while denouncing the market's reluctance to embrace policing functions as an expression of resistance to being regulated. Even if one does not sympathize with the art and antiquities market actors, and elects to approach their arguments against these forms of regulation with a healthy dose of cynicism, one should nevertheless pause and think about the underlying vision of the social world that is being shaped here. For it is ultimately a vision of a total surveillance society where not only everyone *can* and is encouraged to, but the many are to be *mandated* to act as intelligence officers. Effectively, it is a pre-crime society of pre-emptive punishment in the name of de-risking or even elimination of risk altogether under its zero tolerance visions (McCulloch & Wilson, 2016; Arrigo & Sellers, 2021). The separation of the fake from the authentic, both when it comes to objects and when it comes to imposters and fraudsters, becomes a key preoccupation within such a social order. In the art world, the proliferation of these practices is stimulated by the simultaneous obsession with authenticity (as this is the source of ultimate value), 'pristine provenance', and with the fear of the forgery and the fake.

Fakes and forgeries and the quest for authenticity (as certification)

Forgeries and *fakes* bring us even closer to the key discussion of 'due diligence', criminalized and securitized compliance, and the role of anti-policies in the reproduction of the neoliberal ideology and of financial capitalism. This is because the discussion of forgeries and fakes reveals most forcefully the quest for the *authentic* and for *verification* of (self-) identity. Authenticity is key to the understanding of value in the high-end markets of art, antiquities, and luxury. It is prized above all else, and a (genuine) certificate of authenticity which guarantees that the object is what it is claimed to be and that it has been carefully examined and deemed genuine by experts in the field, is meant to offer protection and a guarantee. A guarantee against deception and fraud, an assurance that one's investment is safe and secure, that its provenance is pristine, and therefore its value is likely to increase in the future. The certification of authenticity imbues the object with truth, beauty, order, and purity.

The art and antiquities market, as well as markets for luxury watches or wine, are widely deemed to be flooded by fakes and forgeries, resulting in a high level of demand for authentication services and expertise of all kinds. The Orson Welles docudrama *F for Fake* (1973) on the art forger Elmyr de Hory, explored the tensions between fakery, trickery, authenticity, and expertise, tensions which were similarly raised by the famous Tom Keating affair or 'Watercolorgate' in 1976. The art forger and fakery continue to capture the imagination of the public, as does the perverse system of valuation of works of art in the art market which the fakes bring into plain view. Or as Welles remarks in his film, 'the value depends on opinion, opinion depends on the experts, a faker like Elmyr makes fools of the experts, so who is the expert? Who is the faker?' (27:23); 'it's pretty, but is it rare? … rarity, the chief cause and encouragement of fakery and phoniness in everything' (38:10).

This hints at the market itself being dependent on and generative of forgeries. A similar sentiment can be found in the journalist Geraldine Norman's remarks on Keating:

> In a sense, the art market brings the fakes into existence because it must have goods to turn around. … And the art market sees to it that they continue to confuse. … Auctions, as well as being dumping grounds, are hunting grounds for unrecognized masterpieces. A fake thrown out by one dealer may be pounced on by another as a 'find'. If he realizes his mistake, it may go back once again into auction, only for the same thing to happen. The fake is likely to circulate until someone somewhere gullible enough to believe it genuine and hang it on this wall as a master painting. Or else someone may be found who enjoys its decorative qualities and does not care about the attribution. Thus fakes are eventually distributed and hidden away in private homes the world over. (Keating et al, 1977: 204–6)

Indeed, the public enjoyed the masterfully skilful Cockney forger and art restorer taking the experts and connoisseurs for a ride and sympathized with his assault on the merchants of the art world and the elite buyers. Or as he put it, himself an embodiment of the tension between the love of art and beauty and the commodification of art and the fetishization of the authentic in an economy predicated upon and reproductive of inequality:

> As well as old masters, I had also made a close study of the lives and work of the French Impressionists. It seemed disgraceful to me how many of them had died in poverty. All their lives they had been exploited by unscrupulous dealers and then, as if to dishonour their memory, these same dealers continued to exploit them in death. I was determined

to do what I could to avenge my brothers and it was to this end that I decided to turn my hand to Sexton Blaking. (Keating et al, 1977: 79)

With more than 2,000 of Keating's fakes, or 'Sexton Blakes' in rhyming slang, circulating in the market, many have themselves become rather pricey and coveted 'genuine fakes' selling for tens of thousands of pounds. The irony of it is that 'dodgy paintings in Keating's original style, proudly bearing what-looks-like his signature, are finding their way into the market. If they manage to fool, they can claim £5,000 to £10,000'.[40] Forgeries can be rationalized away in many ways, and raise important questions of what is deemed a crime, for whom, and why in the art world. For our purposes here we can only hint at these issues. But an older remark from Fine (1983) can illuminate some of these underlying tensions and point us back into the direction of the drive to eliminate the impure and the tainted:

> Gilbert Edelson, a lawyer who served as Secretary-Treasurer of the Art Dealers' Association of America, claimed that the key to handling fakes is to remove them from circulation: 'I feel this is reasonable because we already have legislation that calls for the impounding of impure food and drugs. Why shouldn't we have the same kind of statute for impure works of art...?' This rhetoric emphasizes the tainted (historical) object, and directs attention away from the system which permits such objects to be bought and sold at a profit. While the forgers focus blame on the dealers, the dealers denigrate the legitimacy of the work of art. (Fine, 1983: 79)

The problem of the tainted and impure, of fakes and forgeries, is seen as only growing. As the demand for these luxury collectibles and investments has grown, so have the incentives for fakes and forgeries – precisely at the same time as new technologies have enabled both their easier creation and detection. This sits parallel with new ways to manufacture fraudulent documents, be these certificates of authenticity or forged provenance records such as invoices, letters, images, the backdating of documents or falsifying of signatures, and so on. These in turn created demand for new technologies for verification and forensic analysis. While new technologies (on both sides) proliferate, fewer experts, for fears of legal liability, appear willing to put their names down on any definitive certificates. Or as Bonner assessed, alluding again to the idea of the 'wild west':

> If anything, today's art market is even more susceptible to rampant fraud because of a breakdown in the process of art authentication. Starting decades ago, fewer and fewer knowledgeable and impartial experts and academics are willing to express opinions on the genuineness of art

because of the prospect of having to defend themselves in expensive litigation. This, coupled with the potential of a sizeable financial payoff for the successful forger, has made today's art market the 'wild west' for fraud. (Bonner, 2017: 21)

What is also revealing about the cases of forgeries and fakes is that while their quality is indeed of importance in order to succeed in their deception, what is even more important is the ability to skilfully *manufacture the perception of authenticity*. This requires convincing forged documentation, be it a plausible provenance, forensic reports, or scientific analysis.

The iconic case here is that of John Myatt. A forger commissioned by John Drewe, between 1986 and 1996, Myatt gained access to archives and planted fake archival evidence to manufacture provenance and paper trails for his forgeries, even establishing his own Art Research Associates firm. In doing so, he wrought havoc on the British art world and its archives (Carter, 2007). Drewe understood that provenance is key to value in the art market, and that the quality of the provenance holds even more value than the quality of the forgeries, given 'that paintings of even poor quality could be passed off as authentic as long as a convincing paper trail was in place' (Carter, 2007: 79). To imitate this sense of pristine provenance, the notorious Wolfgang Beltracchi created fake provenance from scratch, inventing *Sammlung Jaegers 1920s*, with 'records, exhibition labels, photographic evidence and authenticity certificates created to support the forged art works' (Christopherson, 2016: 139). Then there is the notorious case of the Knoedler gallery in New York, which had to close down in 2011 amidst a lawsuit over the forgeries of Jackson Pollock and Mark Rothko, ending in a settlement for an undisclosed amount in 2012. In this case, Glarifa Rosales worked with a forger from 1996 to 2009 and ' "falsely represented authenticity and provenance" on works sold as being by the Abstract Expressionists' (Amineddoleh, 2015: 423). In another case, Ely Sakhai had been running multi-million-dollar forgery scams which came to light in 2000 once Paul Gaugin's *Vase de Fleurs* showed up for auction at Sotheby's and Christie's at the same time. The success of the scam was predicated on exploiting the obsession with certificates of authenticity, to which we shall turn. As the media reported at the time:

the forger's success may lie in the art world itself – and how deftly he navigated its politics. By avoiding the New York market, he ensured that he'd generate little local heat. Moreover, Japanese art buyers are particularly reliant upon certificates of authenticity; because they're so far from Europe, Tokyo collectors do not have easy access to the experts who can spot a fake Chagall at 50 feet. As a result, 'the Japanese are famous for being kind of obsessed with certificates of authenticity.

They're almost more important than the actual painting,' says Judd Tully, editor-at-large of *Art & Auction*. A forger who transferred a real certificate to a counterfeit could be sure that few Japanese experts would spot the deceit. (Thompson, 2004)

Many more examples could be given; for our purposes it suffices to emphasize the sense of permanent threat surrounding high-value objects circulating in these markets – to which, again, ever higher standards of due diligence are being proposed as a solution (Amineddoleh, 2015). Online discussion forums of antiquities collectors are overwhelmingly characterized by a sense of suspicion, and littered with back-and-forth exchanges providing tips on how to tell the genuine object from the fake and conduct different forms of more or less elaborate forensic analysis. Tips on how to verify certificates of authenticity and other documents; how to perform due diligence on the reputations of dealers and laboratories; how one decides whom to trust and whom to avoid. There is a permanent sense of paranoia, of the possibility that one has just purchased a fake or been betrayed and fooled, that the object is not what it was sold as. But there is also the reverse: purchasing something cheaply hoping to discover (or unintentionally discovering) that it is authentic and thus hitting a jackpot. While outright fakes and forgeries are indeed prevalent, disputed attributions and controversies around variously misattributed artworks and so called 'sleepers' are also of importance, the subject of legal research (Bandle, 2016) and real-world quests by 'sleeper-hunters'[41] keen on discovering these misattributed gems.

From all these concerns we see brand-new markets springing up on top of the old, promising to apply new technological and scientific methods to the question of authenticity. High hopes are being pinned onto the blockchain technologies, and a great number of providers of various authentication-cum-provenance and verification services have cropped up. Alas, these chained records of ownership depend on the starting point being valid, and may thus have more application for brand-new or recent artworks and less for any sort of historical record keeping, which can be easily manipulated (Whitaker, 2019). There are companies such as Verisart by Artory, which allow you to create and sell NFTs as well as certificates of authenticity, or generate secure QR stickers, or engage in tokengating (just like Johnny Depp).[42] Verisart promises that their services will allow you to 'own your story, add value, build trust, prevent fraud', and 'become a verified creator to protect yourself from imposters and scams'.[43] Trust is in technosolutionist scenarios always imagined as an effect of successful verification, authentication, surveillance, and monitoring which promise to guarantee the absence of fraud. Trust becomes a matter of successful crime fighting *through* technologies of authentication. Holographic certificates, secure links and QR codes are *the* preferred solution. Blockchain-secured registration and encrypted certification of artworks and other high-value objects are within this technosolutionist imaginary the state-of-the-art paths to both compliance and market 'integrity'; providing, to cite a collaboration between Artory and Christie's,[44] 'a permanent digital record of the information about the artwork'. The website of ARTtrust captures the promise of these products:

> What's better than a certificate of authenticity? *A secured certificate of authenticity!* Thanks to ARTtrust, you are able to produce a non-forgeable certificate of authenticity for each authentic piece of art. ARTtrust offers artists and art professionals a range of products to secure each artwork and their certificate of authenticity individually. To do so, ARTtrust uses one of the most reliable security technology: the Bubble Tag™. Each Bubble Tag™ is unique and impossible to reproduce. They are used as a fingerprint for the item protected. Bubble Tag™ material is a transparent polymer that generates bubbles at complete random. Bubbles appear with positions, sizes and shapes that cannot be mastered. Each constellation of bubbles is, therefore, unique but also impossible to replicate, even by its original manufacturer.[45]

In a world of omnipresent threats of frauds and fakes, the solution presents itself almost exclusively as one of technological surveillance; it promises to close loopholes and make fraud *technically* impossible. To this effect, it mobilizes biometric metaphors, such as that of the fingerprint – which is both unique and cannot be altered, and which cannot be forged. Other actors, too, play on the popularity of biometric verification, such as Tagsmart Verified, promising to deliver secure DNA Tags.[46] Even the luxury wine industry, facing similar problems, is now proudly presenting its own anti-fraud technologies (as featured on the site of Vinovest, a company promising to democratize fine wine investing by 'leveraging technology to provide access to all'):[47]

> Wine provenance refers to a wine's authenticity, the bottle's origin, proof of ownership, and storage conditions. Fraudsters go to extreme lengths to create counterfeit wine, making it difficult for buyers to distinguish between a fake and an authentic wine bottle. For example, between 2017 and 2019, Stephen Burton and James Wellesley were operating a large-scale wine fraud scheme. They pursued wine investors from the United States to invest $99.4m (according to Wine Spectator) by using bogus wines as collateral for loans. Federal prosecutors charged the fraudsters in New York in March 2022. Luckily, wine specialists can trace the wine's provenance using anti-fraud technology, which helps analyze the label font, artwork, and cork size. This helps them certify

the origin, trail the ownership history, and verify the authenticity of every wine bottle.[48]

ORIGYN, a company heavily invested in the business of fractionalization of artworks for investment, goes even a step further. It offers a 'certification ecosystem' without QR codes or micro-chips. Instead, it uses the 'biometrics' of objects, 'the item's unique characteristics to guarantee the authenticity of luxury watches, leather goods, cars, fine or high jewellery items, yacht, cars and so much more'.[49] It claims to be 'certifying trust' by providing 'a universal solution for the Luxury Industry players' by:

> securing a luxury item's identity, authenticity and ownership data within a Digital Certificate. These Authenticity Biometric Certificates provide unique value opportunities, from increased consumer confidence, exclusive experiences, new ways of interaction, and ultimately, additional revenue streams to new services for owners. ... These Utility NFT certificates provide a universal solution for certifying trust across the luxury industry.[50]

The metadata of physical luxury objects, art, and antiquities are thus to be further monetized, financialized, and the value ultimately transferred onto the certificate. Every material object is to be turned into a digital and traceable asset open to further layers of financial speculation – all in the name of combatting fakes, forgeries, and counterfeits, of course, while trust itself is being 'certified'. While building trust is understood as the elimination of risk through constant proof and evidence of trustworthiness, this trust is also to be monetized. These technological solutions, databases, meta-data, created in the name of trust and pre-emption of crime, fraud, and corruption, precisely enable the 'turning of things into assets' (Birch & Muniesa, 2020). Of course, the 'certification' of trust is the exact opposite of the true meaning of trust, which is an assuredness of belief that is *not* reliant on verification and thereby necessitates an element of risk rather than its elimination. We could not say that a husband or a wife 'trusts' that their spouse remains faithful to them if they demanded that their spouse constantly provide digital and biometric evidence of their fidelity. What is being produced here in this obsession with authenticity is not trust and is certainly not ethics, but rather an insurance product.

In a nutshell, we are told that one simply needs *more* and *better* verification and authentication technologies, and expertise to distinguish the fake from the real, the authentic from the inauthentic, and the corrupt from the pure. Alas, the value of the original, the authentic, and the pure is dependent on the very existence of the fake, forged, and corrupt. Anti-policies cannot function if they successfully eliminate that which they are 'anti-'. While there is indeed nothing wrong with the attempts to authenticate works of art per se, we are witness to a drive of this logic towards the extreme wherein the artwork or object being secured becomes of secondary importance. It is the certificate that is fetishized and takes the place of the unique artwork, becoming more valuable and important than the work itself; a reversal prefigured by the financialization of art and the new creative modes of investment in artworks (Taylor, 2011). If we return to Artory/Winston and their offerings of 'investment vehicles that feature due diligence certification secured on the blockchain and the flexibility and liquidity of tokenization',[51] we are left in no doubt about these developments. The artwork is turned into and often chopped into imaginary small pieces as an investment, while due diligence and certification are the products on sale. Artory/Winston promise not only the old-fashioned returns on investment, but the fetish itself to go with them: after sourcing of the artworks for their portfolio and conducting all the due diligence, recording this is the Artory database: 'Artory then generates a unique, encrypted Due Diligence Certificate securely stored on the blockchain to capture all key data. Artory tokenizes the data and Due Diligence Certificate in a digital representation of ownership. Only investors receive exclusive access to these data and regular market, investment, and diligence updates.'[52]

While these investments are still backed by some real artworks, even if hidden from sight, the NFT art market is possibly the most extreme expression of this fetishization of the certificate. Some would argue that NFTs are not much more than 'glorified certificates'.[53] While the enthusiasm may be waning now as the NFT markets are collapsing following the FTX crash, from a cultural perspective this growing obsession with certificates of authenticity are of great interest. For it appears that traceability, transparency, and visibility for their own sake come to replace the idea of 'art for art's sake'. What used to be imagined as the purity of art, along with the notion of its separation from the world of markets and commodities, is now to be imagined solely in terms of the purity, health, and integrity of the financial markets – markets free of corruption, fraud, crime, and other sorts of dirt. This can explain the obsession with (art reduced to) empty signifiers, with purity, and ultimately with death. For it is emptiness – the art and object being hollowed out or intentionally killed (or at best, stowed away and hidden), materialized in the pure certified financial value – that is being sought. The virtual becomes the real. Or as Taylor summed up, the financialization of art:

> becomes a progressively abstract play of nonreferential signs, abstract financial instruments increasingly create an autonomous sphere of circulation whose end is nothing other than the endless proliferation of monetary and financial signs. When the art of finance becomes the finance of art, art is no longer merely a commodity to be bought and sold, but becomes the currency of exchange fabricated for hedge funds

and private equity funds, where it is traded like any other financial asset. (Taylor, 2011: 1)

Instances in which artworks are being burned are possibly the most revealing, whereby the value of the burnt and now-dead artwork is magically transposed onto the glorified certificate of the NFT. Just consider the 'money-making stunt', the burning of Banksy's work *Morons* which depicts a Christie's auctioneer, that was performed and filmed by the blockchain firm Injective Protocol (Criddle, 2021). The original physical piece by Banksy was bought and minted as an NFT, with the physical piece subsequently being burnt out of existence. As the explanation given in the video explains:

> If you wanna have the NFT and the physical piece, the value would be primarily in the physical piece. By removing the physical piece from existence and only having the NFT we can *ensure* that the NFT through its smart contract ability of the blockchain, will *ensure* that *no one can alter the piece and it is the true piece* that exists in the world, by doing this, the value of the physical piece will then move onto the NFT being *the only way you can have this piece anymore*. (Emphasis added)[54]

Note the emphasis placed on *ensuring*, on the smart contract as the only pure, true way to possess that which is destroyed and continues to exist only as some sort of pure spirit on blockchain. The quest for abstract value, for financial gain, ends in destruction. For the pure world is a dead world. Damien Hirst rather predictably jumped onto this trend as well, burning 1,000 of his pieces.[55] As Crosthwaite argued, using Hirst as a prime example:

> it is precisely the function of the contemporary art market – and of the art auction in particular – to provide an arena in which reserves of capital may be wantonly expended, and that the wastefulness of such acts of prodigality is maximised when the object purchased itself represents, or literally embodies, waste. Hence the prominence today of artworks that entail death, decay, mortification and abjection. (Crosthwaite, 2011: 81)

The paradox, or not, may be that it is precisely by turning to death that one also seeks purity, 'health', and integrity.

Corruption, luxury, and the compliance-industrial complex

In this chapter we have taken a long and winding journey through art theft, looted antiquities, smuggling, forgeries, and fakes, sometimes in ways that do not seem immediately relevant for a book on corruption. While all of these crimes feature prominently in the imaginary of the art and antiquities markets, more and more we see these narratives being overlaid by and integrated into larger concerns around corruption, kleptocracy, and money-laundering. Or else, into issues, which as we have seen throughout this book, have been elevated to the status of national security. Influential reports have contributed to setting these issues on the agenda of the art world. The report, by the US Senate's Permanent Subcommittee on Investigations, on sanctions evasion and money laundering in the art market discussed, among others, the sanctioned oligarchs Arkadii and Boris Rotenberg, as well as the role of auction houses, shell companies, and various intermediaries in the facilitation of laundering of proceeds of crime and corruption (Portman & Carper, 2020). An EU report connected freeports storing high-end art and other goods to the issues of money laundering and financial crime risks (Korver, 2018). These criminal scenarios, taken together, have been utilized to argue that the opacity and secretive nature of the art market, combined with the portability and value of the assets that float through it, creates what Thomas Christ, the board member of the Basel Institute on Governance, describes as 'an ideal playing ground for money laundering' (Bowley & Rashbaum, 2017). Scandals and lawsuits involving cash payments, under and over-valuation, price fixing, record falsification, and black-market transactions feature prominently in arguments for this form of regulation (Shea, 2018).

Again, in the realm of corruption and money-laundering, several scandals emerge as iconic, cited, and recited across policy, regulatory, academic, and popular literature. One of these is the 'Bouvier Affair', involving the Swiss art dealer Yves Bouvier, well-known for his luxury freeport business, and being charged with defrauding wealthy clients, overcharging and money laundering. This came to light as the Russian billionaire Dmitri Rybolovlev brought suit against Bouvier alleging losses of over $1 billion, a battle that has by now been fought over 7 years and in multiple jurisdictions (Noce, 2022a). Then there is the influential case of the Brazilian financier and art collector Edemar Cid Ferreira, charged with money laundering and convicted in 2006 and sentenced to 21 years, famous for his attempt to launder money through art acquisitions, most notably of Jean-Michel Basquiat's *Hannibal* (1981), which he tried to smuggle into the US, along with other paintings, with a declared value of $100. This case was prominently mentioned in The Department of the Treasury's report from February 2022, the *Study of the Facilitation of Money Laundering and Terror Finance Through the Trade in Works of Art.*[56] While this study did not result in any immediate recommendations of the implementation of AML regulation in the US art market akin to the UK and EU regimes, there is no doubt that regulators will be progressively moving into the direction of regulatory harmonization. The report has already been embraced by the compliance industry as indicative of the regulations to come and of the need to embrace more self-regulation and due diligence procedures, as well as training, awareness raising, and data-driven compliance platforms. The sanctions regimes which pertain to all, already pave the way for more or less the same investigative strategies to be applied, even if to different ends. Another popular example, cited across the board, is that of the aforementioned Rotenberg brothers, brought to light by The Permanent Subcommittee on Investigations' report on these sanctioned oligarchs (Portman & Carper, 2020). The report famously alleged that Arkadii Rotenberg, with the help of a Moscow-based dealer Gregory Baltser through his private firm Baltzer, spent $18 million purchasing artworks after the imposition of sanctions. *The Art Newspaper* could report in July 2020 that Baltzer denied any such involvement, stating that:

> The firm 'maintains a strict compliance program, and has never conducted any transaction prohibited by any sanctions list,' it says. 'Baltzer can confirm that neither it nor Gregory Baltzer has ever, at any time, represented or transacted in any way with Boris or Arkady Rotenberg. Baltzer strongly denies any suggestion to the contrary.' (Ludel, 2020)

The same response came from Sotheby's, following revelations of the auction house's links to the sanctioned brothers. In their statement, Sotheby's emphasized that they take 'anti-money laundering and US sanctions policies extremely seriously and voluntarily participated in the Senate subcommittee's investigation' (Ludel, 2020). The Senate subcommittee's report delves in detail into the AML and sanctions compliance performed by the gallerist, as well as Christie's and Sotheby's, revealing some of the ways one can creatively play with and around the concepts of due diligence (Portman & Carper, 2020).

Other corruption scandals, such as 1MDB mentioned in the first chapter, have forever linked the art market and the luxury industry to money laundering, offshore jurisdictions, freeports, images of art world excesses, opulent auctions, financial speculation and more. The art market was revealed as a happy and secretive facilitator of figures such as Jho Low,

> bold-faced art-world names litter the documents and criminal complaints that have amassed as investigations have ramped up in Washington, D.C. Aside from DiCaprio, art-world figures who did business deals with Low include the Sotheby's financial services department, the Nahmad family, the private dealership SNS Fine Art, French mega-collector François Pinault, and former Christie's post-war and contemporary chairman Loïc Gouzer. (Freeman, 2019)

It is in light of these scandals that one argues that the only way to 'root out bad actors within this market and make the industry less attractive to criminals' (Shea, 2018: 668) is by extending the AML legislation from the financial sector to the art market, following the example of real estate markets and precious metals and gems (Baranello, 2021). As we have seen, the notion of due diligence has thus come to encompass due diligence performed on transactions, individuals, and corporate and other entities, in addition to the traditional provenance checks. Peter B. Hardy, former US prosecutor, is even quoted as remarking that 'sometimes, the provenance of the funds can be more critical than the provenance of the art' (Mashberg, 2019: 34). And as we have seen, the logic of authentication, verification, of the fetishization of biometrics, becomes key to crime fighting across the board. Objects and humans are reduced to an object ID or personal ID, their histories tracked and flagged for any risk indicators, harnessed, and analysed by data-driven platforms, compliance, and other experts. Transparency, tracking, databases, training, and risk-management, along with ethical codes and standards, are seen as the only way ahead, the only way to purify the market of these Impurities, of the taint.

The removal of this taint bears the promise of improved reputation and at least the illusion, if not the reality, of cleanliness and licitness. The Belgian diamond industry can be taken as an example here. This previously 'unregulated' sector has been beset by fears of blood and conflict diamonds, exploitation, organized crime, human rights violations, and of 'diamonds tainted by abuse'[57] entering Western markets. Consequently, the industry has become subject to AML and CFT regulations, and introduced various due diligence procedures, which have eventually 'contributed to the reestablishment of the reputation of this market, which has led to commercial benefits: as a "clean" sector the diamond industry attracts business that previously hesitated to engage with this market as it was considered a "money laundering hub"' (Mosna, 2022: 320). The Kimberley Process Certification Scheme was created to ensure the buyers that the diamonds they are purchasing are not *tainted* by atrocities. But as a leading diamond broker, Martin Rapaport remarked in the *New York Times*: 'We use the Kimberley Process as the greatest greenwashing machine the world has ever seen' (Searcey, 2022). Despite this improved reputation – an effect of skilful 'ethics' and compliance-washing – we can read, for instance, of the Russian paramilitary Wagner group – notorious for its mercenaries in Ukraine and linked to looting, extortion, forced labour, rape, and violence – taking over the local diamonds trade and exporting diamonds from the civil war and poverty ridden Central African Republic to Dubai and Antwerp (Ilyushina & Ebel, 2022).

Russia is also a major exporter of diamonds, and in light of the war in Ukraine, calls were made to label these as 'conflict diamonds' under the

Kimberley Process as a source of funding for the war. Russia has been fighting back against these calls together with its allies, and not unexpectedly, no action was taken by the Kimberley Process. While the import of Russian diamonds has been sanctioned by the Western allies, it is no secret that the diamonds tend to easily disappear across global supply chains as they are cut and polished. Or as the *New York Times* put it, 'Because of loopholes and technicalities, so-called ethical diamonds don't really exist, many jewellers acknowledge' (Searcey, 2022). It appears that what matters over reality, above all, is the regulatory hyperreality and its simulations of 'purification' in the quest for 'integrity', which unwittingly keep the system going as it currently exists. After all, can we really lay blame at the feet of 'loopholes'? That it is *because* of the loopholes that all this violence, exploitation and misery continue? The proliferation of compliance demonstrates a fundamental unwillingness to think about the cause of these problems at a deeper level. It indicates a basic reticence to challenge the subjectivities generated by our present political-economic system, an unwillingness to question whether or not this economic system is remotely compatible with ethics or morality, and a tendency to pervert what ethics really is.

The rapidly expanding sanctions regimes following the war in Ukraine, the establishment of the Task Force KleptoCapture, and similar units discussed in the opening chapter, have only accelerated this way of combatting the evil and the corrupt. We are told that closing 'loopholes' and improving upon 'technicalities' will eventually do the trick, while a full-blown war is being fought. And for that, we need more technology, more tracking across global supply chains, and more background checks. Or else, more data-driven compliance (but de facto/pre-emptive/policing) solutions and more authentication and verification, more purification of the social and the material by sorting out the fake from the real, by flagging the sanctioned, the criminal, and otherwise suspicious alike for elimination from any transactions, for 'enhanced due diligence' procedures, and/or for reporting to the authorities. But what happens after one has flagged artworks, antiquities, diamonds, individuals, companies? As a rule, it appears that awfully little happens (at least to the wealthy), with the exception of a few cases that are used to set an 'example'. What happens to an object when it is withdrawn from sale by an auction house? Most likely it shall be sold elsewhere, while the auction house withdrawing it will improve or maintain its reputation as a legitimate market actor, complying with high standard of ethics (while casting doubt over smaller outfits and dealers, effectively insinuating that what is small is often also illicit or at least suspicious, that trust can be placed only in large actors).

The way we have chosen to 'regulate' these markets is by stimulating the proliferation of 'audit cultures' (Strathern, 2000; Shore & Wright, 2015, 2018), by creating and fuelling audit *markets* and an industry that manufactures the hyperreal and the ideological fantasies of compliance. This industry relies on and is unthinkable without the steady stream of revelations, corruption scandals, crime scenarios, conflicts, threats, and risk, and without the anti-policies that have emerged to tackle them. This is an industry that would like us to believe that by expanding the logic of compliance we will be able to control this increasingly uncontrollable world. We simply have to bring things into the light, make transactions 'transparent' by creating all sorts of databases, and endlessly document, record, audit, and create paper trails. Clients and intermediaries, as well as artworks and antiquities, must be subjected to both overt and covert intelligence investigations and risk assessments, we are told, that encompass both the provenance of funds and objects, and generate suspicious activity reports (SARs) for law enforcement and intelligence units. But while we have more data (points) than ever, we seem to be less and less able to make any sense of them (Hansen & Flyverbom, 2015). Nor can we seem to find any vision that may transgress this data obsession that conflates knowledge with information (Tsoukas, 1997).

We must question this quest for control driven by negative visions of eliminating and purging the unwanted, as Hartmut Rosa rightly observed:

> modernity's incessant desire to make the world engineerable, predictable, available, accessible, disposable (i.e. *verfügbar*) in all its aspects ... this very desire alters our relationship to the world ... a fully engineerable world eventually would be a 'dead world' ... this desire for control produces, behind our backs, a world that in the end is utterly uncontrollable in all the relevant aspects. We cannot control our late modern world in any way: politically, economically, legally, technologically, or individually. The drive and desire toward controllability ultimately creates monstrous, frightening forms of uncontrollability. (Rosa, 2021: viii–ix)

Only the dead world is upon this vision a pure world.

This quest to control the world through anti-policies and the privatization and pluralization of the tools of intelligence and law enforcement, leads to the proliferation of agents of purification. And thus, irrespective of how much we tend to view these markets as implicated in one way or another in these crimes and their facilitation, we cannot *not* see them simultaneously as saviours, as instrumental in both crime prevention, detection and intelligence gathering, and in foreign policy, as *partners* to the state in crime-fighting – such as through sanctions regimes, asset freezes, unexplained wealth orders, for example the UK Economic Crime (Transparency and Enforcement) Act 2022.[58] The 'best practice' that has thus been established is to enlist regulated entities and diverse art market participants, including museums, in crime prevention, pre-emption and crime fighting, and in the vey implementation of foreign and security policy, placing both legal and moral duty on these to perform policing functions.

Fixated on the idea of the abuse of the (inherently virtuous) markets by bad actors, this narrow focus *strategically disavows* systemic problems; upon this view, to create a better world we simply need to identify, risk-assess and, if necessary, eliminate, prosecute, and prohibit bad actors from transacting in the market. Securitization and policing come to reign supreme, mirroring the anti-policy par excellence – anti-terrorism. As Chamayou argued, the discourse shifted from 'the classic doctrinal framework of counterinsurgency', which is 'essentially politico-military', to antiterrorism, 'which fundamentally has to do with policing and security' (Chamayou, 2015: 68). This has had significant implication for the way terrorism came to be fought.

> First, there is difference in the way the enemy is conceived. Whereas the first paradigm regards insurgents as the 'representatives of deeper claims at the heart of society' … the second one, by labelling them 'terrorist', regards them above all as 'aberrant individuals,' dangerous figures, quite simply mad, or as incarnations of pure evil … antiterrorism adopts a strictly opposite way of proceeding [to counterinsurgency]: its policing logic individualizes the problem and reduces its objectives to neutralizing, on a case-by-case basis, as many suspects as possible … the solution lies in tracking such people down one by one. … Within the categories of policing, political analysis dissolves. Antiterrorism, which is both moralizing and Manichean abandons any real analysis of the roots of hostility and its own effects upon it. The binary nature of good and evil is no longer just a rhetorical ploy but is imposed as an analytical category, to the detriment of any consideration of the complexity of strategic relations. (Chamayou, 2015: 68–9)

This logic of anti-terrorism can be discerned across the discourse of anti-corruption and other anti-policies, even if never in such a brutal expression. For even in our case, the only thinkable solution to the problems of corruption becomes purification through sorting and elimination of the evil.

This purification delivers legitimacy to those who participate in these forms of (self)-policing, while casting those who lack the same resources to perform spectacular feats of due diligence and auditing as 'shady' (to put it simply, it serves the market interest of large Western market actors). Those deemed 'shady' are typically small businesses: hence, this is not only a technique of legitimization by purification, but also monopolization, privileging the big players with large audit and research teams. We can thus read, for instance, that 'because small businesses often lack the financial and human capital that larger arts organizations can devote to identifying suspicious activity, they may even be more susceptible to being taken advantage of by criminal actors by virtue of their size' (Shea, 2018: 681). By extension, they, too, become suspect in the eyes of the large actors. Those who benefit most from these regulatory regimes are, however, the likes of the Big Four: consulting, audit, compliance, and legal firms. These firms hold disproportionate power not only in translating these regulations into practice, but also in shaping their content. The rise to power of these intermediaries means that their visions and managerial and governance 'best practices' in reality dictate how we should be governed and how the evils of this world should be combatted (Shore & Wright, 2015, 2018; Tsingou, 2018; Ylönen & Kuusela, 2019; Kuldova, 2022a). One thing is clear, there is no such perpetual revenue stream in solving our problems, like there is in perpetuating and intensifying them.

More of the same, please (not)

If these solutions fail, and they indeed do as the failure is systemic and the system itself criminogenic, the solution proposed is more of the same. More regulation, more standards, more reporting, more auditing, more due diligence, more awareness training and education, more certifications of experts, more screening software, more data for more complete databases and so on. And since the new technologies themselves generate their own problems and new opportunities for fraud, there need to be more audits of these new technologies and so on. When researching this field, as one attends conference after conference and webinar after webinar, all delivered by the same compliance and crime fighting experts, one quickly begins to feel as if trapped in an oppressive echo-chamber, where the same formulas are repeated, time and again. The proponents of these solutions, all trained and certified, repeat the same clichés, provide the same examples, and offer the same pseudo-solutions and products. It is a peculiar universe that both accelerates and grows as it manufactures threats and risks, and that at the same time remains fundamentally the same despite this growth, a strange mix of total stasis with frenetic speed and activity.

Asking for an alternative, one receives merely more of the same, only with more words and crafty formulations, but not with any more depth (or any depth at all for that matter). After all, there is simply no time to sit back and ruminate on alternative approaches. One of the authors (Kuldova) has spent considerable time within the compliance universe, undertaking various training and certifications as a form of ethnographic research into the anti-corruption and compliance industry (Kuldova, 2022a). One of the most striking features of this world of compliance was how it imbued subjects and practitioners with the feeling that if they were to sit still and do nothing, even for a day, the world would become uncontrollable. What is impressed upon the subjects and practitioners of compliance, anti-corruption, and AML is that there is no time to think. We simply have to act, and act now. This is reflective of Žižek's view of the neoliberal era as characterized by what he describes as *post-political biopolitics*, whereby old ideological struggles around the big questions of how society is to be organized politically and economically are left behind, and where all that exists is the regulation, security, and administration of everyday life (Žižek, 2008). As Žižek writes, within this depoliticized and sanitized world, 'the only way to introduce passion to this field, to actively mobilise people, is through fear. ... For this reason, bio-politics is ultimately a politics of fear; it focuses on defence from potential victimisation or harassment' (Žižek, 2008: 40).

Indeed, as neoliberalism staggers on in a zombie-like state, are we not increasingly governed through a perpetual politics of emergency? The 2008 global financial crisis; the COVID-19 pandemic; the war in Ukraine; the spectre of climate change; the cost-of-living crisis. It is not just that all of these issues were or are significant crises with sizeable impacts on a global scale. It is that the almost uniform and default response to these issues has been to govern through a state of emergency, and often to mobilise the ultimate emergency discourse: that of war. The response to COVID-19 was steeped in martial metaphors as the world fought the 'war against Covid' (Green & Fazi, 2023). The present cost-of-living crisis that currently plagues large swathes of the world is described in *The New York Times Magazine* as a 'war against inflation' (Steinberger, 2023). The esteemed environmental scholar Andreas Malm advocates a 'war communism' to tackle climate change (Malm, 2020), while the prominent climate change activist Bill McKibben has argued that 'it is not that global warming is *like* a world war. It *is* a world war', and our 'only hope is to mobilize like we did in World War II' (McKibben, 2016). Even those political figures who are least alarmist about the issue of global warming invoke phrases such as the 'fight' or 'battle' against climate change with such regularity that it no longer seems strange. And while the crisis in Ukraine is an actual military war, those of us outside of Ukraine and who are not at war with Russia are invited to *feel* and think as if we are. Corruption, kleptocracy, and money laundering are merely the latest issues to be put on a war footing and governed as an emergency, elevated to the status of a national security imperative which demands that we take swift emergency measures. As Wang Jianxin, a director of publicity within the Communist Party of China's (CPC) Central Commission for Discipline put it: 'The fight against corruption is a life and death struggle. We can only advance, never retreat, and only win, never lose.'[59] Emergency discourses encourage both the rapid formation of a consensus on how best to respond to the emergency, and a strict enforcement of that consensus through the foreclosure of thought and alternatives. To sit back and think about this issue is merely self-indulgent intellectual pirouetting. There is only one way to think of the problem, and that boils down to the negative: to fight against corruption and other crimes by the same procedures that seek to eliminate the suspicious and the tainted from the circulation and transaction in the hopes of the mysterious quality of 'integrity' and 'purity' emerging.

A useful example of just how hegemonic this approach has become is illustrated by a conversation we had with the much-celebrated bot, Open AI's ChatGPT. Since the bot is really a mere linguistic model, a stochastic parrot, delivering the statistically most plausible sequence of words (and known for 'hallucinating' facts that do not exist, such as references to articles never written), we were the more intrigued by what kinds of answers this bot would give to issues of corruption and fraud in the art market. After all, it is a model trained on what could be deemed the hegemonic collective consciousness. Interestingly, several hours spent interrogating this bot – which is fed on much of whatever is out there in the digital realm – results in the experience of the exact same frustration with both the more and the circling around the same anti-policy, governance, and compliance dispositifs. In some sense, nothing can summarize the hegemony of this governance ideology better than the bot. When confronted with the inefficiency of the standard precepts, the answer is always more of the same. Since the conversation captures the sense of entrapment by ideology so well, it is worth including here a brief excerpt from this conversation:

> To address these challenges and improve the integrity of the art market, it may be necessary to consider a range of additional measures, such as:
>
> - Increasing education and awareness about the importance of authenticity and provenance, to help buyers and sellers make informed decisions about the work of art they are considering.
> - Strengthening and enforcing regulations and standards related to the art market, including those related to provenance, authentication, and fair pricing.
> - Increasing cooperation and collaboration among different stakeholders in the art market, including art market professionals, law enforcement agencies, and industry organizations, to better address issues related to fraud and other forms of criminal activity.
> - Developing and implementing new technologies and approaches, such as blockchain and digital authentication, to help improve the accuracy and reliability of authentication and provenance.
>
> *What you are suggesting is effectively more of the same, more of what we already have. Do you have alternatives to this, something completely different as a solution?*
>
> I apologize if my previous responses seemed to suggest that the measures I listed were simply more of the same. While it is true that

many of the measures I listed are already in place in some form, it is also possible that there are opportunities to improve and expand upon these measures in order to more effectively address the challenges and issues facing the art market. One potential alternative approach that could be considered is the use of digital technologies and platforms to improve the transparency and efficiency of the art market. For example, the use of blockchain and other digital technologies could help to improve the accuracy and reliability of authentication and provenance, and could make it easier for buyers and sellers to access and share information about the works of art being exchanged. Another potential alternative approach could be the establishment of more comprehensive and standardized regulations and standards for the art market. This could include the creation of an independent regulatory body or oversight agency to enforce these standards and ensure that the art market is operating fairly and transparently. Finally, it could also be useful to consider alternative approaches to pricing and valuation in the art market. For example, the use of more objective and data-driven approaches to valuation, such as the use of algorithms or machine learning, could help to reduce subjectivity and improve the fairness of pricing in the art market.[60]

The bot has indeed managed to capture key features of this hegemonic governance narrative, and since, being a mere model, it cannot think, it is not surprising that it cannot produce a critique of the premises outlined (which may be suggestive also of the fact that there is no such critique in its training data). It postulates the threats to the 'integrity of the art market'. It emphasises the focus on combatting these threats and enlisting the industry's stakeholders in this fight against crime that undermined the market's integrity. It endlessly repeats the quest for market integrity, and when confronted with the challenge of considering alternative solutions, merely apologises that the 'alternatives' it proposes are simply more of the same, only to immediately fetishize technological and data-driven solutions that are built on the same logic. What is more troubling, is that the same unthinking and the same foreclosure of alternatives dominates the industry and regulatory discourse. The problem is not the unthinking of the bot, but the unthinking of the people (which it does reflect). While quoting this bot at such length may seem unnecessary, it is interesting in that it generates an original text, a meta-text, of all the texts one can read on the commercial websites, blogs, and in reports of the proliferating providers of compliance, due diligence, AML, and sanctions screening services for the art market, in addition to the more traditional legal firms specializing in the art market. It does, indeed, a good job of capturing the ethos of their messaging.

Following the introduction of AML regulations in Europe and the imposition of sanctions on the export of luxury goods to Russia and on select oligarchs, we see more and more providers in this market offering the obligatory AML training, AML audits and various risk assessments. Providers such as Artlogic, ArtAML, or FCS Compliance, mentioned earlier. The latter was set up in 2016 by Jerry Walters, former police officer with Thames Valley and City of London Police,[61] and specializes in financial crime investigations, boasting a team comprising of many former police officers and others who used to be employed in regulatory agencies, in addition to legal experts. The movement of law enforcement, intelligence experts and former regulators from the public sector into the various realms of 'compliance' is more of a rule than an exception. This again testifies to the privatization and pluralization of policing (Boels & Verhage, 2015; O'Reilly, 2015) under the guise of regulation and to the expansion of the logic of crime fighting; we are left without doubt that the fight against the 'corruption' of the integrity of markets is the preferred approach to 'regulating' the social in our times.

There are academic publications emerging on the subjects of AML and compliance in the art world, often digging into the legal details of the various regulations, or into the dynamics of their implementation (Shea, 2018; Hufnagel & King, 2020; Baranello, 2021; Mosna, 2022). But few, if any, seem to be more fundamentally puzzled by this one-sided drive towards the (largely symbolic) elimination of the tainted, illicit, and impure and by the parallel imaginary of the gaps which need to be closed. Most commentators in this sphere are often too busy engaging in the discovery and frenetic uncovering of new gaps, be they in knowledge or regulation, and in keeping preoccupied with the endless filling of these gaps, for these are indeed never to be closed. These gaps appear to be everywhere, not only in regulation or knowledge, but of course in compliance itself; the systems are 'leaky' and far from air-tight, irrespective of how much compliance surveillance tech is used (Kuldova, 2022a). And thus, we can read in Refinitiv's marketing blog post titled 'Crime-fighting value of enhanced due diligence' that:

> Gaps in compliance are enabling the spread of financial crime, including through the absence of formal checks when onboarding third-parties. ... With financial crime still pervasive, insufficient due diligence is at least partly to blame for criminals slipping through the compliance net. ... Respondents further revealed the existence of some significant gaps in formal compliance, with 51 percent of customer, supplier and partner relationships not undergoing any formal due diligence checks at the on-boarding stage. Closing these gaps is crucial if we are to win the war on financial crime.[62]

But it is not only the industry that is set on selling gap-closing technologies and products. Academics appear to be equally seduced by the *gap-mode of conceptualization* and the accompanying rhetoric of *pollution*. A recent example may be the article by Brodie et al, which tries to answer the question of why there is still illicit trade in cultural objects by performing a 'gap analysis to access underperforming practice and policy' (Brodie et al, 2022: 117). The article proceeds along familiar lines. Firstly, the polluting nature of the trade is hyperbolically exaggerated, referring to the joint operations of Interpol, Europol, and World Customs Organizations, the Athena and Pandora operations. The authors then urge us to:

> Imagine these operations as annual sampling exercises undertaken to test the effectiveness of a *clean-up campaign* aimed at *eliminating illicit pollutants* from legitimate trade. The clean-up campaign would be judged ineffectual. The staggering numbers of objects seized and the global reach of the networks involved (103 countries) provide tangible evidence of a global trade that is prospering, not one that is well-regulated, under control, or on the way to eradication ... if the reported arrests and seizures are only *the tip of a much larger dark criminal iceberg*, then the indications are that the illicit trade in cultural objects is very poorly controlled. (Brodie et al, 2022: 117; emphasis added)

From this initial determination of the 'polluting' nature of the illicit markets, we move into the discussion of gaps – gaps that are yet again blamed for the failure to control: 'the fabric of international policy is a thing of gaps, reactions, and piecemeal patches, knit together by the enduring threads of the UNESCO convention ... the cumulative outcome of closing the gaps would be more effective policy and reduced illicit trade' (Brodie et al, 2022: 118).

Gaps in control architectures that allow the pollutants to enter and undermine the integrity of markets are at the heart of the hegemonic regulatory narrative, a narrative that has become so entrenched and so common-sense, that few question it – effectively acting in this respect as stochastic parrots (does this explain the widespread enthusiasm about the capabilities of ChatGPT?). The underlying premise of the integrity of the markets and their assumed inherent good, is never (to be) disputed; the harms of the neoliberal capitalist system which are generative of many of these crimes, are conveniently disavowed. There appears thus to be only one way to handle these always already accelerating issues, and that is by growing and expanding techno-bureaucratic, surveillance and legalistic apparatuses of control and purification and relentlessly filling gaps in our crime-fighting abilities.

And if these efforts fail, as they often do, and if the narrative of gaps to be blamed for this failure turns out too weak, then we turn to corruption – the only plausible answer left is that the control apparatuses themselves became corrupted. We can thus for instance read that 'the limited effectiveness of regulatory systems can be traced to corruption, unwillingness to enforce laws in place, and fragmentation of the control process' (Lane et al, 2008: 251). The fact that none of these apparatuses ever attempt to address the causes, but keep frenetically fighting the proliferating symptoms, does not appear to strike one as in the least odd. Similarly, the fact that this machinery has become driven by purely negative visions, as we have shown, and lacking in any positive vision, beyond the *absence* of crime, strikes only very few as odd. And since the fundamental premises of anti-policies do not strike anyone as odd, the expansion of these (perpetually failing) apparatuses of control also does not raise any 'red flags', to borrow the industry lingo. As Hartmut Rosa sharply observes,

> the basic institutional structure of modern society can be maintained only through constant escalation. A modern society, as I define it, *is one that can stabilize itself only dynamically, in other words one that requires constant economic growth, technological acceleration, and cultural innovation in order to maintain its institutional status quo.* In terms of cultural perception, this escalatory perspective has gradually turned from a promise into a threat. Growth, acceleration, and innovation no longer seem to assure us that life will always get better; they have come instead to be seen as an apocalyptic, claustrophobic menace. ... At both individual and the collective level, what generates this will to escalation is not the promise of improvement in our quality of life, but the unbridled threat that we will lose what we have already attained. ... This game of escalation is perpetuated not by a lust for more, but by the fear of having *less* and *less*. (Rosa, 2021: 9–10; emphasis in original)

This game of escalation precisely drives the expansion of the compliance-industrial complex (Kuldova, 2022a). But as Rosa also observes, 'The ever-growing accumulation of regulations, provisions, and statutes is the manifest expression of our effort to make social life predictable and controllable in the sense of being justiciable – an effort, however, that is at the verge of failing dramatically' (Rosa, 2021: 18).

The modernist impulse to purify, to eliminate the criminal, is mirrored in the aesthetic movement that has, since Adolf Loos, sought to banish, and eliminate ornament. It is worth reminding ourselves that Loos's vision was one deeply influenced by the likes of Lombroso (Canales & Herscher, 2005), whose ideas we now witness being revived in the algorithmic policing systems that seek to spot the criminal based on physiognomic features, what has been termed as 'physiognomic AI' (Stark & Hutson, 2022). The modernist aesthetic impulse to eliminate ornament (as criminal), is mirrored in the anti-policies and regulations that seek to eliminate the informal, the impure, the tainted. It is paradoxical that even the world of art and luxury should succumb to this quest. No longer driven by the visions of creating beauty and making life meaningful, it transforms into a policing apparatus, emptied of ethics, values, and virtue, one that alienates and progressively turns everyone into a potential threat, risk, or suspect. And why? To sustain the reproduction of a system that impoverishes and alienates the many who have to submit to the world of 'total work'; to sustain a system that serves the accumulation of capital in the hands of the few; and to sustain a system that denies the majority the possibility to enjoy the pleasures and virtues of art, handicraft, and leisure which are the very basis of culture (Pieper, 1998), as well as the pleasures of labour endowed by meaning, purpose, and virtue (Morris, 2012); to sustain a criminogenic system whose response to its criminogenicity is not to call that system into question, but to simply cast everyone as a potential threat, potential criminal, or fraud – including those critical of the system, to which the treatment of whistleblowers testifies (Kenny, 2019; Kuldova & Nordrik, 2023). The result is a paranoid, scared, and untrusting world overflowing with heaps of waste and great poverty at the same time. A world where the rich – operating along the same imperatives of the system, and performing these in their extreme form – seek total enclosure in safe and secure apocalyptic bunkers and islands.

The aforementioned Russian oligarch and art collector Dmitry Rybolovlev is a case in point. Since purchasing the Skorpios island in Greece, he has transformed it into a self-sufficient hyper-luxurious secure location, described as a 'giant panic room' by *The Art Newspaper*, where 'Around-the-clock surveillance from security cameras and snipers prevent intruders from crossing. A single cruise ship is permitted to dock at a small public beach, but only when the Rybolovlev family is not there' (Bregman, 2022).

There is likely no better materialization of the ideological fantasy at the heart of neoliberal financial capitalism and its effects. Nor is there a better materialization of its profound emptiness, of the luxurious securitized excess that time and again fails to satisfy, of the hyper-securitized architectures that fail to keep the threat away and the world under control. The ideological fantasy of the perpetual and accelerating battle between compliance and defiance is what permits the disavowal of the real causes of misery and poverty, material and spiritual. Driven by the negative, it fails in delivering any positive vision of a world worth living in, instead, it longs for a pure, dead world. Despite the promises to fight corruption, the corrupt core remains untouched. If we hope for change, we may need to look for ways to traverse this fantasy.

What we need is a *perspectival and cultural shift*: away from anti-policies predicated upon the elimination of the negative and the drive to *combat* threats, towards positive regulatory visions that demand more than the mere elimination of the illicit and the evil, and that are grounded in a recognition of 'complexity and complicity', and impurity (Shotwell, 2016), refusing to engage in elaborate (regulatory) systems of disavowal that only perpetuate, if not accelerate, inequality and injustice. We must not shy away from asking not only how we live together but how we *could* live together (Morris, 2012; Barthes, 2013), not only how we are governed but how we *could* be governed. This would also entail thinking critically of and rethinking ethics, to which we turn next.

4

Luxury, Encasement, and the Emptiness of Anti-Corruption's Ethics

The last intellectual project in the life of the late cultural theorist Steve Redhead was something he termed 'claustropolitan sociology' or 'bunker anthropology' (Redhead, 2011, 2017). An ardent reader of Paul Virilio, he was deeply enamoured with Virilio's off-the-cuff aphorism that life in the 21st-century is moving from 'cosmopolis to claustropolis' (Virilio, 2007). Redhead argued that the extent to which we have embraced a cosmopolitan move toward hyper-sociality, openness, and genuine intersubjective encounters with the Other has always been vastly overstated, and that 'cosmopolitan sociology' was increasingly unable to accurately present and explain social reality. For Redhead, Virilio's aphorism neatly captured a general 'structure of feeling' of life in 21st-century liberal capitalism. That structure of feeling is one of claustrophobia: a sense of being hemmed in, enclosed, pressurized, and besieged by external forces and stimuli. In a liberal-individualistic world of sovereign individuals, we yearn to be encased from the intrusions of the Other. Interactions and encounters with others are increasingly met with either a reluctant dread, annoyance, or a foreboding sense of fear and apprehension (Sennett, 1977). Postmodernism has instilled a pervasive cynicism that prohibits belief in God, science, community, or even love, such that the only thing we believe in is our own cynical non-belief (Winlow & Hall, 2013). Our national, regional, religious, communal, and even familial ties are viewed by many as oppressive weights upon our freedom and individuality, something to be escaped on our individual journeys to full self-realization. Our preference appears to be for a 'capsular civilisation' of solitude over connection with others (Baumgartner, 1988; De Cauter, 2004); and for post-social non-places over a shared commons or community with corresponding social and ethical obligations (Augé, 1995; Raymen, 2016; Kuldova, 2017a).

As Virilio himself suggested – and as evidenced by the technological projects and futuristic fantasies of elites – it seems that what we really want is to get off this planet. Whether it is literally to another location in the universe, such as Elon Musk's project to colonise Mars and make humanity an inter-planetary species, Mark Zuckerberg's desire for us all to live in a virtual Metaverse, or Ray Kurzweil's desire to transcend our mortal form and upload our minds and consciousness to the cloud. In these claustropolitan times, the sense is that we occupy a dying and decaying world, where the very idea of 'society' represents nothing more than a crumbling project that offers little of genuine value, satisfaction, or hope. As Douglas Rushkoff[1] observes, where once such figures 'showered the world with madly optimistic business plans for how technology might benefit human society', now, in true claustropolitan fashion, tech billionaires have 'reduced technological progress to a video game that one of them wins by finding the escape hatch' (Rushkoff, 2022: 4).

The term 'escape', however, is somewhat misleading. 'Escape' conjures up the imagery of breaking free from confinement, of throwing off all shackles and restraints and running free into an open field or plain without rules, walls, or masters. But this is not necessarily the kind of escape that the claustropolitan subject pursues. What claustropolitanism engenders above all else is a desire for *encasement* and *insulation*. It is an escape *inward* behind layers of protection – be they physical, legal, or otherwise. As Rushkoff's *Survival of the Richest* demonstrates, many tech elites, CEOs, and leaders of the financial industry are simply preparing to retreat to their bespoke luxury bunkers and heavily securitized compounds as they anticipate some civilization-threatening Event (Rushkoff, 2022). In recent years, with the emergence of the coronavirus pandemic, the war in Ukraine (Phillips, 2020), and escalating geopolitical tensions between nuclear powers, the luxury bunker industry has reported an enormous surge of market demand for both more modest six-figure bunkers and more extravagant underground residences that stretch into the tens of millions of dollars. Vladimir Putin himself, reports have revealed, commissioned the construction of an emergency bunker beneath the infamous 'Putin's Palace' – his private uber-luxurious dacha on the Black Sea. The bunker itself has approximately 6,500 square feet of living space – the size of a small to middling sized mansion – with two escape tunnels that emerge in the hillside beneath Putin's Palace, and sufficient security, defence systems, and supplies to allow Putin to survive inside for weeks at a time (Schwartz & Carrier, 2023).

Claustropolitan elites and the desire for encasement

Oppidum are a Swiss company who offer to build these more outlandish doomsday properties for ultra-high net-worth individuals (UHNWI).[1]

Upon visiting Oppidum's website, at the time of writing, one is greeted by a welcome video that begins with a shot of a man in a plush living room watching the news, when a 'BREAKING NEWS' headline appears on the television reading 'UNEXPECTED TURN OF EVENTS' followed by 'BLACKOUT WARNING: INCOMING GEOMAGNETIC STORM.'[2] The man quickly reaches for his phone to call what one would assume to be his loved ones, before the shot pans out away from a mansion to reveal the estate's wider grounds, beneath which lies Oppidum's 'L'Heritage' luxury bunker model. A blacked-out SUV drives down a ramp that descends beneath the surface, pulling into a spacious garage peppered with expensive vintage cars. Travelling through a biometrically secured airlock, the viewer is taken on a CGI tour of the property, narrated by a soothing female voice laced with a tinge of excitement at the appropriate moments. We are first greeted with a luxurious expanse of living room space, complete with home theatre and games room where, we are told, 'whatever is happening in the world outside, you can rest easy and live fully in times of tranquillity and times of unrest', with the ability to 'entertain friends, enjoy private time with your family, or just savour having a place to reflect'.

We are then taken to the bunker's private art gallery, which 'keeps your collection in perfect condition and is built to the highest security standard'. Art and sculptures are dotted around the sanitized gallery in a scene reminiscent of the 'Ark of the Art' scene in Alfonso Cuaron's 2006 dystopian classic, *Children of Men*. Particular emphasis is given to the famous *Pericles in Corinthian Helmet* bust, which stands atop a mantle embossed with the Pericles quote: 'Freedom is the possession of those with the courage to defend it'. While a seemingly ironic message when advertising an underground bunker, the choice of quote actually captures the elite's understanding of freedom as an encasement from and mastery over nature, society, and humanity more generally. Amid images of a swimming pool, cigar room, meditation garden, wine cellar, fully equipped gym, dining areas, and lavish bedrooms, we are told of the bunker's security and environmental systems, which consist of blast-proof doors, military-grade security systems, two independent air filtration systems and two back-up power generators which provide constant off-the-grid power in the event of a blackout. There are also emergency batteries which are capable of powering the property independently and are fully charged at all times. All of these systems, we are told, operate 'completely autonomously', and the bunker overall is constructed to 'withstand ballistic, environmental, and civil threats'. However, the prospective buyer is assured that these extensive security measures – which are a harsh reminder of the realities that would be unfolding on the surface – will not disrupt the wider luxurious ambience, as 'all Oppidum systems are carefully integrated into the overall design so that you'll never know it's there. An invisible shield that operates with the same silent dependability of a Swiss watch, unseen and untouched'.

There is an obvious strangeness to the video that is nevertheless easy to overlook. Consider that one would only ever need to use such a bunker in times of great loss, death, destruction, and dangerous unrest, as indicated by the narrator's assurance that the bunker is designed and constructed to withstand 'ballistic, environmental, and civil' threats. This would be a time of great sadness that would engender a corresponding solemnity. Yet this solemnity is completely absent from the video, with the bunker itself entirely divorced from the context of its purpose or 'necessity', if we can use such a term. The video almost positions an End-of-Days event that would force one underground as a time to look forward to with excited anticipation, as an opportunity to kick back, relax, and take a break from the rat race. Never mind mourning the death of millions or the end of civilization. For the UHNWI individual who would own such a bunker, not even the apocalypse can get you down.

The video ends with its core pseudo-ethical justification for such extravagance. As the narrator tells us, 'To protect the people we love and the objects we cherish is the most powerful human instinct. Your Oppidum is the only luxurious answer to this call … this is security without sacrifice, comfort without compromise'. Throughout the website, the prospective buyer is relentlessly reassured of the justness of their purchase, and that they have meritoriously earned the right to such luxurious security through their many years of intrepid entrepreneurialism and effort. 'You have worked hard over many years, taken risks, seized opportunities, made your vision a reality. Your reward is the means to acquire and curate all the beautiful, rare, and precious objects you desire'.

Pushing past limited official and legal definitions, corruption has always been implicitly understood as a dereliction of duty, an absence of public accountability, and a use of power, wealth, and influence to evade the consequences of one's actions (Wedel, 2014). When prosecutors use deferred prosecution and non-prosecution agreements (DPAs/NPAs) against corporations who are guilty of the most egregious crimes, it strikes us as a corruption of the very notion of justice (Garrett, 2014). Similarly, when the banks who crashed the global economy in 2008 were bailed out by governments with huge sums of central bank money, it struck many citizens, academics (Whyte & Tombs, 2015; Tombs, 2016), and even corners of the business press[3] as an instance of blatant corruption and evasion of responsibility. This is particularly so when, in the US, the Treasury drafted in an ex-Goldman Sachs banker to assist in developing the Troubled Asset Relief Programme (Cohan, 2010). The claustropolitan retreat of the elite to their luxury bunkers while society disintegrates is arguably just this mode of corruption on a far grander scale. The power and wealth of the world's elite is not to be deployed to solve or avert growing global crises around climate change, public health, the economy, or geopolitical relations, but merely as a means to evade, shield, and encase themselves from the consequences of a world they have disproportionately helped to create. As Rushkoff, who discussed these disaster plans with tech billionaires, concluded: 'For them [tech elites] the future of technology is about only one thing: escape from the rest of us' (Rushkoff, 2022: 4).

Political economy of neoliberalism as claustropolitan encasement

However, evidence of this desire for encasement goes far beyond the issue of bunkers and in fact permeates our entire culture and economy. In many respects, the luxury bunker is simply an extension of the existing claustropolitan living habits of the super-rich. For decades, the wealthy have opted to reside inside gated communities and domestic fortresses, living 'nodal' lives of concealed mobility in the heart of global cities while never being *part* of them, cloistered from the masses of urban dwellers (Atkinson, 2016, 2020; Kuldova, 2017a). Luxury itself often has a claustropolitan bent. When it comes to property, holiday destinations, modes of personal travel, club memberships, or the ownership and display of art, the more securitized, hidden, and invisible, the better. After all, exclusivity – often a key feature of luxury – is often about inaccessibility, about secrecy. The shell company – that much-maligned financial instrument so crucial to corruption – encases one's wealth and identity in a legally-protected shell, safe from the prying eyes of law enforcement and tax authorities, while the ultimate beneficial owners draw on a small army of professionals and intermediaries who provide further layers of insulation (Michel, 2021; Bullough, 2022). Freeports and Special Economic Zones (SEZs) are another example. Within the demarcated area of the special economic zone or freeport, art, jewellery, fine wine, vintage cars, and other luxury items that are often used for money laundering and other corrupt purposes (Roberts, 2019; Helgadóttir, 2020; Weeks, 2020; Zarobell, 2020; Schwarzkopf & Backsell, 2021) are protected by a legal and regulatory sheath that is distinct from the laws and regulations that govern the rest of the country (Hall et al, 2022).

Indeed, the entire political economy of neoliberalism can be understood along the thematic lines of claustropolitan encasement. As Slobodian has convincingly demonstrated, neoliberalism was not a project of disembedding and 'liberating' the market from society, thereby realizing a utopian 'self-regulated' market (Slobodian, 2018). Rather, neoliberalism was and still is, to use Slobodian's own words, a project of 'encasement' (Slobodian, 2018: 13). The neoliberals built various political and economic institutions, supranational unions, passed laws, and enacted treaties which would encase *dominium* – the realm of property, land, money, and business – from *imperium* – the realm of sovereign governments and territorial states. As he writes, 'Geneva School neoliberals offered a blueprint for globalism based on institutions of multi-tiered governance that are *insulated* from democratic decision making and charged with maintaining the balance between the political world of imperium and the economic world of dominium' (Slobodian, 2018: 12; emphasis added). Neoliberalism was not a laissez-faire market freedom escaping *from* law, institutions, and the state, but an escape from democracy *through* law and managerial discourses, institutions, and the state (Chamayou, 2021); and while globalist neoliberals have drawn on the ethos of cosmopolitanism and multiculturalism as an ethico-cultural justification for their political-economic policies, it has always been primarily driven by a more claustropolitan motivation to encase the economy from the will of the *demos*.

The emergence of the compliance-industrial complex in response to various anti-policies (Kuldova, 2022a), including anti-corruption, is arguably a further example of this metaphor of encasement and bunkerization – of escape, freedom, and sovereignty in the market *through* regulation. As emphasized in the previous chapter, the vast proliferation of compliance measures on corporations looks ostensibly like a form of 'submission' to the state. Financial institutions, corporations, and industries have to engage in FCPA compliance; wider anti-corruption compliance; satisfy AML regulations; implement measures for countering the financing of terrorism (CFT); develop and meet environmental, social, and governance targets (ESG); demonstrate corporate social responsibility (CSR); create and disseminate ethical codes of conduct; stay abreast of directives from supranational governance bodies; update themselves on voluntary guidance, and so on. All of this appears to be evidence of the strong arm of governments bringing the world of money-making to heel, using the powers of the state or supranational body to challenge and curtail corporate sovereignty and perhaps demand higher 'ethical' standards of business. But Kuldova warns us against the mistake of assuming that this explosion of regulatory compliance is an entirely top-down phenomenon reluctantly accepted by industries and markets (Kuldova, 2022a). This would be to overlook the fact that industries themselves seem to be lobbying incessantly *for* regulation, voluntarily developing guidelines, codes of conduct, and expanding their compliance regimes into pervasive governance functions which infiltrate and structure entire organizations and industries.

But why would corporations and industries embrace the growth of compliance? Certainly, there is an element of pre-empting more rigorous state regulation. But the deeper answer, Kuldova argues, lies in the manner in which the various social ills of corruption, kleptocracy, and the financing of terrorism are being fought. Financial institutions, industries, and corporations are being brought in as the first line of defence in the fight against all manner of threats listed previously, with their size, power, centrality to the global economy, and subsequent powers of data and intelligence gathering being utilized as a policing function against illicit flows of money, goods, and services. The result is a wider *regulatory hybridization* in the name of various anti-policies that is resulting in the 'blurring of boundaries between the public and the private, between policy, law enforcement and implementation, and between regulator and regulated' (Kuldova, 2022a: 35). This regulatory hybridization enhances rather than curtails corporate sovereignty. Indeed, as Kuldova writes, what the rise of the compliance-industrial complex entails is the *delegation* of state authority and powers to private actors. With expansive powers to collect data, gather intelligence, investigate, and discipline, industries, corporations, and their employees are simultaneously suspect, police officer, prosecutor, judge, and jury.

In many respects, therefore, modern corporations and industries have transformed into self-contained, self-governing legal bunkers encased within compliance, with a tendency to resolve problems and avert or mitigate the impact of scandals internally rather than in the public legal arena. As Edelman and Suchman have written, such organizations have arguably become 'an entire private legal system in its own right' (Edelman & Suchman, 1999: 985). Janine Wedel has spoken of the 'new' corruption as characterized by 'flexian' individuals who, through wearing multiple hats and simultaneously acting as politicians, informal lobbyists, political advisors, industry leaders and independent academic experts, can blur and move across boundaries seamlessly, exerting influence and achieving ends in a fashion that would strike any ordinary individual as an act of corruption (Wedel, 2014). It seems that large organizations and industries are mirroring this behaviour, with the regulatory hybridization that has occurred as a result of the explosion of compliance scaling up capacities of the individual flexian actor to the organizational level. The Association of Certified Financial Crime Specialists (ACFCS), mentioned earlier, even offers webinars on this subject, a case in point being 'Transition from Government Service to Opportunities in AML, Compliance or Fraud in the Private Sector' which took place on the 11 April 2023 (accessible for members only and featuring intelligence community, law enforcement and military veterans who have successfully transitioned to careers in the financial industry; Kuldova attended this webinar and received, as is common in these events, a certificate of completion and 1.5 CFCS credits); becoming a 'flexian' is being taught, learned, encouraged, and certified.

Regulatory power to the regulated: the luxury superyacht industry

This regulatory hybridization and delegation of state authority not only gives the bunker-corporation or industry (as is the case for other industries, too) powers to internally police themselves, but also enables them to exert increasingly significant influence over the nature, scope, and implementation of regulation in their own industries, thereby shaping the regulatory environment to which they are subject (Edelman & Suchman, 1999; de Oliveira, 2018; Tsingou, 2018). As Kuldova evocatively describes:

> The paradox is that the more criminalized compliance management systems become, at least vis-à-vis those they are designed to control – be it employees, clients, customers, or suppliers – the more we see the proliferation of 'playful' regulatory sandboxes at the top, where regulators become creative sparring partners who jointly 'explore' regulation in the name of innovation rather than acting as 'police' vis-à-vis the regulated entities. ... Overall, we see private sector actors 'entering the international AML/CTF policy-making sphere' and 'significantly influencing global governance and challenging the primacy of the state' (de Oliveira, 2018: 154), and increasingly shaping the very regulation they are to submit to. (Kuldova, 2022a: 62–3)

This trend, where private sector actors and industries are drafted in by regulators as co-collaborators, is arguably the perfect mode of encasement, albeit one which opens the door to the kind of flexian corruption mentioned previously.

A good example of this is provided by the superyacht industry, a section of the luxury economy that has come under significant scrutiny over the past year. Since sanctions were imposed against Russia, the superyacht has become *the* luxury symbol of corruption and kleptocracy, with at least 24 superyachts currently subject to sanctions for their ties to individual Russian oligarchs. A number of these have been arrested or seized in various locations around the world, but even such wide-ranging sanctions make it difficult to arrest these vessels. Like other luxury assets such as real estate and art, superyachts invariably have complex ownership structures, with layers of shell companies disguising the ultimate beneficial owners. But superyachts have an added layer of complexity, often being registered and sailing under the flag of a nation that is different to its owners – called a 'flag of convenience' – while also being highly mobile, evidenced by a number of vessels which 'went dark' when sanctions hit and turned off their AIS tracking systems to avoid detection, quickly sailing to safe havens where sanctions do not apply such as Dubai, Israel, Turkey, and the Maldives.

Given the size, cost, and complexity of these vessels, the superyacht industry has an extremely narrow clientele. All of the superyachts currently subject to sanctions are between 70 and 180 m in length, cost hundreds of millions of dollars to build and purchase and have annual running costs which stretch into the tens of millions of dollars, making ownership of such superyachts off-limits to all but a tiny percentage of the world's wealthiest individuals. The narrow clientele also means that there are only a small handful of major superyacht builders in the world, and these builders derive a significant proportion of their business from parts of the world with high levels of kleptocracy (Transparency International, 2017), particularly at the higher end of the superyacht market. Just over 29 per cent of superyachts over 90 m in length are thought to be owned by Russian oligarchs,[4] with the proportion of high-end superyachts owned by Russian oligarchs more than doubling since 2009 (Transparency International, 2017), a period which coincides with Russia's increased integration into the global financial system as oligarchs sought to legitimize and defend their contestable wealth (Logvinenko, 2021).

The approximately two dozen superyachts that were made subject to sanctions in 2022 were made by just ten superyacht builders, with one company – Lürssen, a superyacht builder based in Germany – responsible for delivering 11 of those vessels, including multiple superyachts that are widely thought to belong to Vladimir Putin. In the aftermath of Russian sanctions, it has been reported that Lürssen actually sent out a questionnaire to its various clients and partners to find out more information about the identity of their clientele, citing a need to answer to authorities on the 'geopolitical situation in Ukraine'.[5] Despite this, Lürssen maintains that they are fully compliant with all laws and regulations.

Heesen, a Dutch superyacht builder, has delivered vessels not only to now-sanctioned Russian oligarchs, but to the Aliyev family – the notoriously corrupt 'First Family' of Azerbaijan – who financed their purchase through the State Oil Company of Azerbaijan (SOCAR) (Ostanin & Di Pietro, 2015). In 2013, Heesen also delivered the $80 m *Galactica Star* to the Nigerian minister for petroleum resources, Diezani Alison-Madueke, who purchased the superyacht through embezzled funds that were generated by £800 m of oil sales to Swiss commodity trading giant Glencore (Blas & Farchy, 2021). As it turns out, between 2008 and 2022 Heesen were owned by Vagit Alekperov, the CEO of Russian energy giant Lukoil via his Cypriot shell company, Morcell Ltd. In 2014 Oceanco, another Netherlands-based superyacht builder, built and delivered the $250 m superyacht *Equanimity* (now renamed *Tranquility*)[6] to Jho Low, the businessman who misappropriated $3.5 bn from the Malaysian sovereign wealth fund as part of the 1MDB (Down, 2018). Oceanco have also delivered superyachts to other figures associated with corruption and kleptocracy, such as Russian oligarchs Igor Sechin and Sergey Guryev. Quite simply, a significant proportion of the top-end of the superyacht industry is underpinned by kleptocratic wealth. Rather fittingly, *Tranquility* is on Oceanco's website marketed with the following line: 'What if You Make Your Own Rules?'[7]

There are innumerable other corruption scandals which implicate the superyacht industry with kleptocrats, brutal dictators, and corrupt figures from around the world. Brokerage firms, charter services, designers and other service providers have not even been discussed. Indeed, the only industry-related business that has been sanctioned is Imperial Yachts, a Monaco-based brokerage firm owned by Russian businessman Evgeniy Kochman who connect their clients with builders, designers, and crew, and generally satisfy various client needs. Imperial Yachts were sanctioned by the US for allegedly brokering the sale of at least one superyacht tied to sanctioned oligarchs who are thought to be Vladimir Putin, Gennedy Timchenko, and Rosneft CEO Igor Sechin, although the company vehemently deny the charges (Forsythe et al, 2022). Their web page, which currently consists solely of a statement in response to the sanctions, claims that: 'Imperial Yachts conducts all its businesses in full compliance with laws and regulations in all jurisdictions in which we operate. We are not involved in our clients' financial affairs. We are in the yacht building, management, sale and charter business. That is our focus and what we do.'[8]

However, these scandalous purchases are not necessarily what is of immediate interest to us here. What is more interesting for the line of argument pursued in this book is how, much like the art and antiquities market discussed in the previous chapter, these superyacht builders have organized and embedded themselves in the superyacht industry's regulatory landscape. Lürssen, Heesen, and Oceanco – along with 20 other superyacht builders – are all members of the Superyacht Builders Association (SYBAss), an organization that represents the shared interests of superyacht builders, and whose members build more than two-thirds of all new superyachts over 40 m.[9] In 2013, SYBAss were granted permanent consultative status at the International Maritime Organization (IMO), a representative agency of the United Nations that regulates all shipping and maritime activities, including the superyacht industry. To quote from their website, SYBAss 'maintain close relationships with regulators', have 'active involvement with regulatory bodies', and 'makes sure that rules which impact superyachts take into account the unique nature of these vessels and the way they are operated'.[10] SYBAss regularly attend IMO committee and subcommittee meetings as well as working groups, and 'actively participates in the development of new proposals or amendments to existing regulations in order to ensure that they take into account the unique nature of the superyacht sector'.[11] Of the ten companies who built and delivered the two-dozen superyachts that are now subject to some combination of UK, EU, or US sanctions, eight were members of SYBAss.[12] This is precisely the defining characteristic of what has been described as 'regulatory capitalism' (Levi-Faur, 2005, 2017; Braithwaite, 2008; Brinks et al, 2021), 'regulatory state' (Veggeland, 2009, 2010), the 'blurring of governance' (Gray, 2006; Solomon, 2010), or 'networked governance' (Bleklie et al, 2011), both by those who would like to see more of it or improve upon it and by those who are critical of its key premises.

In other words, here we have the perfect illustration of this blurring of boundaries between regulator and regulated, characteristic of a compliance-industrial complex that has emerged in response to a series of anti-policies, most notably anti-corruption and AML (Kuldova, 2022a). With its permanent consultative status to the IMO, SYBAss – an organization whose members routinely serve corrupt and kleptocratic clientele and even organizes member companies that have been owned by Russian oligarchs – are actively involved in the development and amendment of the regulation they are subject to in precisely the way in which Kuldova described in the previous excerpt. In an even more absurd extension of the argument made in the previous chapter, companies owned by oligarchs who are heavily implicated in corruption and who draw a significant portion of their top-end business from kleptocratic wealth are now expected to act as crime fighters *against* corruption and kleptocracy. This goes beyond registered lobbyists or even the increase in the practice of shadow lobbying (Wedel, 2014), but provides a formalized and recognized role for corporations to act as collaborators in building and transforming the regulatory environment of their own industry and does so in a way which implies that both regulators and regulated subjects are all on the same team holding the same shared interests. This is perfectly in line with the now hegemonic logic of multistakeholderism (Garsten & Jacobsson, 2012; Garsten & Sörbom, 2018). Multistakeholderism sells us an ideological fantasy of alignment and harmony, a fantasy of *all* – corporations, businesses, investors, venture capitalists and venture philanthropists, academics, scientists, NGOs, foundations, civil society actors, governments, politicians, think tanks, citizens, consumers, etc. – working together for the benefit of all (doing good and fighting crime), in *consensus*, without friction and without any fundamental antagonism (Kuldova, forthcoming); this is precisely what enables the proliferation of 'policies without politics' (Telleria, 2020), while foreclosing alternatives to neoliberal hegemony. The *United States Strategy on Countering Corruption* discussed earlier is a clear example of precisely this logic, enlisting private sector actors as partners in the fight against corruption (White House, 2021b). An even more recent, and even more explicit instance is the US *National Cybersecurity Strategy* (White House, 2023), which emphasizes multistakeholder partnerships and enlists large private actors like Google, Apple, Meta, Amazon, and Microsoft, directly in the task of ensuring national security in the cyberspace, while explicitly lifting any such burden from individuals and small businesses.

Working in close cooperation with the private sector, my Administration has taken steps to protect the American people from hackers, hold bad actors and cybercriminals accountable, and defend against the increasingly malicious cyber campaigns targeting our security and privacy. (White House, 2023: 2)

Together, industry and government must drive effective and equitable collaboration to correct market failures, minimize the harms from cyber incidents to society's most vulnerable, and defend our shared digital ecosystem. (White House, 2023: 9)

This is just to point out that the cases we use from across the luxury sector are not unique, but fall well within hegemonic regulatory trends, where large private actors come to be seen as partners in governance, crime-fighting, and ensuring of national security; in this case, there is little doubt that this further enhances and legitimizes their monopoly power as they become indispensable to the state's security interests and policy.[13]

The luxury yacht industry, in the business of providing privacy, security, and luxury for the ultrarich, while not a likely candidate to protect the nation's security (interests), benefits nonetheless from the same regulatory dispositifs; and, like all businesses, it has to comply with sanctions and perform sanctions screening, precisely in the national security interest.

Along the thematic lines of this chapter, having a hand in shaping and revising the rules one must submit to is arguably the ultimate mode of protective encasement, and it is quite easy to see how defiance *through* compliance can be achieved. After all, as Kuldova shrewdly observes, there is a layered nature to compliance that seems to mirror the methods of money laundering, with layers upon layers of regulations, guidelines, industry standards, and directives adding bewildering levels of complexity in precisely the same way that assets such as superyachts, real estate, and fine art are owned through immensely complex and layered corporate structures (Kuldova, 2022a).

Business ethics, compliance, and Kantian deontology

The growth of compliance has been underpinned by both a long-term rise in the formalization of business ethics and periodic scandals which have spurred calls for the world of business to conduct itself in a more ethical manner (Bloom, 2017; Mees, 2020). Irrespective of their market interests, corporations have a duty to uphold certain non-market ideals and obediently follow rules and regulations set down by external authorities, rules that are supposed to place a handbrake on the amorality of the profit motive. Therefore, at first glance, this blurring of boundaries where regulated subjects insert themselves into and actively shape the rules that they must follow seems to be a *perversion* and a corruption of compliance ethics. But this would be to misunderstand the actual structure of ethics that underpins both compliance and anti-policies, namely that of Kantian deontological ethics. In fact, what we wish to argue is that, rather than being a perversion of ethics, the blurring of regulated and regulator is actually in complete conformity with Kantian deontological ethics, even if it is not consciously derived from it. To understand this point and flesh it out, we must take a closer look at the moral philosophy which implicitly underpins the world of anti-policy, anti-corruption, and compliance, something which is scarcely done in the corruption literature.

Kant's moral philosophical project endeavoured to arrive at a conception of ethics and a way of appraising whether or not something was moral that was timeless and independent of any particular goals, context, religion, culture, historical period, or conception of human flourishing or human happiness (Kant, 2012). For Kant, whether or not something was deemed moral or immoral could not vary across time and space, be subject to particular passions or desires, or be decided by determining whether or not it achieved positive ends for individuals, communities, or society as a whole. This, for Kant, would be to relativize the realm of morality such that there are no moral truths but only particular contextual moral preferences. In Kant's mind, if there is to be any truth to morality, if morality is to have any real purchase, what must be developed is a kind of moral equation that amounts to a truly universal law that is binding upon all free and rational human beings everywhere, independent of space and time. Therefore, Kant held that for any moral precept or imperative to be true, it must be categorical and unconditional in nature, and we discover whether or not something is a genuine categorical moral imperative or morally permissible by subjecting various precepts or actions to what Kant calls the 'universal imperative of duty', which takes the form of 'act as if the maxim of your actions were to become by your will a universal law of nature'. The test of whether or not something is a genuine categorical moral imperative is whether we can consistently universalize it and will that it be a universal law that is unconditionally binding upon all people, including – and perhaps most importantly – ourselves.

Kant contrasts categorical imperatives with hypothetical imperatives which are defined by their conditionality. A hypothetical imperative takes the form of 'you ought to do x, y, and z if ...', with the if being able to take all manner of forms, whether that be if you want to please God, achieve, or increase the happiness of yourself or others, or realize some kind of goal or outcome. By contrast, categorical imperatives have no such conditions. We can do nothing but will them, irrespective of whether we want to, whether it is in our interest to do so, or whether or not it will make us happy or even produce positive outcomes for others. Categorical imperatives, therefore, are entirely tautologous. There can be no reason for adhering to a categorical imperative other than the fact that it is has been determined to be a categorical imperative. This determination is reason enough. To try and provide further reasons for following the rules of morality – such as the benefits it would bring – implies a conditionality that belies its categorical and unconditional status. 'In a sublime tautology', writes Terry Eagleton, 'we should be moral simply because it is moral to be so' (Eagleton, 2009: 113). It is simply our duty to follow moral precepts that satisfy the test of the categorical imperative. As MacIntyre has written, a Kantian response to the question 'Why should I do my duty?' would be simply: 'Because it is your duty' (MacIntyre, 2011).

In this respect, the proliferation of anti-policies that we have spoken of in this book, particularly anti-corruption, are quintessential examples of categorical imperatives. Moral philosophers such as MacIntyre have argued that Kant's moral philosophy is a significant dividing point in the history of ethics, such that when laypeople think about ethics, they do so in a way that is roughly analogous to Kant's conception of it, even if they have never read any moral philosophy (MacIntyre, 2002: 183). It is therefore entirely unsurprising that in a world where the dominant conception of ethics is broadly Kantian, we witness a seemingly endless proliferation of anti-policies. Practices such as corruption are conceived as universal *a priori* evils, the elimination of which is categorically and unconditionally moral. Nobody tries to claim anymore, as some scholars once did, that there are particular situations and contexts in which corruption can be beneficial and permissible (Leff, 1964; Bayley, 1966; Huntington, [1987] 2002). It is true that governments, NGOs, anti-corruption activists and corporations regularly and predictably recite the various social, political, and economic benefits that it is assumed would be derived from eliminating corruption, thereby making it appear as if they were treating the tackling of corruption as a hypothetical imperative. This is an important point that we will return to later in this chapter. But if it was somehow discovered that these benefits would not actually materialize if we were to successfully tackle corruption, it would not cause any of these actors to suggest that we should stop trying to do so or to conclude that corruption was morally permissible.

Indeed, it is openly acknowledged that despite the quite astounding growth of the anti-corruption industry and various anti-corruption measures, they have failed to be effective in tackling corruption or delivering the benefits that anti-corruption was supposed to yield (Johnston, 2012; Johnston & Fritzen, 2021). On the contrary, it has been argued that when it comes to the benefits of anti-corruption – such as justice, transparency, accountability, ethics, and a redistribution of wealth and power to the people – the growth of the compliance-industrial complex and the anti-corruption industry has yielded outcomes opposite to what they were supposed to achieve (Kuldova, 2022a). Corporations are given NPAs and DPAs which hardly seem like meaningful forms of justice (Garrett, 2014). We are awash in an overabundance of data that cannot be meaningfully processed and understood by human beings, and the regulatory landscape has become so complex and engorged as to be utterly incomprehensible, both of which amount to an increase in opacity instead of transparency (Hansen, 2015; Rosa, 2021; Kuldova, 2022a). As a result of this incomprehensibility, there is an increased reliance on technocratic experts and a burgeoning RegTech and SupTech industry which has done more to transfer wealth upwards and concentrate power than it has to distribute it to ordinary people (Han, 2015). Moreover, the increasing use of such technologies to tackle corruption and the suspicion of human judgment means that human actors are scarcely being asked to exercise any ethical agency whatsoever, making it difficult to suggest there has been any genuine ethical renaissance.

Nevertheless, even with the benefits of anti-corruption not being forthcoming – and perhaps *never* being forthcoming – it has not dampened the conviction that corruption must continuously be fought. Or, to put it another way, the benefits of anti-corruption are understood as just that: benefits. They are not *reasons*, for the only reason for tackling corruption is that it is a categorical imperative to fight corruption. In the world of anti-corruption, there is little pragmatic talk of reducing corruption to 'acceptable' levels. As is true of other anti-policies such as anti-racism or anti-fascism, while we know that the total eradication of corruption is impossible, there is simply no tolerable level of it that can be accepted, with law enforcement and regulators regularly speaking of 'zero tolerance' approaches to purify the world of corruption or money laundering, a further indicator that the elimination of corruption is implicitly treated as a categorical imperative.

Morality for Kant is about duty. As Kant writes at the opening of *Groundwork for the Metaphysics of Morals*, 'It is impossible to think of anything at all in the world, or indeed even beyond it, that could be taken to be good without limitation, except a *good will*' (Kant, 2012: 9, emphasis in original). Even if what we happen to want to do or what is in our interest to do passes the test of the categorical imperative, what is most important is that our actions are motivated by duty, rather than performed from any other motives. Even performing a morally good action because it makes us feel good to act in an ethical way does not, in Kant's formulation, make the action moral. What determines the morality of our action is the intention to conform with what we know to be our moral duty. In Kant's mind, we cannot choose our inclinations. All we can do is choose between our inclinations or desires as they happen to be, and what we know our duty to be according to the test of the categorical imperative.

It is for this reason that when we think about ethics, we typically think of it as obedient rule-following. And when we think about rule *following*, it implies that these rules are derived from some external authority or source. But this is not at all what Kant had in mind. For Kant, genuine moral reasoning is the ultimate expression of *autonomy*. At the very opening of his essay, *An Answer to the Question 'What is Enlightenment?'*, Kant describes the 'inability to use one's own understanding without the guidance of another' (Kant, 1991: 1) as a moral and intellectual 'immaturity' and derided the laziness of having 'a book to have understanding in place of me, a spiritual adviser to have a conscience for me, a doctor to judge my diet for me' (Kant, 1991: 1). It is the *choices* we make that make our actions worthy of moral praise or condemnation. If we are simply following rules predetermined by God, a regulator, or a government, there is no moral agency or thought at work here, we are simply doing what we are told. If we act based on our feelings or desires as they happen to be, we are merely slave to our passions. To act in this way is not to act with autonomous and rational moral agency but to succumb to *heteronomy* and allow ourselves to be influenced by forces external to our own reason.

The prominence within deontological ethics of obediently adhering to our duty – and the positioning of duty in opposition to all other desires, interests, goals, or outcomes – makes it easy to overlook the centrality of autonomy in Kant's moral philosophy. Kant's conception of ethics is about making the rational human being an autonomous moral sovereign. In and of itself, the test of the categorical imperative does not hand down any moral edicts. It does not tell us *what* we ought to do – another important point that we will return to later – it simply provides the *means* for evaluating various actions or principles, and it is down to the individual to do the work of figuring out what duty demands of them. Therefore, the individual moral agent obeys nobody but her own rationality and can – or rather *must* – reject all external authorities so as not to fall into the trap of heteronomy. Indeed, the etymological root of the English word autonomy is found in the Greek word *autonomos*, meaning 'having its own laws' or 'making laws for oneself'. It is here that it becomes clearer how the aforementioned blurring of the regulated and regulator in relation to SYBAss and the superyacht industry, while seeming like a perversion or a corruption of ethics, is in fact in deeper conformity with the structure of our culture's predominant conception of ethics than we intuitively realize. As MacIntyre writes, within Kant's ethics, 'the rational being utters the commands of morality to himself' (MacIntyre, 2002: 187). They develop their own moral precepts and submit them to the test of the categorical imperative, with the likes of Elizabeth Anscombe describing such legislating for oneself as absurd, equating it to calling 'each reflective decision a man made *vote* resulting in a majority, which as a matter of proportion is overwhelming, for it is always 1–0' (Anscombe, 1958: 2).

This is what allows deontological ethics to sit so comfortably within a society governed by the political philosophy and ideology of liberal individualism. Not only does the categorical imperative make the individual morally sovereign, but in detaching duty from the fulfilment of any particular social role, social practice, or the achievement of any particular end, it also permits the individual to live in any way they choose and do whatever they happen to want to do, provided that it can pass the test of the categorical imperative. As noted already, the categorical imperative does not tell us what we ought to do in the way that, say, neo-Aristotelian ethics does in its conception of various social roles and practices as having certain associated ethical commitments and goals. Consistent with the anti-policies that are a product of its moral philosophy, Kantian ethics most often produces *negative* ethical injunctions. As MacIntyre argues:

> The typical examples of alleged categorical imperatives given by Kant tell us what *not* to do; not to break promises, tell lies, commit suicide, and so on. But as to what activities we ought to engage in, what ends we ought to pursue, the categorical imperative seems to be silent. Morality sets limits to the ways in which and the means by which we conduct our lives; it does not give them direction. Thus morality apparently sanctions any way of life which is compatible with keeping our promises, telling the truth, and so on. (MacIntyre, 2002: 190)

Furthermore, because we are not told from where or what source we are to derive the maxims which we must submit to the test of the categorical imperative, these maxims can take almost any form. Herein for MacIntyre lies a major problem, for he argues that the test of the categorical imperative is actually a relatively *empty* one because 'with sufficient ingenuity almost every precept can be universalised' (MacIntyre, 2002: 190). All that is required is that these precepts are structured with a sufficient degree of specificity such that 'the maxims will permit me to do what I want while prohibiting others from doing what would nullify the maxim if universalised' (MacIntyre, 2002: 190) to the extent that MacIntyre concludes that the test of the categorical imperative is sufficiently empty that it 'imposes restrictions only on those insufficiently equipped with ingenuity' (MacIntyre, 2002: 191). This is especially the case given that ethics, for Kant, is entirely disconnected from the achievement of any particular outcomes. It matters not if the precepts constructed achieve any positive ends, all that matters is that they can be universalized. This is undoubtedly not what Kant had intended, and such manipulation of the test of the categorical imperative would certainly be a perversion of the *spirit* of Kant's moral philosophy. But it is not a perversion of its structure.

We can therefore quite easily imagine how the blurring of regulated and regulator, whereby the regulated subject has a hand in making regulation for themselves, can allow such regulation to be crafted in such highly specific ways as to permit ethically questionable behaviour and *encase* such behaviour within regulations which do nothing to achieve any positive outcomes in combatting corruption. This is indicated by the previous quotes taken from SYBAss' own website, where SYBAss describes their role as making sure that IMO regulation accounts for the specificity and 'unique' nature of superyachts and the superyacht industry. We can find a similar example of the emptiness of deontological maxims in the Organization for Economic Co-operation and Development's (OECD) much-vaunted 'Public Integrity Indicators' which were first launched in December 2021. These indicators were conceived as a great step forward in the international comparative measurement of corruption risks, pushing past the subjectivism of Transparency International's Corruption Perception Index and 'establishing a new benchmark for government resilience to corruption risks' rooted in 'objective, evidence-based and actionable data'.[14] Most importantly, some of these indicators ostensibly go some way in casting scrutiny on the often overlooked 'flexian' and 'revolving door' corruption described by Wedel (2014), by measuring the frequency with which ministers or top-tier civil servants moved from a ministry to the private sector. But the parameters of these indicators are formulated with such a degree of specificity as to render them entirely useless. The indicators are only accounting for those ministers or civil servants who, within 2 years of leaving their posts, are hired by private sector companies operating in their most recent ministry's area of competency.[15] Poor scores on this indicator are indicative of corruption risks, while positive scores suggest there are little corruption risks to worry about in this area. But given the realities of contemporary politics where politicians move between ministries with great regularity, often holding multiple ministerial offices in a single year, these restrictions are somewhat arbitrary and easy to circumnavigate. When regulations or metrics are connected to reward or sanction – even intangible ones like a corruption risk rating – gaming of those regulations and metrics will inevitably occur (Merry, 2011, 2016; Whitson, 2013; Muller, 2018; Kuldova, 2021a); and endeavouring to measure something like ethics or integrity through performance on metrics or compliance with policy or regulations is likely to produce mere illusions which tell us little about reality.

This kind of gaming and evasion will be particularly prevalent in a culture where the dominant conception of ethics is entirely concerned with the obedient performance of *duty*, and is unconcerned with the achievement of particular ends or the development of moral *character* or particular virtues. The fundamental ethical question for neo-Aristotelian moral philosophy is 'what am I to do if I am to flourish as a human being?' For utilitarian moral philosophy, it is 'what am I to do if I am to achieve the greatest happiness for the greatest number?' For deontological moral philosophy, the fundamental ethical question is 'what am I to do if I am to do right?', and it asks this question in such a way that there is no necessary connection between doing right, faring well, or achieving happiness or any other moral outcome. Indeed, it is somewhat of a paradox that anti-corruption, which is so obsessively and single-mindedly geared toward the achievement of the particular outcome of ending corruption, has endeavoured to do so through the employment of a deontological ethics that is entirely *unconcerned* with the achievement of particular ends of the good of a particular social order. All it is concerned with is whether one's duty according to the categorical imperative has been obediently performed; and we have already demonstrated that duty can be structured in such a way that it does not necessarily prohibit or conflict with forms of behaviour that would be widely considered as corrupt.

Furthermore, this deontological detachment of duty from social roles, offices, or the achievement of shared goods and ends effectively amounts to the severance between morality and desire, and leaves us in a situation where the individual is given no good reasons for adhering to the abstract commands of duty. As MacIntyre outlines, other ethical systems typically operate with a three-part structure (MacIntyre, 2011). There is the individual as they happen to be on the one hand, and the individual as they could be if they realized their *telos* on the other. Ethics – which in MacIntyre's neo-Aristotelian view is a training in the virtues to achieve genuine goods and ends which are shared by humanity – enables the individual to make the transition from the former to the latter. It involves an education of one's desires towards their true Good. Therefore, the individual can always be provided with good reasons for adhering to what morality requires of them, as morality within these frameworks is not seen as distinct from or in opposition to the achievement of human flourishing or happiness, but as integral to its achievement and a necessary spur to its pursuit. But with the deontological detachment of duty from social roles, offices, notions of human flourishing, or the achievement of shared goods and ends, the individual is given no good reasons for adhering to the abstract commands of duty. The cohesive three-part scheme is reduced to a two-part scheme. There is simply, on the one hand, the individual and their desires as they happen to be in their untutored state, and the various maxims of morality on the other, with no apparent relationship between these two parts. Consequently, within this system 'the injunctions of morality, thus understood, are likely to be ones that human nature, thus understood, has strong tendencies to disobey' (MacIntyre, 2011: 55).

This is the precise reason that the duties of avoiding corruption, bribery, fraud, kleptocracy and so on – which are all positioned as categorical imperatives – are subsequently treated as *hypothetical* imperatives in practice. With deontological ethics incapable of providing the subject with good reasons for doing their duty of avoiding and tackling corruption – other than the tautologous 'because it is your duty' – various reasons must be constructed. Consequently, corporations are warned of the reputational and financial damage of corruption scandals, or the benefits of a firm signalling their ethical conduct. In the sphere of political corruption, warnings are given as to how corruption and bribery can discourage foreign investment, hamper social and economic development, or damage trust in government or undermine the integrity of the financial system. This amounts to a transformation of ethics into risk management, and it is striking that when corporations and consulting firms specializing in compliance speak about corruption, they flit seamlessly between the language of ethics and the language of risk management as if the two were entirely interchangeable. In its pages on anti-corruption and integrity in the public sector, the OECD talks of 'risk management to safeguard integrity'.[16] Similarly, the audit, consulting, and financial advisory giant Deloitte, claim that 'the implementation of a fraud and corruption risk management process' can 'proactively promote the ethical culture within your organisation'.[17] It is notable that this merger of ethics and risk is not limited to corruption but is replicated in a wide range of other areas of contemporary life. The ethical approval of academic research has become a bureaucratic risk management exercise rather than a genuine evaluation of the ethical merits and shortcomings of the proposed research methodology (Hall & Winlow, 2012). Similarly in the field of medicine, ethical principles which govern the conduct and decision-making of medical professionals have become intimately entangled with managing risks of litigation and financial loss (Kapp, 1991; Card, 2020); while in the financial services industry, it is suggested that equality, diversity and inclusion (EDI) in the workplace should be seen simultaneously as both an ethical cause and a risk management decision.[18] Properly conceived, ethics and risk are entirely distinct categories. Ethics is about the cultivation of virtues, character, and behaviour that will allow individuals and collectives to discover, pursue, and realize genuine goods shared by humanity. Risk management, on the other hand, is merely the efficient use of resources to avoid negative outcomes on the basis of their likelihood and severity (Beck, 1992). There is an enormous gulf between them. Despite this, the merger of ethics and risk in these various spheres of social, economic, and professional life passes largely without comment, and is not experienced as particularly strange or remarkable. This indicates that there is something deeper about our culture and the way we understand ethics, the human subject, and their relationships to social practices that needs to be revisited.

Anti-corruption and the culture of emotivism

It is at this point that anti-corruption betrays its original Kantian ethical underpinnings, and through compliance, risk, and the infrastructure of regulatory and supervisory technologies, descends into a manipulative emotivism. As a brief recap, emotivism is the theory that all moral judgments are nothing more than expressions of particular preferences, attitudes, or feelings and that there is nothing inherently factual about them. Emotivism has a tendency to flourish in a culture that has abandoned any notion or account of the human *telos*, and where moral disagreements are made up of participants whose rival starting premises, while internally coherent, are so radically incommensurable with one another that they cannot logically defeat the other's argument on its own terms, and thereby become circular in nature. We see this interminable debate all the time on various hot-button topics such as the moral legitimacy of abortion, the justness of war, or the ethical legitimacy of lockdowns during COVID-19 and so on. For instance, when it comes to the topic of abortion, advocates of pro-choice argue from the starting premise of the mother's right to choose. Pro-life advocates, on the other hand, argue for the right of the unborn child, and that the taking of any human life is a sin. On their own terms, each side's arguments are internally coherent and logically follow from the chosen starting premises. They can provide endless reasons for why an individual would agree with their position. But these arguments are only convincing insofar as one already accepts the starting premises on which they are based. In a culture of emotivism, MacIntyre argues, what neither side can do is provide an argument that logically defeats the starting premises of their opponent, and thereby provide good reasons for choosing one set of starting premises over another. 'From our rival conclusions we can argue back to our rival premises; but when we do arrive at our premises argument ceases and the invocation of one premise against another becomes a matter of pure assertion and counter-assertion' (MacIntyre, 2011: 8). Consequently, the debates become interminable, not just in the sense that they go on and on, but in that they can find no resolution. As the emotivist philosopher C.L. Stevenson argued, moral or evaluative statements such as 'this is good' or 'this is bad' amount to nothing more than 'I approve/disapprove of this, do so as well' (Stevenson, 1960).

What this state of affairs involves, and what MacIntyre argues to be the defining feature of a culture of emotivism, is an obliteration of any distinction between manipulative and non-manipulative relations. Since ethical debates can find no terminus in such a culture, there is nothing left to do but for 'one will to align the attitudes, feelings, preferences and choices of another with its own' (MacIntyre, 2011: 28), often through manipulative means. The side who emerges victorious is the side who can coerce the greatest emotive support for their position, harnessing feelings such as guilt, fear, and shame, and appealing to notions of 'freedom' and 'justice' often in highly emotive and entirely opposed ways. Hence the contemporary prevalence of 'naming and shaming' as a strategy in anti-corruption, human rights violations, financial regulation, and so on (Hafner-Burton, 2008; Friman, 2015). In moral debates that descend into emotivism, we often see one side try to smear the character of their opponent, denigrate their intellect, accuse them of some form of bigotry or other evil, and cynically question their true motives to inspire distrust for their opponent among onlookers to the debate. The moral argument is 'won' through force, not reason.

On the face of it, this scenario does not apply to the field of corruption and anti-corruption. After all, is it not true that everyone is uniformly *against* corruption? Where debates do become interminable, however, are around the means for tackling corruption such as bringing an end to the anonymity of shell companies, the duty to complete due diligence and KYC checks and so on. There are those, for example, who defend the use of anonymous shell companies from the starting premise of the right to privacy and the economic freedom to conceal assets for legitimate purposes or for tax planning. Restricting the use of shell companies or demanding a public register of beneficial ownership is viewed as an unconscionable imposition on these rights. The Court of Justice of the European Union, in its ruling of 22 November 2022[19] has even stated that, as *Wealth Briefing* put it, 'it is invalid to use public registers of beneficial ownership as a weapon against money laundering because of the risks of threats to financial privacy. The judgment, which could have big implications for the industry, highlights boundaries between legitimate privacy and illegitimate secrecy'[20]; the ruling invalidated the provision of the 5th EU Anti-Money Laundering Directive which guaranteed public access to data on companies' beneficial owners.

On the other hand, there are those who argue there is no need for such anonymity and that any legitimate use of anonymous shell companies is far outweighed by their facilitation of harmful practices such as kleptocracy, organized crime, money laundering, and tax evasion. Predictably, Transparency International argued that the decision by the Court of Justice of the European Union will set back the fight against cross-border corruption by years.[21] While a far greater number agree with TI, and denounce the use of anonymous shell companies rather than advocate for them, the debate is nevertheless an interminable one. Evidence for this can be seen in governmental or organizational reports or webpages that critically discuss the relationship between corruption and shell companies. In such publications, it has become almost compulsory to open with the caveat or disclaimer that there are numerous legitimate purposes for anonymous shell companies. Nevertheless, the use of shell companies itself has, in emotivist fashion, become tainted with suspicion and transformed into a 'red flag', along with the respective localities and jurisdictions.

Similarly, around the issue of due diligence and KYC, there are large numbers of people who argue that such measures are absolutely imperative. Without them, kleptocrats, organized crime groups, fraudsters and other nefarious actors would be able to launder money and peddle fraudulent goods with impunity. Given that such wealth is accumulated on the back of oppression, physical and political violence, the immiseration of entire nations, and their social and economic infrastructures, such measures possess a strong moral justification. But there are those who oppose the proliferation of due diligence and KYC checks. The CEO of cryptocurrency exchange ShapeShift, Erik Voorhees, has publicly challenged the ethical legitimacy of blanket KYC mandates. Invoking the right to individual liberty and privacy, Voorhees objects to the continued expansion of KYC and due diligence on the grounds that they necessarily involve the surveillance and investigation of the innocent as well as the guilty, in addition to the fact that such measures are often highly ineffective in tackling money laundering. In an interview, he states: 'I can understand the argument that if someone is charged or suspected of a crime that they start losing certain rights from that. But to mandate surveillance and endangerment of all people innocent seems to be completely unethical on its face'.[22]

On its own merits, this argument is logical. Why should innocent people be subjected to pre-emptive forensic investigation and surveillance, to be considered guilty and suspicious until proven innocent and trustworthy? While we may be sceptical about the motivations underpinning such arguments from the likes of Voorhees, we should recall that it was precisely these arguments that were invoked by the political liberal-left in opposition to the vast expansion of intelligence and surveillance powers in the aftermath of 9/11 (Agamben, 2005). That very same political demographic now tends to populate the field of anti-corruption activism and academic scholarship on anti-corruption, and would now reject the arguments they once invoked when they are applied to the issue of anti-corruption.

Therefore, these are largely interminable debates, but in this culture of emotivism, the act of openly challenging measures such as KYC or due diligence is a red flag in itself, suggestive that one is tacitly accepting – or even an active facilitator – of money laundering, fraud, corruption, and kleptocracy, and therefore on the side of Biden's 'bad guys'. To be critical or resistant to strategies of transparency is positioned as tantamount to permitting and being complicit in organized crime, the violation of human rights, the commission of political violence, and the impoverishment of entire nations as their leaders steal their national wealth or sell off their natural resources at a fraction of their true value in exchange for a personal fortune. Critique of measures such as transparency, KYC, and due diligence seem limited to critiques of how successfully and thoroughly they have been implemented and embraced. There is little systemic critique of the measures themselves; and the fact that there appears to be such a consensus on how we tackle corruption – or at least an absence of critique for existing approaches – is a testament to the success and power of these emotivist arguments in foreclosing the boundaries of the debate. It is analogous to the way in which those who questioned the efficacy or moral legitimacy of lockdowns, facemasks, or vaccine mandates during the COVID-19 pandemic were immediately and uniformly labelled conspiracy theorists, COVID-sceptics, or 'covidiots' who were willing to risk the lives of everyone around them and their loved ones (Briggs et al, 2021; Green & Fazi, 2023). They were branded selfish individuals, who placed their personal ability to consume or the health of the economy over and above protecting the lives of citizens.

When we encounter such emotivist arguments in the field of anti-corruption we should always keep in mind that there are vested economic interests at play here and that, as emphasized throughout this book, anti-corruption, AML and compliance are all market *creators* in precisely the same way that the COVID-19 pandemic created new markets or significantly expanded demand in existing markets in the tech and pharmaceutical industries. What is commodified here, however, is law, rulemaking, regulation, and regulatory compliance, the very ways in which we are governed; indeed, the very commodification of regulation and its capture by powerful market interests is precisely where the threat to liberty and justice of the common man lies. To point this out is not conspiracy theorizing, but to simply remind ourselves of the logic of capital and how economic interests seek to maintain, concentrate, and expand its power to accumulate wealth; something which intellectuals and activists from the left have always endeavoured to critique.

We should be clear that we do not raise these points out of any sympathy with the likes of Voorhees's openly libertarian position. Rather, the point we are making is that this form of 'ethics' can only be successful through a manipulative and emotivist coercion. This is far from cultivating a genuine culture of ethics or fostering virtuous moral character among the actors within the world of luxury, business, and finance; and it is the precise opposite of Kant's conception of ethics. For Kant and many other earlier moral philosophers, a relationship informed by morality treats the other as an end in itself, whereas a relationship uninformed by morality treats the other only as a means to some other ends. To treat the other as an end in itself is to provide them with good reasons for acting in a certain way, but to ultimately leave it up to them to evaluate the validity of those reasons. To treat the other as a means is to treat them as a mere implement for achieving my chosen purposes and employ whatever tools of persuasion are available that one believes will be most effective upon them in any given situation (MacIntyre, 2011). Compliance, therefore, is performed not out of any sense of ethical duty, desire to achieve a particular ethical good, or even through belief in the efficacy of these measures in their stated goals, but merely as a means to avoid suspicion and, as suggested in the previous chapter, sustain the ideological fantasy of the essential purity of financial markets. Indeed, MacIntyre argues that one of the chief characters of our culture of emotivism is the bureaucratic manager, and he is careful to distinguish characters from mere social roles (MacIntyre, 2011). Characters are a very special type of social role, for they are 'the moral representatives of their culture and they are so because of the way in which moral and metaphysical ideas and theories assume through them an embodied existence in the social world. *Characters* are the masks worn by moral philosophies' (MacIntyre, 2011: 32–3). Applied to this context, we could argue that the compliance officer and the actors within the compliance industry are the moral *characters* of our time, embodying our emotivist moral culture by crafting incentive and sanction structures to coerce behaviour. As Bukovansky argues in her article, 'The Hollowness of Anti-Corruption Discourse':

> Despite its moral undertones, the bulk of contemporary anti-corruption discourse deploys the language and methodologies of economics and rational choice to render diagnostic assessments of the plight of the corrupt and less developed, and to develop 'cures' based on these forms of analysis (Hopkin, 2002). Advances in incorporating the study of institutions into analyses of economic growth and development, represented by the 'new institutional economics' have led to greater and more refined treatment of variables previously excluded from economic studies of development. Yet the analytical framework has not changed in one important respect: it is a framework wherein self-interested agents respond to a set of incentives in their environment, yielding either positive (wealth and utility enhancing) or negative (wealth and utility detracting) outcomes. Public policies aim to manipulate the incentive structures such self-interested actors face in order to achieve positive collective outcomes or at least minimize negative ones. Corruption control thus becomes a technical matter of effectively manipulating incentive structures. (Bukovansky, 2006: 183)

This descent into emotivism aside, there is a further betrayal of anti-corruption's original Kantian ethical underpinnings. Recall earlier that, despite the characterization of deontological ethics as obedient rule-following, morality for Kant was about the exercise of *autonomy*. If we act simply according to our base desires, feelings, our economic interests, or according to the word of God or some other authority we are not behaving *freely*. Rather, we are behaving *heteronomously* and therefore the only way to truly exercise freedom is through the exercise of moral agency by adhering to our duty which we have determined for ourselves according to the test of the categorical imperative. However, in the absence of being able to provide the subject with good reasons for adhering to their moral duty, and with a significant distrust that human actors will do so (particularly in the world of business and capitalism), what the growth of the compliance industry on the back of anti-corruption has done is to remove the exercise of human judgment and the exercise of moral agency from the picture entirely. This was discussed at length in the previous chapter, where we looked at the rise of artificial intelligence technologies, RegTech, SupTech, and software and databases to which we *interpassively* delegate our moral agency when it comes to money laundering, fakes, forgeries, or fraud; in this sense, these data-driven compliance systems are not merely automating ethics itself, but they are being *ethical on our behalf*, which effectively frees us from ethical and moral responsibility (Pfaller, 2017; Kuldova, 2018b). This would qualify, for Kant, as a failure of autonomy and a retreat into heteronomy. It has even reached a point where the sheer volume and complexity of financial transactions have the compliance industrial complex to render the moral judgment of human beings as risky and flawed (Papantoniou, 2022), with the Basel Committee on Banking Supervision arguing that 'automated processes are less prone to error than [human] manual processes'.[23] This is indeed a widespread argument among technosolutionists, who deem the technical judgement superior to human judgement and discretion, as it is seen as removing emotions and bias, and as the machine does not suffer from changing moods or tiredness (Joh, 2016; Gundhus, 2017; Bullock, 2019; Brayne, 2021). Consequently, there is no ethical or moral agency to speak of whatsoever, and in an extension of a quote cited previously, Kant derides such thinking as a form of moral 'immaturity' in a passage that perfectly encapsulates this point:

> It is so convenient to be immature! If I have a book to have understanding in place of me, a spiritual adviser to have a conscience for me, a doctor to judge my diet for me, and so on, I need not make any efforts at all. I need not think, so long as I can pay; others will soon take the tiresome job over for me. *The guardians who have kindly taken upon themselves the work of supervision will soon see to it that by far the largest part of mankind should consider the step forward to maturity not only as difficult but also as highly dangerous.* Having first infatuated their domesticated animals, and carefully prevented the docile creatures from daring to take a step without the leading strings to which they are tied, they next show them the danger which threatens them if they try to walk unaided. (Kant, 1991: 1–2; emphasis added)

As anti-policy is pursued and its *a priori* evils tackled through compliance, there has been a significant cherry-picking of the features of deontological ethics on the part of market actors and the compliance industry. At the upper-end level of regulation, they have adhered to Kant's conception of morality as an expression of autonomy where the moral subject – be it an individual, business, or organization such as SYBAss mentioned previously – issues moral precepts to themselves. But at the level of operationalization, of actually adhering to what duty demands, there is an abdication of responsibility for autonomy entirely, as the task of ethics is handed over to AI and RegTech or delegated to ethics professionals and integrity managers, which perform similar interpassive functions. There is, therefore, an absolute *emptiness* to this ethics.

The emptiness of anti-corruption ethics

As we have seen, this emptiness is multifaceted. There is the initial emptiness of the test of the categorical imperative itself; the emptiness and absence of the cultivation of moral virtue and character as compliance transforms anti-corruption's 'ethics' into a form of manipulative emotivism; and finally, the emptiness of any moral agency as ethical action is computerized and delegated to automated processes and technologies who 'do ethics' on behalf of humans. While corporations and entire industries talk endlessly of cultivating a 'culture of ethics' and a new era of 'ethical capitalism', what they inevitably produce is reminiscent of what Deneen describes as an 'anticulture' (Deneen, 2018), which he argues 'is the consequence of a regime of standardizing law replacing widely observed informal norms that come to be discarded as forms of oppressions' (Deneen, 2018: 66), or indeed as outright risks and dangers. But this descent into emotivism and its emptiness is a consequence of the central tenets of Kantian ethics that underpin anti-corruption, and its inability to provide subjects with good reasons for following the injunctions of morality; and that this difficulty is itself a consequence of the severance and opposition between morality and economic interest and desire that capitalism has engendered, and which Kant's moral philosophy takes for granted. As MacIntyre has written:

> those concerned with ethics in the last two hundred years, from whatever standpoint, became insufficiently concerned with money and those engaging with money became insufficiently concerned with ethics. What ethics became as a result and what the management of money became as a result are such that we no longer know how to connect them. (MacIntyre, 2016: 12)

Ethics, properly conceived, is about the achievement of the Good. Even Kant, who roundly rejected the idea that ethics was about the achievement of any particular ends, nevertheless concluded that it would be a tragedy if adhering to our deontological duty did not eventually produce happiness or a good society (Kant, 2012). It is, more deeply, about a deliberation on what the Good is, and on the goods *internal* to social practices that are worth pursuing in themselves. The goods internal to academic life, for example, might be truth or knowledge, and this is to be placed in opposition to external goods such as academic prestige, promotions, money and so on.

So, what are the goods internal to politics as a social practice? What are the goods internal to regulation? To art? To cultural heritage? To housing? To energy provision? What virtues and excellences do we need to pursue in order to achieve these internal goods? The very obvious problem that is consistently disavowed is that we occupy a culture where the primary good is that of money; a good that, while external to the achievement of goods internal to various social practices, is today not treated as merely a means to other ends but as an end in itself. And with money being treated as an end in itself, its pursuit often involves the subordination of the goods internal to various social practices, and thereby involves the subordination of ethics itself.

When we think about tackling corruption, and when anti-corruptionists talk about ethics, we think about it in terms of regulation. But as MacIntyre observes, 'debates over regulation commonly have as their aim the prevention of further large-scale crises' (MacIntyre, 2016: 20). The horizon of their aims is how to prevent money laundering, kleptocracy, bribery and so on, without fundamentally altering the economic system we live in or challenging the way in which we think about money, money-making, and various other social practices that produce these ethically and socially challenging problems. But we consistently see the dissatisfactory nature of a rules and regulation-oriented ethical culture whenever a corporation, institution, or politically exposed person is cast under scrutiny surrounding some form of fraud or corruption. The typical response made through rote statements and legal teams is that the conduct under scrutiny did not breach any laws, that they have complied with all regulations, and that their actions fall within the boundaries of governance restrictions. These explanations are never experienced as persuasive, and they do not allay our lingering suspicions that some kind of wrongdoing or ethical failure has taken place. Such arguments are strangely impervious to defeat despite the fact that nobody seems to believe in them, and the implementation of more regulations and rules do not cause anyone to think that the sector or industry is becoming more 'ethical' in any substantive way. Practices such as settlements, e.g., those by the Securities and Exchange Commission (SEC) to resolve FCPA violations, where corporations pay large fines for fraud and corruption but do not admit guilt, only raise more suspicion.[24]

This response is indicative of the fact that, in many ways, we continue to intuitively think in a broadly neo-Aristotelian way, evaluating a particular case or scandal according to the *telos* of its associated practice. The issue, Raymen argues, is that: 'we occupy a culture that is so habituated to conceiving of morality as obedient rule-following and viewing law, morality, and desire as separate and distinct realms that this more teleological thinking lacks any meaningful arena in which it can be formally expressed, taken seriously, and acted upon' (Raymen, 2022: 135). Therefore, as MacIntyre suggests, what we need is not a set of regulations but an approach to ethics that addresses and thinks about the moral dimensions of the *normal* functioning of our economic systems and industries (MacIntyre, 2016). One which considers the proper moral dimensions and *telos* of art, housing, fashion, politics, regulation, or even banking. The fact that many readers would struggle – quite understandably – to conceive of banking as a social practice with a set of internal goods that are separate from, and prior to, the external goods of capital accumulation is a testament to the absence of a space for this kind of ethical thought. But it is only once we think about these things as social practices with a fundamentally moral component – rather than as practices which follow abstract moral rules – that we can even begin to address them as industries and think about their proper moral relationship to money. To do this of course is to rethink luxury as a whole. Indeed, it would require us to rethink the entire foundations of our society and economy, since a global economy founded on such principles would be wholly different to one based on laissez-faire principles, neoliberal principles, or even Keynesian or socialist principles. But it is only through such thinking that ethics can have any meaningful substance. If we fail to do so, both ethics and law will remain empty shells that can encase the corrupt in a thin but durable sheath of morality.

Epilogue: Luxury, Corruption, and the Death Drive

Corruption scandals; globally recognized anti-corruption activists; the luxury art and antiquities market; the role of compliance in sustaining financial capitalism's ideological fantasies; luxury bunkers, and the moral philosophy and ethics that underpin anti-corruption. This book has been made up of a number of seemingly disparate topics. But if there has been anything that unites them – barring luxury and corruption – it has been the themes of emptiness, repetition, sacrifice and lack, all of which happen to be constituent features of the death drive. Therefore, as we close this book, we consider the intellectual and political utility of thinking luxury, corruption, and anti-corruption through the psychoanalytic lens of the death drive, and consider some of its implications.

For those who are only loosely familiar or entirely unfamiliar with Freud's notion of the death drive (and Jacques Lacan's development of it), it is useful to provide some brief conceptual context. Developed in his 1920 work *Beyond the Pleasure Principle*, Freud's exposition of the death drive as the key psychic force in the formation and operation of human subjectivity involved an almost complete U-turn from his previous work (Freud, 1961). Up until this point, both Freud's own work and psychoanalysis in general held that the psyche was governed by the pleasure principle. The death drive, by contrast, involves the tendency of human subjects to repetitiously return to an original or traumatic loss and engage in acts of continual self-sabotage and destruction. What is the original loss of which Freud (and later Lacan) speak?

Initially, as Freud sees it, the human animal is an autoerotic being. It has no object world. There is no distinction between the self and the other, or between subject and object, and there is a degree of satisfaction in this kind of blissful unity with everything in the world. Differentiation between subject and object – and with it the formation of human subjectivity – occurs upon entry into the social world and the socio-symbolic order. For this branch of theoretical psychoanalysis, this differentiation requires an original act of *sacrifice*, a loss of a part of oneself which engenders a split that literally creates both the human subject and the external object world. As a result of this sacrifice and split, the individual comes to experience itself as *lacking*, as missing something which can be reclaimed. The subject begins to take an interest in the object world around it as a result of this original sense of loss, and it is this original sense of loss that gives birth to desire. Desire, theoretical psychoanalysis maintains, is rooted in and circles around this sense of lack, a lack that it is assumed can be filled in and addressed by the object(s) of our desire. Of course we must remember that, in reality, the subject has not lost and is not lacking anything. Its desire, therefore, is not only organized around something that it does not have, but more importantly, something that *does not and cannot exist*, an impossibility (McGowan, 2013). This is what is described in Lacanian terminology as *objet petit a*, or the 'lost object of desire', which is simply the nothingness of lack itself. It is an initial act of sacrifice of something that does not exist that creates the lost object. Consequently, our desire – be it our consumer desires, our economic desires, or our political desires – continuously and repetitiously circle around this phantasmic lost object that can never be captured or reclaimed.

The implications of this for human desire and enjoyment are immense. Plenty of things stand in for the lost object, be it political programmes, commodities, money, careers, achievements and so on. But the moment we acquire these things, we are forced to confront that they are not *the* lost object, since the lost object does not exist. The moment the object is obtained or achieved, it begins to lose its lustre and its appeal. Everyone will have experienced this through shopping, consumerism, the prospect of a new job, a new lover, or transforming their appearance through a new diet or workout. We fetishize and idealise the object of our desire. We imagine acquiring or achieving it and its transformative effects upon our lives. Over time, however, the object of our desire becomes just another commodity among many others, just another job, just another romantic partner with fatal flaws, or just another dissatisfying diet or fitness regime that, even where it has its merits and good points, does not sustain a sense of contentment or satisfaction (Winlow & Hall, 2016). In truth, the entire logic of capitalism is built upon the death drive and this structure of desire and the *promise* of the lost object (McGowan, 2016). The capitalist is driven by the promise of achieving *enough* wealth or profit just as the consumer is driven by the promise of the commodity; promises that always fail to deliver. Nevertheless, we do not give up on our desire. Instead, we continually return to our sense of loss and lack in the dogged belief that it can finally be assuaged.

But what the death drive causes us to do is to continually mislocate where our enjoyment truly lies. We misidentify our enjoyment as residing within the object of desire itself, be it the commodity or money, the promotion, the romantic partner, or the achievement of some political goal or victory. Whereas in truth, as we alluded to in the earliest pages of this book, what we enjoy most is the *prohibition* of the object of our desire and the return to the original sense of loss that gives birth to desire (Žižek,

2012). In order to do so, in order to return to the enjoyment of lack itself (and the prospect of its resolution) the human subject engages in endless self-sabotage, and this compulsion to repeat is the very essence of the death drive. Research has discovered that violent criminals in the course of their psychic life will often return to traumatic experiences of abuse or humiliation, unconsciously seeking out the violent encounter as a means of returning to and (unsuccessfully) resolving this original sense of loss or shame (Winlow, 2014; Ellis et al, 2017). Gamblers routinely place bets fully cognisant of the consequences of their actions, knowing that they are hurting themselves over and over (Schüll, 2012; Raymen & Smith, 2017, 2020). Individuals routinely pursue romantic partners with the same flaws or repeatedly sabotage their relationships in a predictably similar fashion. Freud himself viewed the analysand's resistance to the psychoanalytic cure as evidence for the existence of the death drive, whereby patients would terminate their treatment, engage in regressive behaviour, or act in such a way as to make their continued treatment untenable at precisely the moment that progress was being made (Freud, 1961). Such self-sabotage continually reproduces the lost object and allows it to be enjoyed, and the subject must continually engage in the self-sabotaging and sacrificial acts that produce its lost object irrespective of the damage that it does to that subject's own interests (McGowan, 2013). Subjects of the death drive, therefore, (1) are deeply invested in the prospect of ultimate satisfaction and enjoyment which lies at some point in the future; (2) misidentify the true locus of their enjoyment; and (3) engage in endless self-sabotage and sacrifice. Indeed, it is through loss and sacrifice that objects are imbued with value.

With that brief exposition out of the way, it should by now be clear how this theoretical lens of the death drive is applicable to the issue of luxury, corruption, and anti-corruption, and how it has been implicitly applied to these topics throughout this book. The death drive arguably structures and is present within the actions of the luxury industry, corrupt actors, the compliance industry, the defiance industry, and anti-corruption activists and politicians alike. For the kleptocrat or corrupt oligarch, they dream of a future where they finally have 'enough'. When they have amassed enough wealth and assets, when they have tasted every luxury and indulgence such that they feel satisfied, complete, and no longer plagued by a nagging lack and desire – see Michel's detailed look at the corrupt kleptocrat Teodoro Obiang as a prime example (Michel, 2021) or the excesses of former Ukrainian President Viktor Yanukovych (Kuldova & Østbø, 2023). They repeatedly sacrifice immense amounts of the most precious commodity of all in the capitalist universe – that of money – for empty and superfluous luxury items, and remain perpetually unsated. Like all consumers and capitalists, kleptocrats, oligarchs, organized crime figures and money launderers are in thrall to the illusory promise of capitalism and consumerism, continually misidentifying that the true source of their enjoyment lies in their desire itself and the prohibition of ultimate satisfaction.

This is why a strategy to fight corruption through the theft of enjoyment is arguably foolhardy. In the opening pages of this book, we observed how the anti-corruption sanctions deployed against Russian oligarchs were around the theft of enjoyment. They were imposed to 'deny them the enjoyment of their wealth' (Patrucic & Lozovsky, 2022) and rob them of their 'ill-begotten gains' and their 'luxury toys'. This is precisely why anti-corruption is libidinally appealing. There is great appeal in the idea of stealing the enjoyment of elites, of forcing them to share in a collective not-having, like the rest of us. But it is also precisely where it is doomed to fail. For there has been a misconception of the Russian oligarch as somehow separate from the rest of us, a figure of non-lack who is not subject to the death drive and who possesses a direct relation to enjoyment. As we have established, money and luxury commodities are sublime objects insofar as there is a certain distance between subject and object. The individual must work to acquire money, must save to afford luxury commodities or experiences, and it is this distance which provides money and luxury with its sublimity. Therefore, if anything, the ease with which the kleptocrat or oligarch can access money and luxury goods does not heighten but *diminishes* their enjoyment. We must remember the distinction here between pleasure and enjoyment. Acquisition of the object of our desire is the beginning of pleasure, an experience of intense but short-lived excitation that occurs at the *end* of our enjoyment and actually denotes the *termination* of our enjoyment. This is perhaps one reason why kleptocrats and oligarchs consume so frenetically, because the absence of any prohibitions on their ability to acquire money or goods creates a *crisis* of enjoyment, and in misidentifying the true locus of their enjoyment as residing in the various objects of desire rather than in desire itself, they frantically try to address the problem of this absence of prohibitions through hyper-repetitive and excessive consumerism which never satisfies. Therefore, the vast anti-corruption and AML apparatus not only places prohibitions on such activity, but also means that the corrupt actor must *sacrifice* in order to enjoy the fruits of his corruption. He must be willing to spend a vast excess of time, energy, and money in order to evade and defy these measures, and it is precisely this sacrifice that reconstitutes the privileged object and introduces a prohibition and a barrier that makes it appealing and its prospect enjoyable. Anti-corruption seems to operate on a flawed understanding of corrupt elites as rational economic actors, rather than what they (and we) all are, which is subjects of the death drive. Anti-corruption operates on the belief that by creating these barriers, one can stop the corrupt actor from enjoying; and if one can stop the corrupt actor from enjoying, if one can just make things difficult enough, then one will stop corruption in its tracks. But if anything, and in keeping with the self-sabotaging nature of the death drive, such measures achieve their opposite. They provide the means through which the corrupt actor can enjoy once more, and enjoy better, thereby guaranteeing the continuation of the practices they oppose.

Nevertheless, we cannot seem to transcend this way of thinking. Any regime that endeavours to tackle corruption would seem to need prohibition of some kind at its core; and given that corrupt actors are subjects of the death drive like any others who misidentify the true locus of their enjoyment, simply removing prohibitions on corruption and money laundering is of course not a viable option and would not lead to any positive outcome. Therefore, a seminal question for scholars of corruption is how to construct an anti-corruption regime that does not make the theft of enjoyment its chief target and thereby unintentionally reproduce the privileged lost object that is at the core of the corrupt actor's enjoyment. Quite simply, how can anti-corruption measures deprive corrupt actors of the libidinal space in which they act and enjoy?

We certainly see how the logic of the death drive applies to anti-corruption in numerous other ways. In the first chapter of this book, we suggested that anti-policies and populist political movements that are organized around anti-policy always retain a libidinal attachment to that which they fight. This is particularly the case given that, as anti-policies, they are primarily organized around the negative. They do not necessarily construct a positive vision of the world. Rather, as we have been at pains to stress in this book, their utopia is simply the world as it exists minus the issue that they are 'anti-'. Consequently, for anti-corruption, the continued existence of corruption constitutes the prohibition which allows anti-corruption activists and practitioners to perpetually enjoy the utopia of a world without corruption and the ultimate satisfaction it would deliver. Of course, in reality, the enjoyment and ultimate satisfaction that such a utopia promises would not be forthcoming. Numerous problems would remain, and anti-corruption activists would be forced to confront the essential emptiness of their ideal. Therefore, at an unconscious level, what all anti-policies – including anti-corruption – enjoy most is their failure, which is perhaps one reason among others that the response to their failure is to produce more of the same, as well as the endless manufacturing of new corruption, fraud, and money laundering risks and threats as discussed in several chapters throughout this book. Just as the corrupt oligarch or kleptocrat seems to always need more money and luxury assets, the world of anti-corruption and compliance always demands *more* data, *more* regulation, *more* codes of conduct, *more* ethical guidelines, *more* AML software, *more* ethics training courses, *more* transparency and *more* integrity indicators and metrics. It is arguably not a coincidence that when one looks at such metrics and integrity indicators more closely, there is a quite spectacular emptiness to many of them that seems to mirror the emptiness of the lost object itself. Consistent with the self-sabotaging logic of the death drive, such measures often seem to achieve the opposite of their intention. Efforts toward transparency and knowledge produce an overwhelming abundance of data that generates opacity and a lack of understanding. Compliance regimes that are supposed to engender a culture of ethics and integrity end up diminishing the exercise of moral agency by delegating it to AI or automated processes or stimulate new practices of gaming and evasion; or are employed to *facilitate* corporate wrongdoing, such as in the Wells Fargo cross-selling scandal (Tayan, 2019) or the numerous scandals involving accountancy and audit firms (Shore & Wright, 2015, 2018; Sikka, 2016).

The eradication of corruption would be to eradicate the very basis of the shared identity of the anti-corruption universe, which amounts to an act of self-destruction. Given that anti-corruption has now become an industry *for itself* rather than a movement *in itself* (Johnston & Fritzen, 2021), this unconscious self-sabotage is only likely to intensify and continue. As McGowan writes:

> The good itself, not our failures to achieve it, is the problem. This is the fundamental political insight that psychoanalysis brings to the table. … As we get closer to the ideal of the good, we simultaneously approach the emptiness concealed within the ideal. The notion of the good does not emerge simply from moral reasoning and speculation about the proper arrangement of society. We develop this notion only through the experience of its prohibition. That is to say, the prohibition of the good doesn't form an obstacle to a pre-existing ideal but constitutes the ideal as such. (McGowan, 2013: 6)

As we argued in Chapter 2, the same is arguably true of capitalism and its relationship to anti-corruption. Consider, for instance, the timing with which the term 'good governance' – and by extension corruption – came to the forefront of global political and international development discourse. The absence of explicit limits to capitalism means that capitalism has always required the creation or existence of external limits that enable it to enjoy. For decades, the Soviet Union represented the limit to global liberal-democratic capitalism. Far from being an obstacle which precluded ultimate enjoyment, the Soviet Union arguably functioned as the means through which global capitalist society could enjoy the prospect of an unfettered, truly global capitalism and everything that it promised. The dissolution of the Soviet Union removed such a barrier. The End of History had arrived, and liberal capitalism was declared the political-economic and ideological victor. There were no longer any limits to its project, and its promise could now be fully realized. At this precise moment in April 1992 – merely

4 months after the formal dissolution of the Soviet Union – the World Bank used the term 'good governance' for the first time in its *Governance and Development* report. As we know, good governance is viewed as the ultimate antidote to corruption and its absence the cause of corruption. The World Bank report outlined the various principles of 'good governance' and their integral role in fully realizing and enjoying the benefits of liberal-democratic capitalism, identifying corruption as the primary barrier to this realization and ultimate enjoyment. Through this lens, the World Bank report *unconsciously* introduced a barrier where none otherwise existed so that capitalist society could continue to enjoy. We cannot stress strongly enough the term 'unconsciously' here. We are not for one moment suggesting that this is a conscious ploy enacted by moustache-twisting individuals at the World Bank. Rather, it is precisely the unconscious nature of such actions that structures the enjoyment, and what creates its repetitiousness. Ever since, corruption has consistently been positioned as an obstacle to 'perfected' capitalism, discouraging international economic development and investment and undermining capitalism's competitive and meritocratic ideal through corrupt, kleptocratic, and autocratic authoritarianism. As we outlined in Chapter 2, for the likes of Aleksei Naval'nyi, corruption is what has prohibited post-soviet Russia from becoming sufficiently capitalist, and from enjoying all the benefits that are alleged to follow.

The compliance industry itself is arguably a perfect expression and manifestation of the death drive. The death drive, for Lacan is, in part, the satisfaction that is gained from continuously *missing* the object of its desire, of the subject *not* getting what it wants, such that the object remains prohibited to it and can continue to function as the lost object of desire and retain its promise. As we have emphasized throughout this book, and as others have observed (Johnston & Fritzen, 2021), compliance, as it is applied to anti-corruption, AML, and countering the financing of terrorism, routinely fails in its goals of closing the gaps and the loopholes through which corrupt and illicit money and behaviour taints both financial systems, corporations, and industries. But the compliance industry is not deterred by its failure to close these gaps, by the missing of its object. In this respect, the compliance industry is reminiscent of the character Phil Connors, played by Bill Murray, in the 1993 Hollywood movie *Groundhog Day*. In the film, Connors is caught in a time-loop, forcing him to repeat the same 2 February day over and over again. Aware that he is trapped in a time-loop, he sets himself the task of trying to seduce his colleague Rita Hanson (Andie MacDowell), using his knowledge of the day's events and information derived from previous interactions to win her affections. Each time, Connors sees himself as improving in this endeavour, of getting closer to success, and while he repeatedly fails (even when he gets the interactions right), he derives an enjoyment in the repeated attempt and failure. The compliance industry is arguably the same, repeating the same practices and interactions, perpetually tweaking their approach in miniscule ways in order to manipulate outcomes and continually failing at the achievement of their goal, but nevertheless finding a strange satisfaction in this failure, even using it much like Connors as a positive source of information for improving things next time. In this regard, both Connors and the compliance industry are perfect representations of the death drive.

In a fashion that is reminiscent of this repetitious nature of the death drive, we have repeatedly spoken in this book about how anti-corruption and compliance seeks incessantly to close gaps and holes in the financial system and achieve integrity, wholeness, and purity. There is arguably no better representation of Lacan's notion of the lost object of desire, sacrifice, and his development of the death drive from Freud (Lacan, 2019). The individual subject, as already explained, is endeavouring to fill in the hole, the gap, the lack at the core of subjectivity. It is trying to achieve the impossible of (re)discovering and (re)claiming the lost object that was originally sacrificed and whose loss was constitutive of subjectivity and brought subjectivity into being. Similarly, all symbolic orders (such as capitalism) have a missing signifier, a gap, a signifier that drops out or is sacrificed and whose absence constitutes the symbolic order. In some ways, this missing signifier is to the symbolic order what the lost object is to the individual subject – a constitutive absence or sacrifice that brings it into being – and as we argued in Chapter 1, for capitalism this missing signifier would be ethics. There is a fundamental absence of ethics that, as Bloom has argued, capitalism has always sought to close (Bloom, 2017). A genuine and categorical commitment to ethics is a structuring impossibility within capitalism, an irreducible gap which the capitalist symbolic order has historically circled around and returned since its very inception (Hirschman, 1977; Bloom, 2017; Mees, 2020). As Lacan emphasizes, the death drive satisfies itself by repetitiously *missing* the object of its desire (Lacan, 2019). Just as the subject finds the consumer commodity satisfying so long as it is prohibited to it, capitalism and anti-corruption finds the missing signifier of ethics satisfying so long as it remains missing.

Similarly, it is through this act of sacrifice and loss that we create objects worth desiring and imbue them with some transcendent or sublime value. By engaging in an original act of sacrifice, the subject of the death drive engages in an act of *creation* that produces the lost object of desire, an object that exists only so long as it remains lost. In Chapter 3, we saw the perfect and perverse example of this extended to its logical conclusion in the discussion of corruption, fraud, and anti-corruption in the art and antiquities market. In order to create the sacred purity of the financial system, and in order to create pure, 'authentic' and 'sacred' works of art, the art and antiquities market has to engage in sacrifice. They not only have to sacrifice time, money, and resources on infrastructures of due diligence, KYC, provenance checking, and forensic verification; but ultimately, as in the case of NFTs that were discussed in the latter part of that chapter, they have to engage in the sacrifice of art itself. In order to have a verifiably 'genuine' piece of work, and in order to track and trace the purity of the object's owners, what ultimately had to be sacrificed was the physical piece of art in favour of a securitized digital and 'genuine' NFT. In the name of the sacred of the financial system, and the sacred and authenticity of art, culture itself was sacrificed. The case of the art market and NFTs as it relates to corruption, fraud, and anti-corruption is the perfect expression of the death drive.

This is redolent of Lacan's further development of the death drive. In Seminar VII, *The Ethics of Psychoanalysis*, Lacan sees the death drive as moving *beyond* the existing symbolic order. What the death drive aims at, Lacan argues, is the achievement of a *symbolic death* such that the subject can begin again anew (Lacan, 1992). The self-sabotaging acts of the death drive raze the symbolic field to the ground, enabling something new to be born. As he writes in Seminar VII, Freud's death drive must 'be articulated as a destruction drive, given that it challenges everything that exists. But it is also a will to create from zero, a will to begin again' (Lacan, 1992: 262). We see this with addicts quite often, who drive to hit 'rock bottom' and thereby achieve a symbolic death in which everything associated with their addiction is left in the past and they are born anew as an entirely different subject (Raymen & Smith, 2017); the violent subject returns to their past traumas and abuses and through the violent encounter endeavours to move beyond them and achieve a symbolic death. Similarly, in seeking a pure world – be it a pure financial system, pure corporate integrity, pure industries, or pure objects – the compliance industry inevitably produces the destruction of everything. It razes the symbolic field in the pursuit of the phantasmic lost object of purity and authenticity, with human life and activity increasingly consisting of the empty act of verifying that one is who one says one is, or is doing what one says one has done.

What, then, are we to do with this information? As Todd McGowan writes, 'there is no path leading from the death drive to utopia. The death drive undermines every attempt to construct a utopia; it is the enemy of the good society' (McGowan, 2013: 283). It can be quite difficult to accept the reality of the death drive, for if we accept that the death drive sabotages and undermines every movement toward the good, then we must seemingly abandon the notion of the good itself, something which is seemingly integral to politics. We cannot escape or transcend the death drive, since such an attempt simply reproduces rather than resolves the lost object and still promises an illusory future of ultimate enjoyment and transcendence. Nor can we consciously take up the death drive, for it is a process that remains unconscious. What McGowan argues we can do is reconcile ourselves with the death drive and fully recognize its operation. This, McGowan argues, would not necessarily change anything and in many ways would leave the world entirely as it is. On the other hand, it would change everything. For while such a recognition would not transform the *way* we enjoy, what it would achieve is a transformation in our *relationship* to our enjoyment.

It would force us to recognize where our enjoyment truly lies, rather than misidentifying it as located in a future of ultimate enjoyment that will arrive once every corrupt actor has been weeded out and eradicated, when every suspicious financial transaction has been detected, and when every 'illicit' object has been removed from circulation. Rather than conceiving of the corrupt actor as an *external* limit to a 'perfected' capitalism, corruption would be fully recognized for what it is as an *internal* limit through which capitalist society enjoys. Rather than seeing illicit or fraudulent objects as an obstacle to the achievement of purity and authenticity, it would be recognized that the very existence of these objects is what creates those sacred values of purity and authenticity, and what creates the distinction between genuine and fake. A society that reconciled itself with the death drive would transform the libidinal space in which obscenely wealthy corrupt actors and oligarchs act. After all, the enjoyment of luxury is predicated upon the cultivation of envy. My enjoyment of a luxury car or extravagantly expensive piece of art is dependent upon the envy and admiration of the other, and the impression given to the other that I have a direct and uninhibited access to enjoyment. But a society that recognized the truth of the death drive would eliminate the distinction between figures of lack (us) and figures of non-lack (them). Individual oligarchs and kleptocrats would still consume luxury goods, but they would be entirely deprived of the libidinal space in which they act. It would be a society that would no longer identify ultimate enjoyment in the conquering and obliteration of some external threat, but would simply enjoy its own internal limitations. A society and an anti-corruption strategy organized around a recognition of the death drive would not necessarily have any less corruption to deal with, but it would be a society where the destructive tendencies of the compliance-industrial complex – which are rooted in the fantasy of ultimate enjoyment in the future – would be negated. Many issues remain, but our hope in writing this book has been to reopen what has previously been foreclosed, and begin to critically interrogate that which has been taken to be unassailably good. The alternative is for the field of anti-corruption to ossify and stagnate, trapped in the endless repetitions and failures of the death drive until it has erased everything of human and cultural value.

Notes

Chapter 1

[1]   * All internet links were last accessed 31 May 2023.

'Remarks by President Biden on the Request to Congress for Additional Funding to Support Ukraine', *The White House*, 28 April 2022, https://www.whitehouse.gov/brief ing-room/speeches-remarks/2022/04/28/remarks-by-president-biden-on-the-request-to-congress-for-additional-funding-to-support-ukraine/

[2]   '$300 Million Yacht of Sanctioned Russian Oligarch Suleiman Kerimov Seized by Fiji at Request of United States', *The United States Department of Justice*, 5 May 2022, https://www.justice.gov/opa/pr/300-million-yacht-sanctioned-russian-oligarch-suleiman-keri mov-seized-fiji-request-united

[3]   '$300 Million Yacht of Sanctioned Russian Oligarch Suleiman Kerimov Seized by Fiji at Request of United States', *The United States Department of Justice*, 5 May 2022, https://www.justice.gov/opa/pr/300-million-yacht-sanctioned-russian-oligarch-suleiman-keri mov-seized-fiji-request-united

[4]   '"Rich Also Cry": Russia's Sanctioned Oligarchs Lose Luxuries', *France 24*, 10 May 2022, https://www.france24.com/en/live-news/20220510-rich-also-cry-russia-s-san ctioned-oligarchs-lose-luxuries

[5]   ACF: The Anti-Corruption Foundation, https://acf.international/

[6]   Pope Francis @Pontifex (2017) [Twitter] 9 December. https://twitter.com/Pontifex/sta tus/939472199878103041

[7]   'The Rich and Powerful Are Using Their Superyachts for Secret Meetings Far from Prying Eyes', *Business Insider*, 26 May 2023, https://www.businessinsider.com/super-rich-yachts-secret-meetings-at-sea-far-from-spies-2023-5

[8]   'Luxury Goods, Frequently Asked Questions', *European Comission*, 2 May 2022, https://finance.ec.europa.eu/system/files/2022-08/faqs-sanctions-russia-luxury-goods_en.pdf

[9]   'Over One Billion Dollars Wonder on Wheels! Rolls Royce Ghosts, Porsches, Ferraris, Aventadors … Efcc Still Abandons Seized Luxury Cars to Rust and Rot', *This Day*, 15 April 2018, https://www.thisdaylive.com/index.php/2018/04/15/over-one-billion-doll ars-wonder-on-wheels-rolls-royce-ghosts-porsches-ferraris-aventadors-efcc-still-aband ons-seized-luxury-cars-to-rust-and-rot/

[10]   'Porsche, Corvettes Crushed as Philippines' Duterte Shows Toughness on Tax-Dodging', *The Wire*, 6 February 2018, https://thewire.in/external-affairs/porsche-corvettes-crushed-philippines-duterte-corruption

[11]   'In Bengaluru Anti-Corruption Raids, Focus on Luxury Watches, Bungalows', *NDTV*, 22 March 2022, https://www.ndtv.com/bangalore-news/in-bengaluru-anti-corrupt ion-raids-focus-on-luxury-watches-bungalows-2835602

12 'Zandile Gumede Raid: Here's The Insane Collection of Luxury Cars Seized' [video], *The South African*, 10 October 2019, https://www.thesouthafrican.com/news/zandile-gumede-luxury-cars-co-accused-raid-hawks/

13 'Najib Razak: $225M Worth of Goods Seized from Former Malaysian PM's Residences', *CNN*, 27 June 2018, https://edition.cnn.com/2018/06/27/asia/malaysia-najib-razak-police-intl/index.html

14 'Malaysian Court Orders Govt to Return Luxury Items Seized from Ex-PM Najib', *Benar News*, 11 August 2021, https://www.benarnews.org/english/news/malaysian/malaysian-govt-has-to-return-luxury-goods-to-najib-11082021152439.html

15 'Malaysia's Top Court Sends Ex-PM Najib to Prison on Corruption Charges', *France 24*, 23 August 2022, https://www.france24.com/en/asia-pacific/20220823-malaysia-s-top-court-sends-ex-pm-najib-to-prison-on-corruption-charges

16 *National Security Memorandum/NSSM-1*, 3 June 2021, https://irp.fas.org/offdocs/nsm/nssm-1.pdf p 2.

17 'Fact Sheet: U.S. Strategy on Countering Corruption', *The White House*, 6 December 2021, https://www.whitehouse.gov/briefing-room/statements-releases/2021/12/06/fact-sheet-u-s-strategy-on-countering-corruption/

18 'The UK's Global Anti-Corruption Sanctions: Key Points to Note', *Ashurst*, 7 May 2021, https://www.ashurst.com/en/news-and-insights/legal-updates/the-uk-global-anti-corruption-sanctions---key-points-to-note/

19 'Paul Massaro on the US Strategy for Fighting Kleptocracy', Episode 87, *KickBack – The Global Anti-Corruption Podcast*, 24 January 2023, https://open.spotify.com/episode/28LcyxLkVQPl8snBpmKuPa?si=ke1TnDWcRYSzyCDwBmGYxQ (18:20).

20 'Paul Massaro on the US Strategy for Fighting Kleptocracy', Episode 87, *KickBack – The Global Anti-Corruption Podcast*, 24 January 2023 https://open.spotify.com/episode/28LcyxLkVQPl8snBpmKuPa?si=ke1TnDWcRYSzyCDwBmGYxQ (0:20).

21 'Frederik Obermaier on the Suisse Secrets', Episode 77, *KickBack – The Global Anti-Corruption Podcast*, 9 May 2022, https://soundcloud.com/kickback-gap/77-frederik-obermaier-on-the-suisse-secrets

22 'Fighting Financial Crime with AI', Itera, https://www.itera.com/fighting-financial-crime-with-ai (4:18).

23 'OECD Public Integrity Indicators', OECD, https://oecd-public-integrity-indicators.org/

24 'The Zero Tolerance to Corruption Policy: Rebuilding Ethics and Integrity, 2019, Republic of Uganda', https://www.igg.go.ug/media/files/publications/Zero_Tolerance_to_Corruption_Policy_ZTP_2019.pdf

25 'Siemens Business Is Clean Business', *Siemens*, https://new.siemens.com/global/en/company/sustainability/compliance.html

26 'UNODC and Siemens AG Strengthen Partnership for Business Integrity', *UNDOC*, 2 August 2021, https://www.unodc.org/unodc/en/frontpage/2021/August/unodc-and-siemens-ag-strengthen-partnership-for-business-integrity.html

27 'Who We Are', *Transparency International*, https://www.transparency.org/en/who-we-are

28 'Russian Oligarchs Hide Money in Plain Sight in Luxury New York City Condos', *Newsweek*, 14 March 2022, https://www.newsweek.com/russian-oligarchs-hide-money-plain-sight-luxury-new-york-city-condos-1687503

29 'Dekleptification Guide', *USAID*, https://www.usaid.gov/sites/default/files/2023-02/USAID-Dekleptification-Guide.pdf p 2.

30 'Dekleptification Guide', *USAID*, https://www.usaid.gov/sites/default/files/2023-02/USAID-Dekleptification-Guide.pdf p 55.

31 'Dekleptification Guide', *USAID*, https://www.usaid.gov/sites/default/files/2023-02/USAID-Dekleptification-Guide.pdf p 71.

32 'Dekleptification Guide', *USAID*, https://www.usaid.gov/sites/default/files/2023-02/USAID-Dekleptification-Guide.pdf pp 71–2.

Chapter 2

1 'Дворец для Путина' (Putin's Palace), *Navalny.com*, https://palace.navalny.com

2 'Дворец для Путина. История самой большой взятки' ('Putin's Palace. The History of the Biggest Bribe') [video], *YouTube*, 19 January 2021, https://www.youtube.com/watch?v=ipAnwilMncI (53:30).

3 'Is There Such a Thing as Rules Based Order?' *Financial Times*, 20 April 2023 https://www.ft.com/content/664d7fa5-d575-45da-8129-095647c8abe7

4 See, for instance, discussions around the proposed US Enablers Act which was blocked by the US Senate in December 2022, which was envisioned as closing the last gap by imposing due diligence and compliance obligations onto lawyers, accountants, art dealers and other professionals in an attempt to combat the very same actors as enablers of corruption, money laundering, and other offences; 'US Senate Blocks Major Anti-Money Laundering Bill, the Enablers Act', *ICIJ*, 12 December 2022 https://www.icij.org/investigations/pandora-papers/us-senate-blocks-major-anti-money-laundering-bill-the-enablers-act/

5 See, for instance, the recent UN report by Mary Lawlor, 'Report of the Special Rapporteur on the situation of human rights defenders', which argues that the protections applicable to human rights defenders should be extended to anti-corruption activists, since they, too, are human rights defenders; *Reliefweb*, 8 February 2022, https://reliefweb.int/report/world/heart-struggle-human-rights-defenders-working-against-corruption-report-special

6 'Remarks of President Joe Biden – State of the Union Address As Prepared for Delivery', *The White House*, 1 March 2022, https://www.whitehouse.gov/briefing-room/speeches-remarks/2022/03/01/remarks-of-president-joe-biden-state-of-the-union-address-as-delivered/

7 Bono during the Forbes 400 Philanthropy Summit in 2014 remarking on the 'transparency revolution' he is part of, with the support of Bill and Melinda Gates Foundation. 'Bono: Transparency is the Vaccine against Corruption' [video], *YouTube*, https://www.youtube.com/watch?v=0xvwbeyAr4g 0:42

8 'Memorandum on Establishing the Fight against Corruption as a Core United States National Security Interest', *The White House*, 3 June 2021, https://www.whitehouse.gov/briefing-room/presidential-actions/2021/06/03/memorandum-on-establishing-the-fight-against-corruption-as-a-core-united-states-national-security-interest/

9 'What Is Corruption?', *Transparency International*, https://www.transparency.org/en/what-is-corruption

10 'Hearings Before the Subcommittee on Multinational Corporations of the Committee on Foreign Relations, United States Senate, Ninety-Third Congress on the International Telephone and Telegraph Company and Chile, 1970–71', *U.S. Government Printing Office*, Washington, 1978, https://babel.hathitrust.org/cgi/pt?id=mdp.39015003294462&view=1up&seq=3&q1=million pp 65–70.

11 For the statistics, see: 'DOJ and SEC Enforcement Actions per Year', *Foreign Corrupt Practices Act Clearinghouse*, Stanford Law School, https://fcpa.stanford.edu/statistics-analytics.html

12 'Навальный внесен в реестр террористов и экстремистов Росфинмониторинга' ('Naval'nyi Is Included in Rosfinmonitoring's Register of Terrorists and Extremists'), *Interfax*, 25 January 2022 https://www.interfax.ru/russia/818220

13 'Statement on Alexei Navalny's Status as Prisoner of Conscience', *Amnesty International*, 7 May 2021, https://www.amnesty.org/en/latest/news/2021/05/statement-on-alexei-navalnys-status-as-prisoner-of-conscience/

14 'Navalny Must be Freed, European Rights Court Tells Russia', *BBC News*, 17 February 2021, https://www.bbc.com/news/world-europe-56102257

15 'Lech Wałęsa zgłosił kandydaturę Aleksieja Nawalnego do Pokojowej Nagrody Nobla' ('Lech Wałęsa Announced the Nomination of Aleksei Naval'nyi for the Nobel Peace Prize'), *Wyborcza*, 4 February 2021, https://wyborcza.pl/7,75398,26753260,lech-wal esa-zglosil-kandydature-aleksieja-nawalnego-do-pokojowej.html

16 'Flere fredsprisforslag før fristen gikk ut' ('Several Nominations for the Nobel Peace Prize before the Deadline'), *Aftenposten*, 1 February 2021, https://www.aftenposten.no/norge/ politikk/i/jBL23A/flere-fredsprisforslag-foer-fristen-gikk-ut

17 'Стань националистом!' ('Become a Nationalist!') [video], *YouTube*, 17 October 2007, https://www.youtube.com/watch?v=ICoc2VmGdfw&t=25s

18 Memorial Human Rights Centre (dissolved in April 2022 under the Russian 'foreign agent' law, the site is not being updated since 5 April 2022) https://memohrc.org/ru/ pzk-list

19 'Amnesty Declares Russia's Udaltsov a Prisoner of Conscience', *Radio Free Europe Radio Liberty*, 10 August 2011, https://www.rferl.org/a/russia_udaltsov_prisoner_of_conscie nce/24292629.html

20 'Удальцов прекратил голодовку, чтобы его не кормили насильно' ('Udal'tsov Ended the Hunger Strike to Avoid Force-Feeding'), *Vesti.ru*, 19 August 2014, https:// www.vesti.ru/article/1834377

21 'ЕСПЧ присудил компенсацию Удальцову и Развозжаеву' ('ECHR Awarded Compensation to Udal'tsov and Razvozzhaev'), *Radio Liberty*, 19 November 2019, https:// www.svoboda.org/a/30279984.html

22 'Alexei Navalny awarded the European Parliament's 2021 Sakharov Prize', *News European Parliament*, Press Release, 20 October 2021, https://www.europarl.europa.eu/news/en/ headlines/priorities/sakharov-2021/20211014IPR14915/alexei-navalny-awarded-the-european-parliament-s-2021-sakharov-prize

23 At least in the US, but also in many other countries, political scandals are measured against it, and around the world, many scandals and purported scandals have been named after it, using the suffix '-gate', sometimes also ironically.

24 'Putin "Purges" 150 FSB Agents in Response to Russia's Botched War with Ukraine', *The Times*, 11 April 2022, https://www.thetimes.co.uk/article/putin-purges-150-fsb-age nts-in-response-to-russias-botched-war-with-ukraine-lf9k6tn6g

25 ' "Ящик Пандоры открыть легко": последнее слово Улюкаева целиком' (' "Pandora's Box Is Easy to Open": Uliukaev's Final Statement in Full'), *BBC Russian Service*, 7 December 2017, https://www.bbc.com/russian/features-42265348

26 In fact, at 62 years, he compared the prosecutor's demand for 10 years of imprisonment to a death sentence. Uliukaev was released in May 2022.

27 'Коррупция в высших эшелонах власти' ('Corruption in the Highest Echelons of Power'), *Levada Center*, 7 May 2019, https://www.levada.ru/2019/05/07/korruptsiya-v-vysshih-eshelonah-vlasti/

28 'Президенту Медведеву объяснили, как украсть триллион' ('President Medvedev Explained How to Steal a Trillion'), *Vedomosti*, 1 November 2010, https://www.vedomo sti.ru/politics/articles/2010/11/01/ukrast_trillion

29 'Единорос Пехтин ушел из Госдумы после разоблачений Навального' ('United Russia Deputy Pekhtin Resigned from the State Duma after Naval'nyi's Revelations'), *Lenta*, 20 February 2013, http://lenta.ru/articles/2013/02/20/pekhtin/

30 'ФБК: 79 расследований в одном ролике' ('FBK: 79 Investigations in One Video') [video], *YouTube*, 5 August 2020, https://www.youtube.com/watch?v=s3-Us7eGTvk

31 'Реакция общества на фильм «Фонда борьбы с коррупцией»') ('Society's Reaction to the Film by the Foundation for the Combatting of Corruption'), *Levada Center*,

23 December 2015, https://www.levada.ru/2015/12/23/reaktsiya-obshhestva-na-film-fonda-borby-s-korruptsiej/

32 https://whatstat.ru/channels/news_politics. Shortly after the start of the full-scale war in Ukraine, TV Dozhd's website was blocked, and the channel suspended its activities. On 18 July 2022, it reappeared on social media, having relocated to Latvia, only to be deprived of the license after a few months due to allegedly pro-Putin content. In early 2023, the channel was granted a license in the Netherlands.

33 'Таинственный остров Медведева' ('Medvedev's Mysterious Island') [video], *YouTube*, 10 April 2020, https://www.youtube.com/watch?v=EIoHkq84Lc0&list=PLuBu40P6jU CZtTMNc8Pd_AHun5AjGmOKK&index=52 (00:20).

34 'Ответ Алишеру Усманову' ('Reply to Alisher Usmanov') [video], *YouTube*, 29 May 2017, https://www.youtube.com/watch?v=sM8_EvVD4iw&list=PLuBu40P6jUCZtT MNc8Pd_AHun5AjGmOKK&index=240 (12:15); 'Ответ генералу Золотову' ('Reply to General Zolotov') [video], *YouTube*, 18 October 2018, https://www.youtube.com/watch?v=_2KfjJ-7914

35 'Вы готовы ловить жуликов за руку?' ('Are you Ready to Catch the Crooks Red-Handed?') [video], *YouTube*, 13 February 2018, https://www.youtube.com/watch?v= eHllKhSyxPM&list=PLuBu40P6jUCZtTMNc8Pd_AHun5AjGmOKK&index=168 (08:40).

36 'Фальшивая популярность Путина. Доказательства' ('Putin's False Popularity. Proof') [video], *YouTube*, 5 April 2018, https://www.youtube.com/watch?v=sXVH0Cai iE0&list=PLuBu40P6jUCZtTMNc8Pd_AHun5AjGmOKK&index=153

37 'Взятка Хлопонину. Доказательства' ('Bribe for Khloponin. Proof') [video], *YouTube*, 18 May 2018, https://www.youtube.com/watch?v=emUezdwXhyY&list=PLuBu40P6jU CZtTMNc8Pd_AHun5AjGmOKK&index=144 (00:10).

38 'Взятка Хлопонину. Доказательства' ('Bribe for Khloponin. Proof') [video], *YouTube*, 18 May 2018, https://www.youtube.com/watch?v=emUezdwXhyY&list=PLuBu40P6jU CZtTMNc8Pd_AHun5AjGmOKK&index=144 (03:20).

39 'Зам Собянина украла миллиарды. И выборы' ('Sobyanin's Deputy Stole Billions. And the Elections') [video], *YouTube*, 1 August 2019, https://www.youtube. com/watch?v=vuz2_FEKOPU&list=PLuBu40P6jUCZtTMNc8Pd_AHun5AjGm OKK&index=84 (16:40).

40 'Засекреченные миллиарды премьера Мишустина' ('Prime Minister Mishustin's Secret Billions') [video], *YouTube*, 28 January 2020, https://www.youtube.com/watch?v= fyPWPTYf-b0&list=PLuBu40P6jUCZtTMNc8Pd_AHun5AjGmOKK&index=59

41 'Дворец для Путина. История самой большой взятки' ('Putin's Palace. History of the Biggest Bribe') [video], *YouTube*, 19 January 2021, https://www.youtube.com/watch?v=ipAnwilMncI (59:00).

42 'Золотое безумие. Реальные фотографии дворца Путина' ('Golden Madness. Real Photos from Putin's Palace') [video], *YouTube*, 20 January 2022, https://www.yout ube.com/watch?v=OjYl1xvssJY (40:00).

43 '«Хотите, поговорю о Боге?» Последнее слова [sic] Навального на апелляции по делу «Ив Роше» сообщают «Открытые медиа»' ('"Do You Want Me to Talk about God?" Naval'nyi's Last Words at the Yves Rocher Appeal, Reported by Open Media'), *Open Media*, 20 February 2021, https://openmedia.io/news/n1/my-sudebn uyu-sistemu-mozhem-krutit-na-lyuboj-chasti-tela-kuda-ty-lezesh-poslednee-slovo-navalnogo-na-sude/

44 'Russia: Blogger Navalny Tries to Prove That Fighting Regime Is Fun', 27 October 2010, *Global Voices*, https://globalvoices.org/2010/10/27/russia-blogger-alexey-nava lny-on-fighting-regime/

45 'ЦРУ, Ротенберг и ёршик. Как пропагандисты отмазывают Путина' ('CIA, Rotenberg and Toilet Brush. How the Propagandists Whitewash Putin') [video], *YouTube*, 12 February 2021, https://www.youtube.com/watch?v=IYD-0XqDazQ

46 'Таинственная распаковка. К вам есть вопросы' ('Mysterious Unboxing. Questions for You') [video], *YouTube*, 3 April 2018, https://www.youtube.com/watch?v=aTYT R4evX54&list=PLuBu40P6jUCZtTMNc8Pd_AHun5AjGmOKK&index=154

47 'Как друг Путина Сергей Чемезов осваивает бюджет на поставке лекарственных средств' ('How Putin's Friend Sergei Chemezov Appropriates the Budget for the Supply of Medicines') [video], *YouTube*, 16 June 2016, https://www. youtube.com/watch?v=K5JOMsAD2RU&list=PLuBu40P6jUCZCYqaGjUbSoxApA SjvnzDG&index=279, 'Любовь против полицейского картеля' ('Love vs Police Cartel') [video], *YouTube*, 10 August 2017, https://www.youtube.com/watch?v=OBk9 YlCtp6E&list=PLuBu40P6jUCZtTMNc8Pd_AHun5AjGmOKK&index=216, 'Пять историй о борьбе с коррупцией в госзаказе' ('Five Stories about the Fight against Corruption in Public Procurement') [video], *YouTube*, 5 February 2018, https://www. youtube.com/watch?v=kfcWRxdAPjI&list=PLuBu40P6jUCZtTMNc8Pd_AHun5 AjGmOKK&index=172

48 'Выдвижение Алексея Навального' ('Nomination of Aleksei Naval'nyi') [video], *YouTube*, 25 December 2017, https://www.youtube.com/watch?v=Szh-L13G CMQ&list=PLuBu40P6jUCZtTMNc8Pd_AHun5AjGmOKK&index=185

49 'Москва выбирает забастовку избирателей. 28 января' ('Moscow Chooses a Voters' Boycott') [video], *YouTube*, 28 January 2018, https://www.youtube.com/watch?v=zWG9 hnnQnhk&list=PLuBu40P6jUCZtTMNc8Pd_AHun5AjGmOKK&index=174

50 'Мифы и враньё о пенсионной реформе' ('Myths and Lies about the Pension Reform') [video], *YouTube*, 9 July 2018, https://www.youtube.com/watch?v=cX5BXqz8 0Eo&list=PLuBu40P6jUCZtTMNc8Pd_AHun5AjGmOKK&index=131 'Пенсионная реформа – сплошной обман' ('The Pension Reform Is a Complete Scam') [video], *YouTube*, 27 September 2018, https://www.youtube.com/watch?v=-7xO3gOuVzA&list= PLuBu40P6jUCZtTMNc8Pd_AHun5AjGmOKK&index=115

51 'Это и есть коррупция' ('This Is Corruption') [video], *YouTube*, 14 August 2018, https://www.youtube.com/watch?v=BwHnL8MIbp0&list=PLuBu40P6jUCZtTMNc8 Pd_AHun5AjGmOKK&index=126 (00:20).

52 'Как мы делали «Димона»: ответы на вопросы и инсайды' ('How We Made "Dimon": Answers to Questions and Inside Information') [video], *YouTube*, 21 March 2017, https://www.youtube.com/watch?v=2AWyNwLI9oM&list=PLuBu40P6jUCZtT MNc8Pd_AHun5AjGmOKK&index=268

53 '26 марта все на улицу: он нам не Димон' ('On March 26, Everyone to the Streets: He Is Not Dimon to Us') [video], *YouTube*, 23 March 2017, https://www.yout ube.com/watch?v=-Kh0zUkX7cs&list=PLuBu40P6jUCZtTMNc8Pd_AHun5AjGm OKK&index=264

54 '12 июня. Объясняю на уточках' ('12 June. I Explain Using Ducks') [video], *YouTube*, 11 June 2017, https://www.youtube.com/watch?v=0ubR-1JeJCs&list=PLuBu40P6jU CZtTMNc8Pd_AHun5AjGmOKK&index=234

55 'Конкурс на миллион' ('Million Contest') [video], *YouTube*, 4 June 2017, https:// www.youtube.com/watch?v=GVmG1Vyzbjk&list=PLuBu40P6jUCZtTMNc8Pd_A Hun5AjGmOKK&index=238

56 'Последнее слово Навального. Россия будет счастливой' ('Naval'nyi's Last Statement. Russia Will Be Happy') [video], *YouTube*, 20 February 2021, https://www. youtube.com/watch?v=XPBaJVBV9kI&list=PLuBu40P6jUCZtTMNc8Pd_AHun5 AjGmOKK&index=30 (13:10).

57 'Алексей Навальный: «Мы возродили политику. И это круто»' ('Aleksei Naval'nyi: "We Have Revived Politics. And It's Cool"'), *The New Times*, 26 August 2013, https://newtimes.ru/articles/detail/70195/

58 Conversely, state media go to great lengths in portraying him as a choleric. For instance, TV footage of him in court rendered his voice almost suspiciously highly pitched. According to the reporter, when the defamation case was being heard, Naval'nyi behaved hysterically: 'Навальный устроил истерику на суде по делу о клевете на ветерана ВОВ' ('Naval'nyi Raised Hysteria in Court during the Hearings on the Case of Defamation of the Veteran of the Great Patriotic War'), *Ren TV 5*, February 2021, https://ren.tv/news/v-rossii/799521-navalnyi-ustroil-isteriku-na-sude-po-delu-o-klev ete-na-veterana-vov

59 'Как я заработал денег на дурачках с LifeNews' ('How I Made Money by Fooling LifeNews') [video], *YouTube*, 18 August 2017, https://www.youtube.com/watch?v= U3RLzg5RL3Y&list=PLuBu40P6jUCZtTMNc8Pd_AHun5AjGmOKK&index=213

60 'Расследование нападения на Навального приостановлено' ('The Investigation into the Attack on Naval'nyi Is Suspended'), *BBC News Russia*, 13 July 2017, https://www.bbc.com/russian/news-40593391

61 'Из Барнаула. То ли Маска, то ли Аватар, то ли Шрек' ('From Barnaul. Either Mask, or Avatar, or Shrek'), *Navalny.com*, 23 March 2017, https://navalny.com/p/5287/

62 'Иван Бегтин о «РосПил.Инфо»' ('Ivan Begtin about "RosPil.Info"'), *Polit.ru*, 17 February 2011, https://polit.ru/news/2011/02/17/balagan/

63 'Я позвонил своему убийце. Он признался' ('I Called My Assassin. He Confessed') [video], *YouTube*, 21 December 2020, https://www.youtube.com/watch?v=ibqiet6Bg38

64 'Дворец для Путина' ('Putin's Palace'), *Navalny.com*, https://palace.navalny.com

65 'Рогозин предложил расстрелять собственного сына (и себя)' ('Rogozin Proposed to Shoot His Own Son (and Himself)') [video], *YouTube*, 18 August 2021, https://www.youtube.com/watch?v=WF_0wmTwaYE

66 'Кто захватил столицу Сибири и как её освободить' ('Who Captured the Capital of Siberia and How to Free It') [video], *YouTube*, 31 August 2020, https://www.yout ube.com/watch?v=hx48jaOroRQ

67 'Как живут цари госкорпораций' ('How the Kings of State Corporations Live') [video], *YouTube*, 11 October 2018, https://www.youtube.com/watch?v=Rl7i79_UyU4

68 'Паразиты' ('Parasites') [video], *YouTube*, 10 March 2020, https://www.youtube.com/ watch?v=RfCZm_rdfZM

69 'Путинский пропагандист в Булонском лесу' ('Putin's Propagandist in the Bois de Boulogne') [video], *YouTube*, 15 May 2018, https://www.youtube.com/watch?v=JLMe EylCGyk&list=PLuBu40P6jUCZtTMNc8Pd_AHun5AjGmOKK&index=145 (05:15).

70 'Олигарх Усманов отказывается платить налоги в России' ('Oligarch Usmanov Refuses to Pay Taxes in Russia') [video], *YouTube*, 20 October 2016, https://www.yout ube.com/watch?v=Qq4RNwfJDSY&list=PLuBu40P6jUCZtTMNc8Pd_AHun5AjGm OKK&index=301

71 'Потупчик не предлагать' ('Don't Recommend Potupchik') [video], 6 February 2012, https://navalny.livejournal.com/673497.html (01:30).

72 'Где берутся деньги и куда они уходят' ('Where Does Money Come from and Where Does It Go?') [video], *YouTube*, 25 July 2017, https://www.youtube.com/watch?v=jle2 YsPnrlg&list=PLuBu40P6jUCZtTMNc8Pd_AHun5AjGmOKK&index=221

73 'Штаб Навального в Краснодаре: кто эти люди и чем они будут заниматься' ('Naval'nyi's Headquarters in Krasnodar: Who Are These People and What Will They Do'), 13 March 2017, https://kuban.rbc.ru/krasnodar/13/03/2017/58c6434e9a7947a26 9ceec81

74 'Без Навального: как ФБК работает без своего лидера' ('Without Naval'nyi: How FBK Works Without Its Leader'), *BBC Russian News*, 11 September 2020, https://www.bbc.com/russian/features-54119390

75 'Неутомимый оптимист' ('Tireless Optimist'), *The New Times*, 6 June 2012, https://newtimes.ru/articles/detail/53086

76 '16 смелых' ('16 Brave Ones'), 30 May 2012, https://navalny.livejournal.com/708361.html

77 'Владимир Ашурков: Оппозиция как бизнес-проект' ('Vladimir Ashurkov: Opposition as a Business Project'), *Vedomosti.ru*, 12 December 2012, https://www.vedomosti.ru/opinion/articles/2012/12/12/samye_perspektivnye_investicii

78 'Тим Кук против Сечина и Миллера' ('Tim Cook vs. Sechin and Miller') [video], *YouTube*, 12 January 2017, https://www.youtube.com/watch?v=AYHnay-Z_DA&list=PLuBu40P6jUCZCYqaGjUbSoxApASjvnzDG&index=250 02:00

79 'Распаковка гаджета за 10 млрд рублей' ('Unpacking a Gadget at the Cost of 10 Billion Rubles') [video], *YouTube*, 30 November 2017, https://www.youtube.com/watch?v=6dIjeUB51-s (03:45).

80 'Кто захватил столицу Сибири и как её освободить' ('Who Captured the Capital of Siberia and How to Free It') [video], *YouTube*, 31 August 2020, https://www.youtube.com/watch?v=hx48jaOroRQ (04:20).

81 'Кто захватил столицу Сибири и как её освободить' ('Who Captured the Capital of Siberia and How to Free It') [video], *YouTube*, 31 August 2020, https://www.youtube.com/watch?v=hx48jaOroRQ (01:30).

82 'Что произошло в Армении и что нужно делать нам' ('What Happened in Armenia and What We Need to Do') [video], *YouTube*, 25 April 2018, https://www.youtube.com/watch?v=BqD0umu1mRA&list=PLuBu40P6jUCZtTMNc8Pd_AHun5AjGmOKK&index=150 (06:30).

83 'Russia's Maverick Tech Prodigy Durov Says His $5 Billion App Telegram Can't Be Bought', *The Moscow Times*, 12 December 2017, https://www.themoscowtimes.com/2017/12/12/russias-maverick-tech-prodigy-durov-says-his-5-billion-app-telegram-cant-be-bought-a59904

84 'Путин привел Телеграмм в пример взаимодействия властей с соцсетями' ('Putin Cited Telegram as an Example of Interaction between the Authorities and Social Networks'), *RIA Novosti*, 30 June 2021, https://ria.ru/20210630/telegram-1739219120.html

85 'Панельная дискуссия с участием представителей IT-индустрии' ('Panel Discussion with Representatives of the IT Industry'), *Russian Government News*, 9 July 2020, http://government.ru/news/39995/

86 'О мессенджере Телеграмм' ('About the Telegram Messenger'), *The Federal Service for Supervision of Communications, Information Technology and Mass Media (Roskomnadzor)*, 18 June 2020, https://rkn.gov.ru/news/rsoc/news73050.htm

87 'Навальный опубликовал программу экономических реформ' ('Naval'nyi Published a Program of Economic Reforms'), *Vedomosti.ru*, 13 December 2017, https://www.vedomosti.ru/politics/articles/2017/12/13/745161-navalnii-programmu

88 'Алексей Навальный опубликовал подробную предвыборную программу. К ней есть вопросы' ('Aleksei Naval'nyi Has Published a Detailed Election Program. There Are Questions'), *Meduza*, 13 December 2017, https://meduza.io/slides/aleksey-navalnyy-opublikoval-podrobnuyu-predvybornuyu-programmu-k-ney-est-voprosy

89 'Либералы VS Силовики. Рублёвские дачи министра и генерала' ('Liberals v. Siloviki. Rublevskoe Chaussee Dachas of the Minister and the General') [video], *YouTube*, 24 April 2019, https://www.youtube.com/watch?v=QR3vJ0Wl4_k&list=PLuBu40P6jUCZtTMNc8Pd_AHun5AjGmOKK&index=94 (0:49).

90   'Спасение повара Путина' ('Saving Putin's Chef') [video], *YouTube*, 21 November 2017, https://www.youtube.com/watch?v=gAufSaa8S4o&list=PLuBu40P6jUCZtT MNc8Pd_AHun5AjGmOKK&index=192 (05:45).

91   'Спасение повара Путина' ('Saving Putin's Chef') [video], *YouTube*, 21 November 2017, https://www.youtube.com/watch?v=gAufSaa8S4o&list=PLuBu40P6jUCZtT MNc8Pd_AHun5AjGmOKK&index=192 (04:25).

92   'Фантастические твари и сколько они получают' ('Fantastic Beasts and How Much They Earn') [video], *YouTube*, 28 April 2021, https://www.youtube.com/watch?v=5QDt ACuZRp8&list=PLuBu40P6jUCZtTMNc8Pd_AHun5AjGmOKK&index=25

93   'Поздравляю Путина с новым государственным праздником' ('Congratulations to Putin on The New State Holiday') [video], *YouTube*, 21 September 2017, https:// youtu.be/-5wh7CZGdnY

94   'Яхта. Самолёт. Девушка. Запретная любовь за ваш счёт' ('Yacht. Airplane. Girl. Forbidden Love at Your Expense') [video], *YouTube*, 2 December 2019, https://www. youtube.com/watch?v=bkdzT5cOiSQ&list=PLuBu40P6jUCZtTMNc8Pd_AHun5 AjGmOKK&index=62

95   'Программа Алексея Навального' ('Aleksei Naval'nyi's Programme') [video], *YouTube*, 13 December 2017, https://www.youtube.com/watch?v=a2psViamdq8&list=PLuBu40 P6jUCZtTMNc8Pd_AHun5AjGmOKK&index=189 (00:19).

96   'Разбираем конституцию РФ как новый iPhone' ('We Analyse the Constitution of the Russian Federation as a New iPhone'), *Navalny.com*, 12 December 2015, https:// navalny.com/p/4609/

97   'Зам Собянина украла миллиарды. И выборы' ('Sobyanin's Deputy Stole Billions. And the Elections') [video], *YouTube*, 1 August 2019, https://www.youtube. com/watch?v=vuz2_FEKOPU&list=PLuBu40P6jUCZtTMNc8Pd_AHun5AjGm OKK&index=84 (03:10).

98   'Томск в плену у депутатской мафии' ('Tomsk Is in Held Prisoner by a Mafia of Parliamentarians') [video], *YouTube*, 3 September 2020, https://www.youtube. com/watch?v=y7rMbcKBW-E&list=PLuBu40P6jUCZtTMNc8Pd_AHun5AjGm OKK&index=38 (37:10).

99   'Дворец для Путина' ('Putin's Palace'), *Navalny.com*, https://palace.navalny.com

100 'Последнее слово Навального. Россия будет счастливой' ('Naval'nyi's Last Statement. Russia Will be Happy') [video], *YouTube*, 20 February 2021, https://www. youtube.com/watch?v=XPBaJVBV9kI&list=PLuBu40P6jUCZtTMNc8Pd_AHun5 AjGmOKK&index=30

101 'Яхта. Самолёт. Девушка. Запретная любовь за ваш счёт' ('Yacht. Airplane. Girl. Forbidden Love at Your Expense') [video], *YouTube*, 2 December 2019, https://www. youtube.com/watch?v=bkdzT5cOiSQ&list=PLuBu40P6jUCZtTMNc8Pd_AHun5 AjGmOKK&index=62 (28:15).

102 'Яхты, взятки и любовница. Что скрывает министр Лавров' ('Yachts, Bribes and a Mistress: What Is Minister Lavrov Hiding?') [video], *YouTube*, 16 September 2021, https://www.youtube.com/watch?v=xNa5XknuXkQ&list=PLuBu40P6jUCZtTMNc8 Pd_AHun5AjGmOKK&index=9 (30:10).

103 'Финальная битва между добром и нейтралитетом' ('The Final Battle between Good and Neutrality') [video], *YouTube*, 18 April 2021, https://www.youtube. com/watch?v=nIQSS7_44wQ&list=PLuBu40P6jUCZtTMNc8Pd_AHun5AjGm OKK&index=26 (07:00).

104 'Екатерина Шульман: Практический Нострадамус, или 12 умственных привычек, которые мешают нам предвидеть будущее' ('Ekaterina Shulman: Practical Nostradamus, or 12 Mental Habits That Prevent Us from Predicting the Future'),

Vedomosti.ru, 24 December 2014, https://www.vedomosti.ru/opinion/articles/2014/12/24/prakticheskij-nostradamus

Chapter 4

1. 'Livestream: Visionary: The Paul G. Allen Collection Part I' [video], Christie's *You Tube*, 10 November 2022, https://www.youtube.com/watch?v=4B62L9x1jmU
2. 'The State of Food Security and Nutrition in the World 2022', *Food and Agriculture Organization of the United Nations*, https://www.fao.org/3/cc0639en/online/sofi-2022/key-messages.html
3. 'G20 Must Tackle the "Cost of Profit" Crisis Causing Chaos Worldwide, says Oxfam', *Oxfam*, 14 November 2022, https://www.oxfam.org.nz/news-media/g20-must-tackle-the-cost-of-profit-crisis/
4. '"Dr. Doom" Roubini: The Art Market Is "Shady"' [video], CNN Business *You Tube*, 11 May 2015, https://www.youtube.com/watch?v=bca9ECcSlBs
5. 'Dekleptification Guide', *USAID*, https://www.usaid.gov/sites/default/files/2023-02/USAID-Dekleptification-Guide.pdf
6. 'Who We Are', *Transparency International*, https://www.transparency.org/en/who-we-are
7. 'Fact Sheet: Establishing the Fight against Corruption as a Core U.S. National Security Interest', *The White House*, 3 June 2021, https://www.whitehouse.gov/briefing-room/statements-releases/2021/06/03/fact-sheet-establishing-the-fight-against-corruption-as-a-core-u-s-national-security-interest/
8. 'Other People's Money', Chapter 5, *Louis D. Brandeis School of Law Library*, https://louisville.edu/law/library/special-collections/the-louis-d.-brandeis-collection/other-peoples-money-chapter-v
9. This is a recurrent way of speaking about cryptocurrencies, see, for instance, this article titled: 'EU Agrees to Tame "Wild West" with New Crypto Market Rules', *Reuters*, 1 July 2022, https://www.reuters.com/markets/europe/eu-seeks-deal-ground-breaking-rules-regulate-crypto-2022-06-30/
10. 'Treasury Announces Two Enforcement Actions for over $24m and $29m against Virtual Currency Exchange Bittrex, Inc.', *US Department of Treasury*, 11 October 2022, https://home.treasury.gov/news/press-releases/jy1006
11. 'Treasury Announces Two Enforcement Actions for over $24m and $29m against Virtual Currency Exchange Bittrex, Inc.', *US Department of Treasury*, 11 October 2022, https://home.treasury.gov/news/press-releases/jy1006
12. 'A Framework for OFAC Compliance Commitments', *Department of the Treasury*, https://ofac.treasury.gov/media/16331/download?inline p 6.
13. 'Remediation', *Online Etymological Dictionary*, https://www.etymonline.com/word/remediation
14. 'The Art Market Is a Scam (and Rich People Run It)' [video], Wendover Productions, *You Tube*, 5 October 2021, https://www.youtube.com/watch?v=ZZ3F3zWiEmc
15. 'Fine Art Isn't about Art. It's about Evading Taxes' [video], Jake Tran, *You Tube*, 30 April 2021, https://www.youtube.com/watch?v=3L1an9JU3Nk
16. 'International Anti-Corruption Day 2022: Stop Kleptocrats and Protect the Common Good', *Transparency International*, 9 December 2022, https://www.transparency.org/en/news/international-anti-corruption-day-2022-stop-kleptocrats-protect-common-good
17. 'Gardner Museum Theft: An Active and Ongoing Investigation', *Isabella Stewart Gardner Museum*, https://www.gardnermuseum.org/organization/theft
18. 'The 25 Greatest Art Heists of All Time', *ARTnews*, 11 February 2021, https://www.artnews.com/list/art-news/artists/greatest-art-heists-of-all-time-1234583441/van-gogh-singer-laren-museum/

19 To take an example, see, for instance, the Art Guard provider: https://www.artguard. net/private-collections/

20 For an overview see, for example, the United States Government Accountability Office's Report to Congressional Requesters: 'Cultural Property': Protection of Iraqi and Syrian Antiquities', August 2016: https://www.si.edu/Content/Pdf/About/GAO/GAO.16.673-Antiquities-Looting-Final-report-2016.pdf

21 'Museums: Last Week Tonight with John Oliver (HBO)' [video], LastWeekTonight *YouTube*, 3 October 2022, https://www.youtube.com/watch?v=eJPLiT1kCSM

22 'Спецотдел (2002)' (Special Department), https://www.kino-teatr.ru/kino/movie/ros/6709/annot/

23 'John Oliver Roasts Museums in Episode on Looted Art', *Hyperallergic*, 4 October 2022, https://hyperallergic.com/766138/john-oliver-roasts-western-museums-in-episode-on-looted-art/

24 'The Art Loss Register' https://www.artloss.com/

25 'International Claim Database' (formerly the Art Claim Database) https://www.internationalclaim.com/

26 'The Watch Register' https://www.thewatchregister.com/

27 'ID-Art Mobile App', *INTERPOL*, https://www.interpol.int/en/Crimes/Cultural-heritage-crime/ID-Art-mobile-app

28 'Documenting ISIL's Antiquities Trafficking: The Looting and Destruction of Iraqi and Syrian Cultural Heritage: What We Know and What Can Be Done', *US Department of State*, 29 September 2015, https://2009-2017.state.gov/e/eb/rls/rm/2015/247610.htm; reports such as these are often reused in compliance training webinars to document the risk and the scale of the problem.

29 'FinCEN Informs Financial Institutions of Efforts Related to Trade in Antiquities and Art', *FinCEN*, 9 March 2021, https://www.fincen.gov/sites/default/files/2021-03/FinCEN%20Notice%20on%20Antiquities%20and%20Art_508C.pdf

30 'Frequently Asked Questions: Interim Final Rule – Anti-Money Laundering Programs for Dealers in Precious Metals, Stones, or Jewels', *FinCEN*, https://www.fincen.gov/sites/default/files/shared/faq060305.pdf

31 'The Need for Prosecuting Participants in the Illegal Antiquities Trade', *Conflict Antiquities*, report by Clooney Foundation for Justice, 8 June 2022, https://cfj.org/report/the-need-for-prosecuting-participants-in-the-illegal-antiquities-trade/

32 'Art and Antiquities', course by Manchester CF, financial intelligence and compliance training company, https://www.manchestercf.com/art-and-antiquities-3/

33 'Financial Crimes Task Force', *The Antiquities Coalition*, https://theantiquitiescoalition.org/developing-implementing-solutions/financial-crimes-task-force/

34 Sayari, a leading provider of sanctions risk intelligence, https://sayari.com/

35 Lexis Nexis Risk Solutions https://risk.lexisnexis.com/global/en

36 Refinitiv World-Check Risk Intelligence https://solutions.refinitiv.com/world-check-kyc-screening

37 'Art Market Guidelines', *Responsible Art Market*, http://responsibleartmarket.org/art-market-guidelines/

38 The recent German Supply Chain Act imposing due diligence obligations in respect to human rights violations, slavery, forced labour, minimum wage, the environment and more that came in effect on 1 January 2023, is a case in point and a prime example of the expansion of this logic into ever new domains, and likely to become a trend-setting legislation. It expands on the UN Guiding Principles on Business and Human Rights to modern slavery and mirrors other supply chain due diligence regulations such as the Modern Slavery Act in the UK and Australia, Transparency Act in Norway, and similar EU regulation being finalized.

39 'Perspectives', *CINOA*, the International Federation of Art and Antique Dealer Associations, https://www.cinoa.org/cinoa/perspectives

40 'When Is a Fake Not a Fake? When It's a Genuine Forgery', *The Guardian*, 2 July 2005, https://www.theguardian.com/money/2005/jul/02/alternativeinvestment.jobsandmoney

41 'The Art of Spotting "Sleepers," the Misattributed Masterpieces That Earn Dealers Millions', *Artsy*, 29 September 2017, https://www.artsy.net/article/artsy-editorial-art-spotting-sleepers-misattributed-masterpieces-earn-dealers-millions

42 'Verisart', https://verisart.com/tokengating

43 'Protect Your Creations. Fight Fraud. Build Trust. Add Value', *Verisart*, https://verisart.com/our-certificates

44 'Provenance Revealed: Galerie Steinitz Sale Will Be Recorded on the Blockchain', *Salon Privé Magazine*, 16 September 2022, https://www.salonprivemag.com/galerie-steinitz-sale/

45 'Secure Certificates of Authenticity with Cutting-Edge Technology', *ARTtrust*, https://www.arttrustonline.com/artcertificate/secure/

46 'Tagsmart', https://www.tagsmart.com/dna-tags

47 'Vinovest: About Us', *Vinovest*, https://www.vinovest.co/about-us

48 'Wine Provenance: What Is It and Why Is It Important to Investors?', *Vinovest*, https://www.vinovest.co/blog/wine-provenance

49 'For the First Time in History, an Object Becomes Proof of Its Own Authenticity', *Origyn Foundation*, https://web.archive.org/web/20230321074236/https://www.origyn.com/luxury

50 'For the First Time in History, an Object Becomes Proof of Its Own Authenticity', *Origyn Foundation*, https://web.archive.org/web/20230321074236/https://www.origyn.com/luxury

51 'Invest in the Art You Love, Trust the Art You Own', *Artory/Winston*, https://www.artory-winston.com/

52 'Investment Opportunities at a Glance', *Artory/Winston*, https://www.artory-winston.com/#artory-investment-opportunities

53 'Selling NFTs as an Artist: A Gold Mine or a Quick Sand?', *Information Prime*, 24 January 2022, https://informationprime.wordpress.com/2022/01/24/selling-nfts-as-an-artist-a-gold-mine-or-a-quick-sand/

54 'Authentic Banksy Art Burning Ceremony (NFT)' [video], Burnt Finance, *YouTube*, 4 March 2021, https://www.youtube.com/watch?time_continue=67&v=C4wm-p_VFh0&feature=emb_logo 00:30–00:50.

55 'Artists Are Burning Their Work for NFTs', *PetaPixel*, 12 October 2022, https://petapixel.com/2022/10/12/artists-are-burning-their-work-for-nfts/

56 'Study of the Facilitation of Money Laundering and Terror Finance through the Trade in Works of Art', *Department of Treasury*, February 2022, https://home.treasury.gov/system/files/136/Treasury_Study_WoA.pdf

57 'Diamond Trade Still Fuels Human Suffering', *Human Rights Watch*, 10 May 2018, https://www.hrw.org/news/2018/05/10/diamond-trade-still-fuels-human-suffering

58 'Research Briefing: Economic Crime (Transparency and Enforcement) Act 2022', *UK Parliament, House of Commons Library*, 23 March 2022, https://commonslibrary.parliament.uk/research-briefings/cbp-9486/

59 'Fight against Corruption: A Life and Death Struggle That We Must Win: Official', *Global Times*, 25 October 2022, https://www.globaltimes.cn/page/202210/1277881.shtml

60 Chat with OpenAI's GPT, December 28, 2022.

61 'About Us', *FCS Compliance*, https://fcscompliance.co.uk/company-overview/

[62] 'Crime-fighting value of Enhanced Due Diligence', *Refinitiv*, 8 October 2019, https://www.refinitiv.com/perspectives/regulation-risk-compliance/crime-fighting-value-of-enhanced-due-diligence/

Chapter 5

[1] There is also a widely reported upon The Oppidum, an ultra-luxury bunker in an undisclosed location in the Czech Republic, near Český Brod, strategically situated in central Europe and adapted from a 77,500 square-foot former military bunker from the Soviet era. The website has been deleted, the last capture by Wayback Machine is from 25 June 2022, available here: https://web.archive.org/web/20220625022952/http://www.theoppidum.com/ While the bunker has been widely reported upon, it is unclear whether it ever existed in the form presented in media; some Czech media have even disputed its existence. It has been linked to the former Czech Intelligence Chief, Andor Šándor. See for instance: 'Apokalyptická pevnost pro miliardáře v Česku: Bezpečnost boháčů řídí Andor Šándor' ('Apocalyptic Bunker for Billionaires: The Security for the Rich Is Managed by Andor Šándor'), *Blesk*, 11 November 2015, https://www.blesk.cz/clanek/zpravy-udalosti/354886/apokalypticka-pevnost-pro-miliardare-v-cesku-bezpecnost-bohacu-ridi-andor-sandor.html

[2] 'Oppidum', https://oppidum.ch/en

[3] See for instance: 'Corruption and the Global Financial Crisis', *Forbes*, 27 January 2009, https://www.forbes.com/2009/01/27/corruption-financial-crisis-business-corruption09_0127corruption.html or 'Secrets and Lies of the Bailout', *Rolling Stone*, 4 January 2013, https://www.rollingstone.com/politics/politics-news/secrets-and-lies-of-the-bailout-113270/

[4] 'The Numbers behind Russian-Owned Superyachts', *Superyacht News*, 24 March 2022, https://www.superyachtnews.com/business/the-numbers-behind-russian-owned-superyachts

[5] 'Luxury Yachtmaker to the Oligarchs Checks Up On Who Its Customers Are', *Bloomberg*, 7 April 2022, https://www.bloomberg.com/news/articles/2022-04-07/germany-s-yachtmaker-to-the-oligarchs-asks-who-its-customers-are

[6] 'What if You Make Your Own Rules', *Oceanco*, https://www.oceancoyacht.com/fleet/tranquility/

[7] 'What if You Make Your Own Rules', *Oceanco*, https://www.oceancoyacht.com/fleet/tranquility/

[8] 'Imperial', https://www.imperial-yachts.com/

[9] 'SYBAss Members Account for 56% of Yachts over 40m under Construction (Dec 2022)', *SYBAss*, https://sybass.org/membership/our-members/

[10] 'Sybass Makes Sure That Rules Which Impact Superyachts Take into Account the Unique Nature of These Vessels and the Way They Are Operated', *SYBAss*, https://sybass.org/our-work/regulation/

[11] 'Sybass Makes Sure That Rules Which Impact Superyachts Take into Account the Unique Nature of These Vessels and the Way They Are Operated', *SYBAss*, https://sybass.org/our-work/regulation/

[12] The ten companies who built and delivered these vessels are as follows: Lürssen, Heesen, Oceanco, Feadship, Nobiskrug, Fincantieri, Amels, Princess Yachts Ltd, San Lorenzo, Dunya. The only two non-SYbass members of this group are Princess Yachts Ltd and Dunya. For a list of SYBass's full membership, see the following link: 'SYBAss Members Account For 56% Of Yachts Over 40m Under Construction (Dec 2022)', *SYBAss*, https://sybass.org/membership/our-members/

[13] The enthusiasm for this form of regulation, or rather, delegation of power and enlisting of services in the name of national security, on the part of the industry, can be discerned

in industry media. As an example here, we can take Microsoft's Blue Security Podcast, and the 19 March 2023 episode on the White House National Cybersecurity Strategy, *YouTube*, 20 March 2023 https://www.youtube.com/watch?v=BxG155ryP5I

[14] 'About the OECD Public Integrity Indicators', *OECD*, https://oecd-public-integrity-indicators.org/about

[15] 'Post Employment Integrity In Practice (Ministers)', *OECD*, https://oecd-public-integrity-indicators.org/indicators/1000097/subindicators/1000414

[16] 'Risk management to safeguard integrity', *OECD*, https://www.oecd.org/governance/ethics/risk-management-integrity.htm

[17] 'Forensic: Fraud and Corruption Risk Management', *Deloitte*, https://www2.deloitte.com/za/en/pages/risk/articles/fraud-and-corruption-risk-management.html

[18] 'Promoting EDI is more than a cause, it should be managed as a risk', *BSC Consulting*, 11 November 2021, Wayback Machine, https://web.archive.org/web/20230129130120/https://www.bcsconsulting.com/blog/promoting-edi-is-more-than-a-cause-it-should-be-managed-as-a-risk/ (BSC Consulting is now part of Accenture and the original site is deleted).

[19] 'Judgment Of The Court (Grand Chamber) 22 November 2022', *InfoCuria*, Case-Law, https://curia.europa.eu/juris/document/document.jsf?text=&docid=268059&pageIndex=0&doclang=en&mode=lst&dir=&occ=first&part=1&cid=1291

[20] 'Public Registers Of Beneficial Ownership Violate Human Rights – EU Court', *Wealth Briefing*, 24 November 2022, https://www.wealthbriefing.com/html/article.php?id=196292

[21] 'EU Court of Justice Delivers Blow to Beneficial Ownership Transparency', *Transparency International*, 22 November 2022, https://www.transparency.org/en/press/eu-court-of-justice-delivers-blow-to-beneficial-ownership-transparency

[22] 'Why this CEO argues against KYC norms for Bitcoin', *AMB Crypto*, 9 April 2021, https://ambcrypto.com/why-this-ceo-argues-against-kyc-norms-for-bitcoin/

[23] 'Principles for the Sound Management of Operational Risk', *Basel Committee on Banking Supervision*, June 2011, https://www.bis.org/publ/bcbs195.pdf, p 23.

[24] 'SEC Extracts Fines, But Not Confessions', *The Center for Public Integrity*, 24 March 2011, https://publicintegrity.org/inequality-poverty-opportunity/sec-extracts-fines-but-not-confessions/

References

Adam, G. (2006). The Nazi Bounty Hunters: War Loot Claims Become Big Business. The Art Newspaper. 1 December. https://www.theartne wspaper.com/2006/12/01/the-nazi-bounty-hunters-war-loot-claims-bec ome-big-business

Agamben, G. (2005). *State of Exception*. University of Chicago Press.

Alexeeva, L. (1985). *Soviet Dissent: Contemporary Movements for National, Religious, and Human Rights*. Wesleyan University Press.

Almohamad, A. (2021). The Destruction and Looting of Cultural Heritage Sites by ISIS in Syria: The Case of Manbij and its Countryside. *International Journal of Cultural Property*, 28(2), 221–60.

Amicelle, A., & Iafolla, V. (2018). Suspicion-in-The-Making: Surveillance and Denunciation in Financial Policing. *The British Journal of Criminology*, 58(4), 845–63.

Amineddoleh, L. (2015). Purchasing Art in a Market Full of Forgeries: Risks and Legal Remedies for Buyers. *International Journal of Cultural Property*, 22, 419–35.

Anderson, E. (2017). *Private Government: How Employers Rule Our Lives (and Why We Don't Talk about It)*. Princeton University Press.

Anscombe, G.E.M. (1958). Modern Moral Philosophy. *Philosophy*, 33(124), 1–19.

Antonova, N. (2021). Dissidents Aren't Saints. Foreign Policy. 5 March. https://foreignpolicy.com/2021/03/05/alexei-navalny-amnesty-priso ner-conscience-dissidents-saints/

Arrigo, B., & Sellers, B. (Eds) (2021). *The Pre-Crime Society: Crime, Culture and Control in the Ultramodern Age*. Bristol University Press.

Åslund, A. (2019). *Russia's Crony Capitalism: The Path from Market Economy to Kleptocracy*. Yale University Press.

Atkinson, R. (2016). Limited Exposure: Social Concealment, Mobility and Engagement with Public Space by the Super-Rich in London. *Environment and Planning A: Economy and Space*, 48(7), 1302–17.

Atkinson, R. (2020). *Alpha City: How London Was Captured by the Super-Rich*. Verso.

Augé, M. (1995). *Non-Places: An Introduction to Supermodernity*. Verso.

Averre, D. (2007). 'Sovereign Democracy' and Russia's Relations with the European Union. *Demokratizatsiya*, 15(2), 173–90.

Bacio-Terracino, J. (2010). Linking Corruption and Human Rights. *Proceedings of the Annual Meeting (American Society of International Law)*, 104, 243–6.

Bækken, H. (2018). *Law and Power in Russia: Making Sense of Quasi-Legal Practices*. Routledge.

Baker, S. (2022). Seizing a Russian Superyacht Is Much More Complicated Than You Think. Bloomberg. 7 November. https://www.bloomberg.com/news/features/2022-11-07/russian-oligarch-s-seized-yachts-are-costing-tax-payers-millions

Bandle, A.L. (2016). *The Sale of Misattributed Artworks and Antiques at Auction*. Edward Elgar.

Baranello, A.M. (2021). Money Laundering and the Art Market: Closing the Regulatory Gap. *Seton Hall Legislative Journal*, 45(3), 695–737.

Barberis, J., Arner, D.W., & Buckley, R.P. (2019). *The RegTech Book: The Financial Technology Handbook for Investors, Entrepreneurs and Visionaries in Regulation*. Willey & Sons.

Barthel, F. (2022). *The Triumph of Broken Promises: The End of the Cold War and the Rise of Neoliberalism*. Harvard University Press.

Barthes, R. (2013). *How to Live Together: Novelistic Simulations of Some Everyday Spaces* (K. Briggs, Trans.). Columbia University Press.

Bataille, G. (1993). *The Accursed Share: Volumes II and III*. Zone Books.

Baudrillard, J. (1994). *Simulacra and Simulation*. University of Michigan Press.

Baumgartner, M.P. (1988). *The Moral Order of a Suburb*. Verso.

Baumol, W.J., Litan, R.E., & Schramm, C.J. (2007). *Good Capitalism, Bad Capitalism, and the Economics of Growth and Prosperity*. Yale University Press.

Bayley, D.H. (1966). The Effects of Corruption in a Developing Nation. *Western Political Quarterly*, 19(4), 719–32.

Beck, U. (1992). *Risk Society: Towards a New Modernity*. Sage.

Bellows, A. (2020). Regaining U.S. Global Leadership on Anticorruption. Carnegie Endowment. 1 July. https://carnegieendowment.org/2020/07/01/regaining-u.s.-global-leadership-on-anticorruption-pub-82170

Belton, C. (2020). *Putin's People: How the KGB Took Back Russia and Then Took on the West*. Farrar, Straus and Giroux.

Benjamin, R. (2019). *Race After Technology: Abolitionist Tools for the New Jim Code*. Polity Press.

Bernstein, J. (2018). *Secrecy World: Inside the Panama Papers, Illicit Money Networks, and the Global Elite*. Picador Press.

Berry, C. (1994). *The Idea of Luxury: A Conceptual and Historical Investigation*. Cambridge University Press.

Besteman, C., & Gusterson, H. (Eds) (2019). *Life By Algorithms: How Roboprocesses Are Remaking Our World*. University of Chicago Press.

Birch, K., & Muniesa, F. (2020). Introduction: Assetization and Technoscientific Capitalism. In K. Birch & F. Muniesa (Eds), *Assetization* (pp 1–41). The MIT Press.

Birkenfeld, B.C. (2020). *Lucifer's Banker: Uncensored*. Republic Book Publishers.

Blas, J., & Farchy, J. (2021). *The World for Sale: Money, Power, and the Traders Who Barter Earth's Resources*. Oxford University Press.

Bleklie, I., Enders, J., Lepori, B., & Musselin, C. (2011). NPM, Network Governance and the University as a Changing Professional Organization. In T. Christensen & P. Lagreid (Eds), *The Ashgate Research Companion to New Public Management* (pp 161–76). Ashgate.

Bloom, P. (2017). *The Ethics of Neoliberalism: The Business of Making Capitalism Moral*. Routledge.

Boels, D., & Verhage, A. (2015). Plural Policing: A State-of-the-Art Review. *Policing: An International Journal of Police Strategies & Management*, 39(1), 2–18.

Bonner, J.M. (2017). Let Them Authenticate: Deterring Art Fraud. *UCLA Entertainment Law Review*, 24, 18–50.

Boser, U. (2010). *The Gardner Heist: The True Story of the World's Largest Unsolved Art Theft*. Harper Paperbacks.

Bove, T. (2022). Prepare for a 'Long and Ugly' Recession, says Dr. Doom, the Economist Who Predicted the 2008 Crash. Fortune. 21 September. https://fortune.com/2022/09/21/long-ugly-recession-dr-doom-nour iel-roubini/

Bowley, G., & Rashbaum, W.K. (2017). Has The Art Market Become an Unwitting Partner in Crime? The New York Times. 19 February. https://www.nytimes.com/2017/02/19/arts/design/has-the-art-market-become-an-unwitting-partner-in-crime.html

Boyer, P.S. (1992). *When Time Shall Be No More: Prophecy Belief in Modern American Culture*. Belknap Press of Harvard University Press.

Braithwaite, J. (2008). *Regulatory Capitalism: How it Works, Ideas for Making it Better*. Edward Elgar.

Brayne, S. (2021). *Predict and Surveil: Data, Discretion and the Future of Policing*. Oxford University Press.

Bregman, A. (2022). Russian Oligarch and Art Collector Creates Bond-style Lair on Greek Island. The Art Newspaper. 4 November. https://www.theartnewspaper.com/2022/11/04/russian-oligarch-and-art-collector-crea tes-bond-style-lair-on-greek-island

Briggs, D., Telford, L., Lloyd, A., Ellis, A., & Kotzé, J. (2021). *Lockdown: Social Harm in the COVID-19 Era*. Palgrave.

Brinks, D., Dehm, J., Engle, K., & Taylor, K. (Eds) (2021). *Power, Participation and Private Regulatory Initiatives: Human Rights Under Supply Chain Capitalism*. University of Pennsylvania Press.

Brodie, N., & Tubb, K.W. (Eds) (2002). *Illicit Antiquities: The Theft of Culture and the Extinction of Archaeology*. Routledge.

Brodie, N., Kersel, M.M., Mackenzie, S., Sabrine, I., Smith, E., & Yates, D. (2022). Why There Is Still an Illicit Trade in Cultural Objects and What Can We Do about It. *Journal of Field Archaeology*, 47(2), 117–30.

Brown, E., & Cloke, J. (2004). Neoliberal Reform, Governance and Corruption in the South: Assessing the International Anti-corruption Crusade. *Antipode*, 36(2), 272–94.

Brown, T. (2016). Sustainability as Empty Signifier: Its Rise, Fall, and Radical Potential. *Antipode*, 48(1), 115–33.

Budraitskis, I. (2022). *Dissidents Among Dissidents*. Verso.

Bukovansky, M. (2006). The Hollowness of Anti-Corruption Discourse. *Review of International Political Economy*, 13(2), 181–209.

Bukovsky, V. (1988). *To Build a Castle: My Life as a Dissenter*. Ethics & Public Policy Center.

Bullock, J.B. (2019). Aritficial Intelligence, Discretion, and Bureaucracy. *American Review of Public Administration*, 49(7), 751–61.

Bullough, O. (2018). *Moneyland: Why Thieves and Crooks Now Rule the World and How to Take it Back*. Profile Books.

Bullough, O. (2022). *Butler to the World: How Britain Became the Servant of Tycoons, Tax Dodgers, Kleptocrats and Criminals*. Profile Books.

Burgis, T. (2020). *Kleptopia: How Dirty Money Is Conquering the World*. HarperCollins Publishers.

Burnell, P.J. (2010). Is There a New Autocracy Promotion? Fride: European Think Tank *for* Global Action. 10 March. https://www.files.ethz.ch/isn/130597/WP96_Autocracy_ENG_mar10.pdf

Burnham, B. (1975). *The Art Crisis: How Cynical Materialism has Brought Crime and Fraud into the World of Art, and Eroded the Foundations on Which it Rests*. Collins.

Burris, D.S. (2020). Keynote: Restoration of a Culture: A California Lawyer's Lengthy Quest to Restitute Nazi-Looted Art. *North Carolina Journal of International Law*, 45(2), 277–332.

Buzan, B., Wæver, O., & de Wilde, J. (1998). *Security: A New Framework for Analysis*. Lynne Rienner Publishers.

Camdessus, M., & Naím, M. (2000). A Talk with Michel Camdessus about God, Globalization, and His Years Running the IMF. *Foreign Policy Analysis*, 32–45.

Campbell, B., & Manning, J. (2014). Microaggression and Moral Cultures. *Comparative Sociology*, 13(6), 692–726.

Campbell, P. (2013). The Illicit Antiquities Trade as a Transnational Criminal Network: Characterizing and Anticipating Trafficking of Cultural Heritage. *International Journal of Cultural Property*, 20(2), 113–53.

Canales, J., & Herscher, A. (2005). Criminal Skins: Tattoos and Modern Architecture in the Work of Adolf Loos. *Architectural History*, 48, 235–56.

Card, A.J. (2020). What Is Ethically Informed Risk Management? *AMA Journal of Ethics*, 22(11), 965–75.

Carter, R.G.S. (2007). Tainted Archives: Art, Archives, and Authenticity. *Archivaria* 63, 75–86.

Cascone, S. (2015). Dr. Doom Warns of Art-World Money Laundering in Davos. Artnet News. 26 January. https://news.artnet.com/market/dr-doom-warns-of-art-world-money-laundering-in-davos-232958

Ceva, E., & Ferretti, M.P. (2021). *Political Corruption: The Internal Enemy of Public Institutions*. Oxford University Press.

Chamayou, G. (2015). *Drone Theory*. Penguin.

Chamayou, G. (2021). *The Ungovernable Society: A Genealogy of Authoritarian Liberalism*. Polity.

Chappell, D., & Polk, K. (2019). Art Theft: An Examination of its Various Forms. In S. Hufnagel & D. Chappell (Eds), *The Palgrave Handbook of Art Crime* (pp 109–32). Palgrave Macmillan.

Chellaney, B. (2022). Why Sanctions Against Russia May Not Work. The Hill. 2 May. https://thehill.com/opinion/international/3473500-why-sanctions-against-russia-may-not-work/

Christopherson, T. (2016). Due Diligence. In J. Hackforth-Jones & I. Robertson (Eds), *Art Business Today: 20 Key Topics* (pp 136–47). Lund Humphries.

Cohan, W.D. (2010). Mystery Men of the Financial Crisis. The New York Times. 4 February. https://archive.nytimes.com/opinionator.blogs.nytimes.com/2010/02/04/mystery-men-of-the-financial-crisis/

Constable, S. (2022). Why Sanctions on Russia Won't Work. Time. 23 February. https://time.com/6150607/why-sanctions-on-russia-wont-work/

Constable, S. (2023). Sanctions On Russia Still Aren't Working. Forbes. 25 February. https://www.forbes.com/sites/simonconstable/2023/02/25/sanctions-on-russia-still-arent-working/

Criddle, C. (2021). Banksy Art Burned, Destroyed and Sold as Token in 'Money-Making Stunt'. BBC Tech. 9 March. https://www.bbc.com/news/technology-56335948

Crosthwaite, P. (2011). What a Waste of Money: Expenditure, the Death Drive, and the Contemporary Art Market. *New Formations*, 72, 80–93.

Dawisha, K. (2011). Is Russia's Foreign Policy That of a Corporatist-Kleptocratic Regime? *Post-Soviet Affairs*, 27(4), 331–65.

Dawisha, K. (2015). *Putin's Kleptocracy: Who Owns Russia?* Simon and Schuster.

De Cauter, L. (2004). *The Capsular Civilisation: On the City in the Age of Fear*. NAi Pub.

de Oliveira, I.S. (2018). The Governance of the Financial Action Task Force: An Analysis of Power and Influence throughout the Years. *Crime, Law and Social Change*, 69(2), 153–72.

Deneen, P. (2018). *Why Liberalism Failed*. Yale University Press.

Dietzler, J. (2013). On 'Organized Crime' in the Illicit Antiquities Trade: Moving Beyond the Definitional Debate. *Trends in Organized Crime*, 16(3), 329–42.

Djankov, S. (2015). Russia's Economy Under Putin: From Crony Capitalism to State Capitalism. Peterson Institute for International Economics. September. https://www.piie.com/publications/policy-briefs/russias-econ omy-under-putin-crony-capitalism-state-capitalism

Dollbaum, J.M., & Semenov, A. (2021). Navalny's Digital Dissidents: A New Dataset on a Russian Opposition Movement. *Problems of Post-Communism*, 1–10.

Dollbaum, J.M., Semenov, A., & Sirotkina, E. (2018). A Top-Down Movement with Grass-Roots Effects? Alexei Navalny's Electoral Campaign. *Social Movement Studies*, 17(5), 618–25.

Dollbaum, J., Lallouet, M., & Noble, B. (2021). *Navalny: Putin's Nemesis, Russia's Future?* Hurst.

Dörry, S., & Hesse, M. (2022). Zones and Zoning: Linking the Geographies of Freeports with ArtTech and Financial Market Making. *Geoforum*, 134, 165–72.

Douglas, M. (2001). *Purity and Danger: An Analysis of Concepts of Pollution and Taboo*. Routledge.

Down, A. (2018). Yacht Allegedly Bought with Stolen Cash Returned to Malaysia. OCCRP: Organized Crime and Corruption Reporting Project. 8 August. https://www.occrp.org/en/daily/8440-yacht-allegedly-bought-with-stolen-cash-returned-to-malaysia

Dupuy, J.-P. (2013). *The Mark of the Sacred*. Stanford University Press.

Dupuy, J.-P. (2014). *Economy and the Future: A Crisis of Faith*. Michigan State University Press.

Eagleton, T. (2009). *Trouble with Strangers: A Study of Ethics*. Blackwell.

Edelman, L.B., & Suchman, M.C. (1999). When the 'Haves' Hold Court: Speculations on the Organizational Internalization of Law. *Law & Society Review*, 33(4), 941–91.

Eisinger, J., Jeff, E., & Kiel, P. (2021). The Secret IRS Files: Trove of Never-Before-Seen Records Reveal How the Wealthiest Avoid Income Tax. Pro Publica. 8 June. https://www.propublica.org/article/the-sec ret-irs-files-trove-of-never-before-seen-records-reveal-how-the-wealthi est-avoid-income-tax

Ellis, A., Winlow, S., & Hall, S. (2017). Throughout My Life I've Had People Walk All Over Me: Trauma in the Lives of Violent Men. *The Sociological Review*, 65(4), 699–713.

Epstein, M. (1993). *The Origins and the Meaning of Russian Postmodernism*. National Council for Soviet and East European Research.

Etkind, A. (2022). *Alexey Navalny: A Hero of the New Time*. New Perspectives.

Featherstone, M. (2020). The Libertine: Criminal Luxury, the Sadean System, and Materialist Horror. In S. Hall, T. Ø. Kuldova, & M. Horsley (Eds), *Crime, Harm and Consumerism* (pp 39–53). Routledge.

Felices-Luna, M. (2016). Entrepreneurialism, Corruption and Moral Order in the Criminal Justice System of the Democratic Republic of Congo. In D. Whyte & J. Wiegratz (Eds), *Neoliberalism and the Moral Economy of Fraud* (pp 129–41). Routledge.

Felsted, A. (2022). The Rich Are Living in a Different Economic World. Bloomberg. 12 October. https://www.bloomberg.com/opinion/articles/2022-10-12/lvmh-boosted-by-americans-and-strong-dollar-in-europe-luxury-still-going-strong

Fine, G.A. (1983). Cheating History: The Rhetorics of Art Forgery. *Empirical Studies of the Arts*, 1(1), 75–93.

Fisher, M. (2009). *Capitalist Realism: Is There No Alternative?* Zero Books.

Fitzpatrick, S. (2005). *Tear Off the Masks!* Princeton University Press.

Fletcher, G. (2016). Fakes, Forgeries and Thefts. In J. Hackforth-Jones & I. Robertson (Eds), *Art Business Today: 20 Key Topics* (pp 106–14). Lund Humphries.

Fomin, I., & Nadskakuła-Kaczmarczyk, O. (2022). Against Putin and Corruption, for Navalny and the "Revolution"? The Dynamics of Framing and Mobilization in the Russian Political Protests of 2017–18. *Communist and Post-Communist Studies*, 55(1), 99–130.

Forsberg, P.B., & Severinsson, K. (2015). Exploring the Virus Metaphor in Corruption Theory: Corruption as a Virus? *Ephemera: Theory & Politics in Organization*, 15(2), 453–63.

Forsythe, M., Pianigiani, G., & Barnes, J.E. (2022). The Middlemen at the Heart of an Oligarch-Industrial Complex. The New York Times. 1 June. https://www.nytimes.com/2022/06/01/world/europe/russia-oligarchs-yachts-middlemen.html

Foucault, M. (2008). *The Birth of Biopolitics: Lectures at the Collège de France, 1978–1979*. Palgrave Macmillan.

Frasen, L., & LeBaron, G. (2019). Big Audit Firms as Regulatory Intermediaries in Transnational Labor Governance. *Regulation & Governance*, 13(2), 260–79.

Freeman, N. (2019). How the World's Biggest Financial Scandal Ensnared the Art World. Artsy. 17 January. https://www.artsy.net/article/artsy-editorial-worlds-financial-scandal-ensnared-art

Freud, S. (1961). *Beyond the Pleasure Principle*. W.W.W. Norton & Company.

Friman, H.R. (Ed) (2015). *The Politics of Leverage in International Relations*. Palgrave Macmillan.

Frischmann, B., & Selinger, E. (2018). *Re-engineering Humanity*. Cambridge University Press.

Fukuyama, F. ([1992] 2006). *The End of History and the Last Man*. Simon and Schuster.

Fukuyama, F. (2022). Francis Fukuyama: Putin's War on the Liberal Order. Financial Times. 4 March. https://www.ft.com/content/d0331b51-5d0e-4132-9f97-c3f41c7d75b3

Gabriel, C. (2018). The Rise of Kleptocracy: Malaysia's Missing Billions. *Journal of Democracy*, 29(1), 69–75.

Garrett, B.L. (2014). *Too Big to Jail: How Prosecutors Compromise with Corporations*. The Belknap Press of Harvard University Press.

Garsten, C., & Jacobsson, K. (2011). Transparency and Legibility in International Institutions: The UN Global Compact and Post-Political Global Ethics. *Social Anthropology*, 19(4), 378–93.

Garsten, C., & Jacobsson, K. (2012). Post-Political Regulation: Soft Power and Post-Political Visions in Global Governance. *Critical Sociology*, 39(3), 421–37.

Garsten, C., & Sörbom, A. (2018). *Discreet Power: How the World Economic Forum Shapes Market Agendas*. Stanford University Press.

Gel'man, V. (2015). *Authoritarian Russia: Analyzing Post-Soviet Regime Changes*. University of Pittsburgh Press.

Gessen, M. (2016). Alexey Navalny's Very Strange Form of Freedom. *The New Yorker*. 15 January. https://www.newyorker.com/news/news-desk/alexey-navalnys-very-strange-form-of-freedom

Gessen, M. (2021). The Evolution of Alexey Navalny's Nationalism. *The New Yorker*. 15 February. https://www.newyorker.com/news/our-columnists/the-evolution-of-alexey-navalnys-nationalism

Glazunova, S. (2020). 'Four Populisms' of Alexey Navalny: An Analysis of Russian Non-systemic Opposition Discourse on Youtube. *Media and Communication*, 8(4). https://doi.org/10.17645/mac.v8i4.3169

Godkin, E.L. (1868). Commercial Immorality and Political Corruption. *The North American Review*, 107(220), 248–66.

Goldstein, M. (2022). Seizing an Oligarch's Assets Is One Thing. Giving Them to Ukraine Is Another. New York Times. 8 May. https://www.nytimes.com/2022/05/08/business/russia-oligarch-yacht-assets.html

Graham, J.-L. (2014). Art Exchange? How the International Art Market Lacks a Clear Regulatory Framework. In V. Vadi & H.E.G.S. Schneider (Eds), *Art, Cultural Heritage and the Market: Ethical and Legal Issues* (pp 319–40). Springer.

Gray, G.G. (2006). The Regulation of Corporate Violations: Punishment, Compliance, and the Blurring of Responsibility. *British Journal of Criminology*, 46(5), 875–92.

Green, T., & Fazi, T. (2023). *The Covid Consensus: The Global Assault on Democracy and the Poor? A Critique from the Left*. Hurst.

Gundhus, H. (2017). Discretion as an Obstacle: Police Culture, Change, and Governance in a Norwegian Context. *Policing: A Journal of Policy and Practice*, 11(3), 258–72.

Hadiz, V.R. (2006). Corruption and Neo-liberal Reform: Markets and Predatory Power in Indonesia and Southeast Asia. In R. Robison (Ed), *The Neo-Liberal Revolution* (pp 79–97). Palgrave McMillan.

Hafner-Burton, E.M. (2008). Sticks and Stones: Naming and Shaming the Human Rights Enforcement Problem. *International Organization*, 62(Fall), 689–716.

Hale, H.E. (2015). *Patronal Politics: Eurasian Regime Dynamics in Comparative Perspective*. Cambridge University Press.

Hall, A., Antonopoulos, G.A., Atkinson, R., & Wyatt, T. (2022). Duty Free: Turning Criminological Spotlight on Special Economic Zones. *British Journal of Criminology*, 63(2), 265–82.

Hall, S. (2012). *Theorizing Crime and Deviance: A New Perspective*. SAGE.

Hall, S. (2014). The Socioeconomic Function of Evil. *The Sociological Review*, 62(S2), 13–31.

Hall, S., & Wilson, D. (2014). New Foundations: Pseudo-Pacification and Special Liberty as Potential Cornerstones for a Multi-Level Theory of Homicide and Serial Murder. *European Journal of Criminology*, 11(5), 635–55.

Hall, S., & Winlow, S. (2012). What Is an 'Ethics Committee'? *The British Journal of Criminology*, 52(2), 400–16.

Hall, S., Winlow, S., & Ancrum, C. (2008) *Criminal Identities and Consumer Culture: Crime, Exclusion and the New Culture of Narcissism*. Routledge.

Han, B.-C. (2015). *The Transparency Society*. Stanford University Press.

Hansen, H.K. (2015). Numerical Operations, Transparency Illusions and the Datafication of Governance. *European Journal of Social Theory*, 18(2), 203–20.

Hansen, H.K., & Flyverbom, M. (2015). The Politics of Transparency and the Calibration of Knowledge in the Digital Age. *Organization*, 22(6), 872–89.

Hardy, S.A. (2020). Criminal Money and Antiquities: An Open Source Investigation into Transnational Organized Cultural Property Crime. In K. Benson, C. King, & C. Walker (Eds), *Assets, Crimes and the State: Innovation in 21st Century Legal Responses* (pp 154–67). Routledge.

Harlan, C., & Pitrelli, S. (2022). Russian Oligarchs Loved Luxe Sardinia. Now They're Frozen Out of Paradise. The Washington Post. 17 May. https://www.washingtonpost.com/world/2022/05/16/oligarchs-emer ald-coast-sardinia/

Harvey, D. (2003). *The New Imperialism*. Oxford University Press.

Harvey, D. (2005). *A Brief History of Neoliberalism*. Oxford University Press.

Haslam, J. (2022). Why Russian Sanctions Won't Topple Putin. The Spectator. 27 April. https://www.spectator.co.uk/article/can-sanctions-topple-putin-/

Haugh, T. (2017). The Criminalization of Compliance. *Notre Dame Law Review*, 92(3), 1215–70.

Hebel, C., Hoppenstedt, M., & Rosenbach, M. (2021). The Telegram Billionaire and His Dark Empire. Spiegel International. 11 June. https://www.spiegel.de/international/world/the-telegram-billionaire-and-his-dark-empire-a-f27cb79f-86ae-48de-bdbd-8df604d07cc8

Hedlund, S. (2002). *Russia's Market Economy: A Bad Case of Predatory Capitalism*. Routledge.

Heidenheimer, A.J., & Johnston, M. (2002). *Political Corruption: Concepts and Contexts*. Transaction Publishers.

Helgadóttir, O. (2020). The New Luxury Freeports: Offshore Storage, Tax Avoidance, and 'Invisible' Art. *Environment and Planning A: Economy and Space*, 55(4), 1020–40.

Hirschman, A.O. (1977). *The Passions and the Interests: Political Arguments for Capitalism Before Its Triumph*. Princeton University Press.

Hochuli, A., Hoare, G., & Cunliffe, P. (2021). *The End of the End of History: Politics in the Twenty-First Century*. Zero Books.

Hoekstra, A., & Kaptein, M. (2021). The Integrity of Integrity Programs: Toward a Normative Framework. *Public Integrity*, 23(2), 129–41.

Hoffman, P. (2021). *Countering the Corrupt: The What, Who, Where, Why and How-to of Countering Corruption*. SiberInk.

Hollingsworth, M., & Lansley, S. (2010). *Londongrad: From Russia with Cash, The Inside Story of Oligarchs*. Fourth Estate.

Holmes, L. (2015). *Corruption: A Very Short Introduction* (Vol. 426). Oxford University Press.

Hong, S.-h. (2020). *Technologies of Speculation: The Limits of Knowledge in a Data-driven Society*. New York University Press.

Hook, D. (2017). What Is 'Enjoyment as a Political Factor'? *Political Psychology*, 38(4), 605–20.

Horsley, M., Kotzé, J., & Hall, S. (2015). The Maintenance of Orderly Disorder: Modernity, Markets and the Pseudo-Pacification Process. *Journal on European History of Law*, 6(1), 18–29.

Horvath, R. (2005). *The Legacy of Soviet Dissent: Dissidents, Democratisation and Radical Nationalism in Russia*. Routledge.

Hufnagel, S., & Chappell, D. (2019). *The Palgrave Handbook on Art Crime*. Palgrave Macmillan.

Hufnagel, S., & King, C. (2020). Anti-Money Laundering Regulation and the Art Market. *Legal Studies* 40(1), 131–50.

Huntington, S.P. ([1987] 2002). Modernization and Corruption. In A.J. Heidenheimer & M. Johnston (Eds), *Political Corruption: Concepts and Contexts* (pp 253–64). Transaction Publishers.

Huss, O., & Pozsgai-Alvarez, J. (2022). Strategic Corruption as a Threat to Security and the New Agenda for Anti-Corruption. Corruption, Justice and Legitimacy. 16 March. https://www.corruptionjusticeandlegitimacy.org/post/strategic-corruption-as-a-threat-to-security-and-the-new-agenda-for-anti-corruption

Hutchison, J.L. (1980). Materiality and Internal Accounting Controls under the Foreign Corrupt Practices Act. *Arizona State Law Journal*, 40, 931–51.

Hyatt, J. (2022). Oligarch Yacht Hunting Is Energizing the Battle Against Financial Corruption. *Forbes*. 26 April. https://www.forbes.com/sites/johnhyatt/2022/04/26/oligarch-yacht-hunting-is-energizing-the-battle-against-financial-corruption/

Ihenacho, P. (2023). Benin Bronzes: Whose Restitution Is This, Anyway? The Art Newspaper. 31 May. https://www.theartnewspaper.com/2023/05/31/benin-bronzes-whose-restitution-is-this-anyway

Ilyushina, M., & Ebel, F. (2022). Russian Mercenaries Accused of Using Violence to Corner Diamond Trade. The Washington Post. 6 December. https://www.washingtonpost.com/world/2022/12/06/wagner-group-mercenaries-africa-diamonds/

Jameson, F. (1984). Postmodernism, or The Cultural Logic of Late Capitalism. *New Left Review*, 1(146), 53–92.

Jeong, H.-G. (2019). United Nations Sanctions on North Korea's Luxury Goods Imports: Impact and Implications. *Asian Economic Policy Review*, 14, 214–33.

Joh, E.E. (2016). The New Surveillance Discretion: Automated Suspicion, Big Data, and Policing. *Harvard Law & Policy Review*, 10, 15–43.

Johnston, M. (2012). Why Do So Many Anti-Corruption Efforts Fail? *NYU Annual Survey of American Law*, 67, 467–96.

Johnston, M., & Fritzen, S. (2021). *The Conundrum of Corruption: Reform for Social Justice*. Routledge.

Just, P. (2007). Law, Ritual and Order. In K. von Benda-Beckmann & F. Pirie (Eds), *Order and Disorder* (pp 112–31). Berghahn Books.

Kajsiu, B. (2016). *A Discourse Analysis of Corruption: Instituting Neoliberalism Against Corruption in Albania, 1998–2005*. Routledge.

Kajsiu, B. (2021). Public or Private Corruption? The Ideological Dimension of Anti-Corruption Discourses in Colombia, Ecuador and Albania. *Journal of Extreme Anthropology*, 5(2), 27–51.

Kaleem, A. (2022). Citizen-Led Intelligence Gathering under UK's Prevent Duty. In H. Ben Jaffel & S. Larsson (Eds), *Problematising Intelligence Studies: Towards A New Research Agenda* (pp 73–95). Routledge.

Kant, I. (1991). *An Answer to the Question 'What Is Enlightenment?'* Cambridge University Press.

Kant, I. (2012). *Groundwork of the Metaphysics of Morals*. Cambridge University Press.

Kapp, M.B. (1991). Are Risk Management and Healthcare Ethics Compatible? *Journal of Healthcare Risk Management*, 11(1), 2–7.

Katzarova, E. (2019). *The Social Construction of Global Corruption: From Utopia to Neoliberalism*. Palgrave Macmillan.

Kazun, A. (2019). To Cover or Not to Cover: Alexei Navalny in Russian Media. *International Area Studies Review*, 22(4), 312–26.

Kazun, A., & Semykina, K. (2020). Presidential Elections 2018: The Struggle of Putin and Navalny for a Media Agenda. *Problems of Post-Communism*, 67(6), 455–66.

Keating, T., Norman, G., & Norman, F. (1977). *The Fake's Progress: Tom Keating's Story*. Hutchinson & Co.

Kenny, K. (2019). *Whistleblowing: Toward A New Theory*. Harvard University Press.

Kerr, J. (2016). *The Securitization and Policing of Art Theft*. Routledge.

Khan, U., & Dhar, R. (2006). Licensing Effect in Consumer Choice. *Journal of Marketing Research*, 43(2), 259–66.

Kimmage, D. (2009). Russia: Selective Capitalism and Kleptocracy (Undermining Democracy: 21st Century Authoritarians). Freedom House. June. https://freedomhouse.org/sites/default/files/russia.pdf

Klebnikov, P. (2000). *Godfather of the Kremlin: The Decline of Russia in the Age of Gangster Capitalism*. Houghton Mifflin Harcourt.

Koehler, M. (2012). The Story of the Foreign Corrupt Practices Act. *Ohio State Law Journal*, 73(5), 929–1013.

Kolstø, P. (2014). Russia's Nationalists Flirt with Democracy. *Journal of Democracy*, 25(3), 120–34.

Korver, R. (2018). Money Laundering and Tax Evasion Risks in Free Ports. European Parliamentary Research Service. October. https://www.europarl.europa.eu/cmsdata/155721/EPRS_STUD_627114_Money%20laundering-FINAL.pdf

Kotzé, J., & Lloyd, A. (2022). *Making Sense of Ultra-Realism*. Emerald Publishing House.

Kramer, D.J. (2022). Defeating Putin in Ukraine Is Vital to the Future of Democracy. *Journal of Democracy*. May. https://www.journalofdemocracy.org/defeating-putin-in-ukraine-is-vital-to-the-future-of-democracy/#author

Krastev, I. (2004). *Shifting Obsessions: Three Essays on the Politics of Anticorruption*. CEU Press.

Krastev, I. (2006). 'Sovereign Democracy', Russian-Style. *Insight Turkey*, 8(4), 113–17.

Krastev, I., & Holmes, S. (2012). Putinism Under Siege: An Autopsy of Managed Democracy. *Journal of Democracy*, 23(3), 33–45.

Krastev, I., & Holmes, S. (2017). Курс на подражание (Heading for Imitation). Russia in Global Affairs. 31 January. https://globalaffairs.ru/articles/kurs-na-podrazhanie/

Kuldova, T. (2016). *Luxury Indian Fashion: A Social Critique*. Bloomsbury.

Kuldova, T. (2017a). Guarded Luxotopias and Expulsions in New Delhi: Aesthetics and Ideology of Outer and Inner Spaces of an Urban Utopia. In T. Kuldova & M.A. Varghese (Eds), *Urban Utopias: Excess and Expulsion in Neoliberal South Asia* (pp 37–52). Palgrave Macmillan.

Kuldova, T. (2017b). The Sublime Splendour of Intimidation: On the Outlaw Biker Aesthetics of Power. *Visual Anthropology*, 30(5), 379–402.

Kuldova, T. (2018a). The 'Ethical Sell' in the Indian Luxury Fashion Business. In V. Pouillard & R. Blaczczyk (Eds), *European Fashion: The Creation of a Global Industry* (pp 263–82). Manchester University Press.

Kuldova, T. (2018b). Interpassive Phenomena in Times of Economic Subordination: From Self-Playing Games via Cryptocurrency Mining to Dressing Up in Subversion. *Continental Thought & Theory: A Journal of Intellectual Freedom*, 2(1), 32–49.

Kuldova, T. (2019). *How Outlaws Win Friends and Influence People*. Palgrave Macmillan.

Kuldova, T. (2020). Luxury Brands in the Wrong Hands: Of Harleys, Harm, and Sovereignty. In S. Hall, T. Kuldova, & M. Horsley (Eds), *Crime, Harm and Consumerism* (pp 90–107). Routledge.

Kuldova, T.Ø. (2020). Imposter Paranoia in the Age of Intelligent Surveillance: Policing Outlaws, Borders and Undercover Agents. *Journal of Extreme Anthropology*, 4(1), 45–73.

Kuldova, T.Ø. (2021a). The Cynical University: Gamified Subjectivity in Norwegian Academia. *Ephemera: Theory & Politics in Organization*, 21(3), 1–29.

Kuldova, T.Ø. (2021b). Luxury and Corruption. In P.-Y. Donzé, V. Pouillard, & J. Roberts (Eds), *The Oxford Handbook of Luxury Business* (pp 547–70). Oxford University Press.

Kuldova, T.Ø. (2022a). *Compliance-Industrial Complex: The Operating System of a Pre-Crime Society*. Palgrave Pivot.

Kuldova, T.Ø. (2022b). Thinking the Delirious Pandemic Governance by Numbers with Samit Basu's Chosen Spirits and Prayaag Akbar's Leila. *Journal of Postcolonial Writing*, 58(2), 167–82.

Kuldova, T.Ø. (forthcoming). Philanthrocapitalism and the Compliance-Industrial Complex, In S. Haydon, T. Jung, & S. Russell (Eds.), *Edward Elgar Handbook on Philanthrocapitalism*. Edward Elgar.

Kuldova, T.Ø., & Nordrik, B. (2023). Workplace Investigations, the Epistemic Power of Managerialism, and the Hollowing Out of the Norwegian Model of Co-determination. *Capital & Class*. https://doi.org/10.1177/03098168231179971.

Kuldova, T.Ø., & Østbø, J. (2023). Mezhyhirya Residence Museum: Novi Petrivtsi, Ukraine. In A. Lynes, C. Kelly, & J. Treadwell (Eds), *50 Dark Destinations: Crime and Contemporary Tourism* (pp 200–6). Policy Press.

Kupka, P., & Naxera, V. (2023). Looking Back on Corruption: Representations of Corruption and Anti-corruption in Czech Party Manifestos between 1990–2017. *Sociální Studia/Social Studies*, 20, 1–22.

Lacan, J. (1992). *The Ethics of Psychoanalysis 1959–1960, Book VII* (D. Porter, Trans.). Routledge.

Lacan, J. (1993). *The Psychoses: The Seminars of Jacques Lacan Book III*. Routledge.

Lacan, J. (2001). *Écrits: A Selection*. Routledge.

Lacan, J. (2019). *The Four Fundamental Concepts of Psychoanalysis: The Seminar of Jacques Lacan Book XI*. Routledge.

Laclau, E. (2005). *On Populist Reason*. Verso.

Lakoff, G., & Johnson, M. (2003). *Metaphors We Live By*. University of Chicago Press.

Lane, D.C., Bromley, D.G., Hicks, R.D., & Mahoney, J.S. (2008). Time Crime: The Transnational Organization of Art and Antiquities Theft. *Journal of Contemporary Criminal Justice*, 24(3), 243–62.

Laporte, D. (2000). *History of Shit*. MIT Press.

Laruelle, M. (2014). Alexei Navalny and Challenges in Reconciling 'Nationalism' and 'Liberalism'. *Post-Soviet Affairs*, 30(4), 276–97.

Laruelle, M. (2021). *Is Russia Fascist? Unraveling Propaganda East and West*. Cornell University Press.

Laruelle, M. (2022). So, Is Russia Fascist Now? Labels and Policy Implications. *The Washington Quarterly*, 45(2), 149–68.

Ledeneva, A.V. (2006). *How Russia Really Works: The Informal Practices that Shaped Post-Soviet Politics and Business*. Cornell University Press.

Ledeneva, A.V. (2013). *Can Russia Modernise? Sistema, Power Networks and Informal Governance*. Cambridge University Press.

Lee, S. (2022). *Decolonize Museums*. OR Books.

Leff, N.H. (1964). Economic Development through Bureaucratic Corruption. *American Behavioral Scientist*, 8(3), 8–14.

Lerman, R., & Kelly, H. (2022). Schadenfreude at Sea: The Internet Is Watching with Glee as Russian Oligarchs' Yachts are Seized. The Washington Post. 10 March. https://www.washingtonpost.com/technology/2022/03/10/russian-oligarch-yacht-tracking/

Levi-Faur, D. (2005). The Global Diffusion of Regulatory Capitalism. *Annals AAPSS*, 598, 12–32.

Levi-Faur, D. (2017). Regulatory Capitalism. In P. Drahos (Ed), *Regulatory Theory: Foundation and Applications* (pp 289–302). ANU Press.

Light, F., & Sauer, P. (2021). True Beliefs and Opportunism: Navalny's Tangled Political Development. The Moscow Times. 19 April. https://www.themoscowtimes.com/2021/02/01/true-beliefs-and-opportunism-navalnys-tangled-political-development-a72797

Lipman, A. (2021). How the Top 1% Evade Taxes – and Get Away with It. *Chicago Policy Review*. 15 November. https://chicagopolicyreview.org/2021/11/15/how-the-top-1-evade-taxes-and-get-away-with-it/

Lipman, M., & McFaul, M. (2001). 'Managed Democracy' in Russia: Putin and the Press. *Harvard International Journal of Press/Politics*, 6(3), 116–27.

Loginov, M. (2011). The Navalny Effect. Open Democracy. 7 June. https://www.opendemocracy.net/en/odr/navalny-effect/

Logvinenko, I. (2021). *Global Finance, Local Control: Corruption and Wealth in Contemporary Russia*. Cornell University Press.

Loiseau, N., & Meijer, P. (2022). Russian Corruption Is an Urgent Security Threat. Foreign Policy. 5 July. https://foreignpolicy.com/2022/07/05/russia-corruption-security-threat/

Lordon, F. (2014). *Willing Slaves of Capital: Spinoza & Marx on Desire*. Verso.

Loucaides, D. (2023). The Kremlin Has Entered the Chat. Wired. 2 February. https://www.wired.com/story/the-kremlin-has-entered-the-chat/

Ludel, W. (2020). Senate Investigation Finds Art Market Secrecy Allowed Russian Billionaire Brothers, Friends of Putin, to Evade Government Sanctions. The Art Newspaper. 30 July. https://www.theartnewspaper.com/2020/07/30/senate-investigation-finds-art-market-secrecy-allowed-russian-billionaire-brothers-friends-of-putin-to-evade-government-sanctions

Mácha, J., & Zouhar, J. (2020). Arnošt Kolman's Critique of Mathematical Fetishism. In R. Schuster (Ed), *The Vienna Circle in Czechoslovakia* (pp 135–50). Springer.

MacIntyre, A. (2002). *A Short History of Ethics*. Routledge.

MacIntyre, A. (2011). *After Virtue: A Study in Moral Theory*. Bloomsbury.

MacIntyre, A. (2016). The Irrelevance of Ethics. In A. Bielskis & K. Knight (Eds), *Virtue and Economy: Essays on Morality and Markets* (pp 7–22). Routledge.

Mackenzie, S. (2011). The Market as Criminal and Criminals in the Market: Reducing Opportunities for Organised Crime in the International Antiquities Market. In S. Manacorda & D. Chappell (Eds), *Crime in the Art and Antiquities World: Illegal Trafficking in Cultural Property* (pp 69–85). Springer.

Mackenzie, S. (2022). Criminology Towards the Metaverse: Cryptocurrency Scams, Grey Economy and the Technosocial. *The British Journal of Criminology*, 62(6), 1537–52.

Makortoff, K. (2022a). How Swiss Banking Secrecy Enabled an Unequal Global Financial System. *The Guardian*. 22 February. https://www.theguardian.com/news/2022/feb/22/how-swiss-banking-secrecy-global-financial-system-switzerland-tax-elite

Makortoff, K. (2022b). Swiss Consider Amending Banking Secrecy Laws Amid UN Pressure. *The Guardian.* 2 May. https://www.theguardian.com/news/2022/may/02/swiss-consider-amending-banking-secrecy-laws-amid-un-pressure

Malm, A. (2020). *Corona, Climate, Chronic Emergency: War Communism in the Twenty-First Century.* Verso Books.

Manacorda, S., & Chappell, D. (Eds) (2011). *Crime in the Art and Antiquities World: Illegal Trafficking in Cultural Property.* Springer.

Mandeville, B. ([1732] 1988). *The Fable of the Bees or Private Vices, Publick Benefits.* The Online Library of Liberty. https://oll.libertyfund.org/title/kaye-the-fable-of-the-bees-or-private-vices-publick-benefits-vol-1

Manzetti, L., & Wilson, C.J. (2007). Why do Corrupt Governments Maintain Public Support? *Comparative Political Studies,* 40(8), 949–70.

Marquette, H. (2003). *Corruption and Development: The Role of the World Bank.* Palgrave Macmillan.

Marten, K. (2015b). Informal Political Networks and Putin's Foreign Policy: The Examples of Iran and Syria. *Problems of Post-Communism,* 62(2), 71–87.

Marx, K. (1973). *Grundrisse.* Penguin.

Mashberg, T. (2019). The Art of Money Laundering. Finance & Development, September, 31–4.

Massaro, P. (2017). Russia's Weaponization of Corruption (and Western Complicity). Commission on Security and Cooperation in Europe (CSCE). 6 June. https://www.csce.gov/international-impact/russia-s-weaponization-corruption-and-western-complicity?page=2

Mau, V. (1996). *The Political History of Economic Reform in Russia, 1985–1994.* Centre for Research into Communist Economies.

Mavelli, L. (2020). Neoliberalism as Religion: Sacralization of the Market and Post-truth Politics. *International Political Sociology,* 14(1), 57–76.

May, C. (2011). The Rule of Law: What Is It and Why Is It 'Constantly on People's Lips'? *Political Studies Review,* 9(3), 357–65.

Mazurek, S.K. (2019). The Invisible Crime: Exploring How Perceptions of Victimhood and the Art Market May Influence Art Fraud Reporting. *International Journal of Cultural Property,* 26, 413–36.

McCarthy, L.F. (2014). How Can We Fight the Scourge of Corruption? World Economic Forum. 24 January. https://www.weforum.org/agenda/2014/01/corruption-public-enemy-number-one-2/

McCulloch, J., & Wilson, D. (2016). *Pre-Crime: Pre-Emption, Precaution and the Future.* Routledge.

McGoey, L. (2012). Philanthrocapitalism and its Critics. *Poetics,* 40, 185–99.

McGoey, L. (2014). The Philanthropic State: Market-State Hybrids in the Philanthrocapitlist Turn. *Third World Quarterly,* 35(1), 109–25.

McGoey, L. (2015). *No Such Thing as a Free Gift: The Gates Foundation and the Price of Philanthropy*. Verso.

McGowan, T. (2013). *Enjoying What We Don't Have: The Political Project of Psychoanalysis*. University of Nebraska Press.

McGowan, T. (2016). *Capitalism and Desire: The Psychic Costs of Free Markets*. Columbia University Press.

McGowan, T. (2019). *Emancipation After Hegel: Achieving a Contradictory Revolution*. Columbia University Press.

McKibben, B. (2016). A World at War: We're Under Attack from Climate Change – and Our Only Hope Is to Mobilize Like We Did In WWII. The New Republic. 15 August. https://newrepublic.com/article/135684/declare-war-climate-change-mobilize-wwii

Mees, B. (2020). *The Rise of Business Ethics*. Routledge.

Melnykovska, I., Plamper, H., & Schweickert, R. (2012). Do Russia and China Promote Autocracy in Central Asia? *Asia Europe Journal*, 10(1), 75–89.

Merry, S.E. (2011). Measuring the World: Indicators, Human Rights, and Global Governance. *Current Anthropology*, 52(S3), S83–S95.

Merry, S.E. (2016). *The Seductions of Quantification: Measuring Human Rights, Gender Violence, and Sex Trafficking*. University of Chicago Press.

Methmann, C.P. (2010). 'Climate Protection' as Empty Signifier: A Discourse Theoretical Perspective on Climate Mainstreaming in World Politics. *Millennium: Journal of International Studies*, 39(2), 345–72.

Michel, C. (2021). *American Kleptocracy: How the U.S. Created the World's Greatest Money Laundering Scheme in History*. St. Martin's Press.

Michelutti, L. (2010). Wrestling with (Body) Politics: Understanding 'Goonda' Political Styles in North India. In P. Price & A.E. Ruud (Eds), *Power and Influence in India: Bosses, Lords and Captains* (pp 44–69). Routledge.

Miller, G., & Belton, C. (2022). Russia's Spies Misread Ukraine and Misled Kremlin as War Loomed. Washington Post. 19 August. https://www.washingtonpost.com/world/interactive/2022/russia-fsb-intelligence-ukraine-war/

Miller, R.A. (2008). *The Erotics of Corruption: Law, Scandal, and Political Perversion*. State University of New York Press.

Minchenko Consulting (2019). Политбюро 2.0 И Антиистеблишментная Волна (Politbureau 2.0 and the Anti-Establishment Wave). Minchenko Consulting http://www.minchenko.ru/netcat_files/userfiles/PB_2.0_I_ANTIISTEBLIShMENTNAYa_VOLNA_04.06.19_LAST.pdf

Mitchell, A., & Sikka, P. (2011). *The Pin-Stripe Mafia: How Accountancy Firms Destroy Societies*. Association for Accountancy & Business Affairs. https://www.publishwhatyoupay.no/sites/default/files/import/PIN_STRIPE_MAFIA_ACCOUNTANCY_FIRMS.pdf

Moen-Larsen, N. (2014). 'Normal Nationalism': Alexei Navalny, LiveJournal and 'the Other'. *East European Politics*, 30(4), 548–67.

Moore, B. (2000). *Moral Purity and Persecution in History*. Princeton University Press.

Morozov, E. (2013). *To Save Everything, Click Here*. Public Affairs.

Morris, W. (2012). *The Collected Works of William Morris*. Cambridge University Press.

Mosna, A. (2022). Give Art Market Regulation a Chance. *Maastricht Journal of European and Comparative Law*, 29(3), 304–27.

Motyl, A.J. (2012). Fascistoid Russia: Putin's Political System in Comparative Context. In S. Stewart, M. Klein, & H.-H. Schröder (Eds), *Presidents, Oligarchs and Bureaucrats: Forms of Rule in the Post-Soviet Space* (pp 125–40). Routledge.

Motyl, A.J. (2016). Putin's Russia as a Fascist Political System. *Communist and Post-Communist Studies*, 49(1), 25–36.

Muller, J.Z. (2018). *The Tyranny of Metrics*. Princeton University Press.

Murray, M.H., Vindman, A., & Bustillos, D.C. (2021). Assessing the Threat of Weaponized Corruption. Lawfare. 7 July. https://www.lawfareblog.com/assessing-threat-weaponized-corruption

Nathans, B. (2015). Talking Fish: On Soviet Dissident Memoirs. *The Journal of Modern History*, 87(3), 579–614.

Nathans, B. (2021). To The Success of Our Hopeless Cause: The Many Lives of Soviet Dissidents. CREECA Lecture Series Podcast. https://podcasts.apple.com/no/podcast/to-the-success-of-our-hopeless-cause-the-many/id1286768316?i=1000537514846

National Security Archive (2020). Allende and Chile: 'Bring Him Down'. *National Security Archive*. https://nsarchive.gwu.edu/briefing-book/chile/2020-11-06/allende-inauguration-50th-anniversary

Naylor, R.T. (2011). *Crass Struggle: Greed, Glitz, and Gluttony in a Wanna-Have World*. McGill-Queen's University Press.

Nemeth, E. (2007). Cultural Security: The Evolving Role of Art in International Security. *Terrorism and Political Violence*, 19(1), 19–42.

Nieto Martín, A. (2022). *Global Criminal Law: Postnational Criminal Justice in the Twenty-First Century*. Palgrave Macmillan.

Noce, V. (2022a). Billionaire Battle Rages on as Geneva Court Overturns Dismissal of Dmitry Rybolovev's Fraud Case Against Art Dealer Yves Bouvier. The Art Newspaper. 28 July. https://www.theartnewspaper.com/2022/07/28/geneva-court-overturns-dismissal-of-dmitry-rybolovevs-fraud-case-against-art-dealer-yves-bouvier

Noce, V. (2022b). Egyptian Antiquities Connected to International Trafficking Ring Seized From Metropolitan Museum in New York. The Art Newspaper. 1 June. https://www.theartnewspaper.com/2022/06/01/egyptian-antiquities-connected-to-international-trafficking-ring-seized-at-metropolitan-museum-in-new-york

Noce, V. (2022c). Exclusive: German Museums Latest to be Implicated in Far-Reaching Criminal Investigation Into Antiquities Trafficking. *The Art Newspaper*. 30 August. https://www.theartnewspaper.com/2022/08/30/german-museums-latest-to-be-implicated-in-far-reaching-criminal-investigation-into-antiquities-trafficking

Oates, S., & Rostova, N. (2023). The More Things Change, the More the Frame Remains the Same: Comparing American and Russian Coverage of Dissident Alexei Navalny. In J.O. Hearns-Branaman & T. Bergman (Eds), *Journalism and Foreign Policy: How the US and UK Media Cover Official Enemies* (pp 31–48). Routledge.

Obermaier, F., & Obermayer, B. (2017). *The Panama Papers: Breaking the Story of How the Rich and Powerful Hide Their Money*. Oneworld Publications.

Offe, C. (2009). Governance: An 'Empty Signifier'? *Constellations*, 16(4), 550–62.

Okara, A. (2007). Sovereign Democracy: A New Russian Idea or a PR Project? *Russia in Global Affairs*, 5(3), 8–20.

Olaison, L., & Sørensen, B.M. (2014). The Abject of Entrepreneurship: Failure, Fiasco, Fraud. *International Journal of Entrepreneurial Behaviour & Research*, 20(2), 193–211.

Olivieri, V. (2019). Unsolved Art Thefts. In S. Hufnagel & D. Chappell (Eds), *The Palgrave Handbook on Art Crime* (pp 133–48). Palgrave Macmillan.

O'Neil, C. (2016). *Weapons of Math Destruction: How Big Data Increases Inequality and Threatens Democracy*. Crown.

O'Reilly, C. (2015). The Pluralization of High Policing: Convergence and Divergence at the Public-Private Interface. *The British Journal of Criminology*, 55(4), 688–710.

Orr, C. (2020). The Solzhenitsyn Affair: Yuri Andropov's Personal Obsesssion. *Journal of Intelligence and Cyber Security*, 3(2), 56–71.

Ostanin, I., & Di Pietro, L. (2015). Azerbaijan: Aliyev Family, Friends Cruise Aboard SOCAR Super Yachts. *OCCRP: Organized Crime and Corruption Reporting Project*. 1 September. https://www.occrp.org/en/corruptistan/azerbaijan/2015/09/01/aliyev-family-friends-cruise-aboard-socar-super-yachts.en.html

Østbø, J. (2017). Securitizing 'Spiritual-moral values' in Russia. *Post-Soviet Affairs*, 33(3), 200–16.

Østbø, J. (2020). Corrupt and Honorable, Gangster and Nobleman: Naval'nyi, Zolotov, and the Conflicting Moral Cultures in Russian Politics. *Cultural Politics*, 16(2), 171–91.

Oushakine, S.A. (2001). The Terrifying Mimicry of Samizdat. *Public Culture*, 13(2), 191–214.

Owen, D. (2021). Confronting the Challenge of Weaponized Corruption in the Black Sea Region and Beyond. *Foreign Policy Research Institute*. 5 November. https://www.fpri.org/article/2021/11/confronting-the-challenge-of-weaponized-corruption-in-the-black-sea-region-and-beyond/

Pacini, C., Swingen, J.A., & Rogers, H. (2002). The Role of the OECD and EU Conventions in Combating Bribery of Foreign Public Officials. *Journal of Business Ethics*, 37(4), 385–405.

Papantoniou, A.A. (2022). RegTech: Steering the Regulatory Spaceship in the Right Direction. *Journal of Banking and Financial Technology*, 6, 1–16.

Pasculli, L., & Ryder, N. (2019). Corruption and Globalisation: Towards an Interdisciplinary Scientific Understanding of Corruption as a Global Crime. In L. Pasculli & N. Ryder (Eds), *Corruption in the Global Era: Causes, Sources and Forms of Manifestation* (pp 3–24). Routledge.

Pasquale, F. (2015). *The Black Box Society: The Secret Algorithms that Control Money and Information*. Harvard University Press.

Patalakh, A. (2018). On the Possible Foreign Policy of the Post-Putin Russia: The Case of Alexei Navalny's Viewpoints on Foreign Affairs. *Central European Journal of International Security Studies*, 12(1), 9–31.

Patrucic, M., & Lozovsky, I. (2022). Sanctioning an Oligarch Is Not So Easy: Why the Money Trail of Alisher Usmanov, One of Russia's Wealthiest Men, Is Difficult to Follow. OCCRP: Organized Crime and Corruption Reporting Project. 22 March. https://www.occrp.org/en/asset-tracker/sanctioning-an-oligarch-is-not-so-easy-why-the-money-trail-of-alisher-usmanov-one-of-russias-wealthiest-men-is-difficult-to-follow

Pearson, Z. (2001). An International Human Rights Approach to Corruption. In P. Larmour & N. Wolanin (Eds), *Corruption and Anti-Corruption* (pp 30–61). Asia Pacific Press.

Pee, R., & Schmidli, W.M. (2018). *The Reagan Administration, the Cold War, and the Transition to Democracy Promotion*. Springer.

Perlman, R.L., & Sykes, A.O. (2017). The Political Economy of the Foreign Corrupt Practices Act: An Exploratory Analysis. *Journal of Legal Analysis*, 9(2), 153–82.

Persson, A., Rothstein, B., & Teorell, J. (2013). Why Anticorruption Reforms Fail: Systemic Corruption as a Collective Action Problem. *Governance*, 26, 449–71.

Petraeus, D., & Whitehouse, S. (2019). Putin and Other Authoritarians' Corruption Is a Weapon – and a Weakness. The Washington Post. 8 March. https://www.washingtonpost.com/opinions/2019/03/08/putin-other-authoritarians-corruption-is-weapon-weakness/

Pfaller, R. (2008). *Das Schmutzige Heilige und die Reine Vernunft: Symptome der Gegenwartskultur*. Fischer Taschenbuch Verlag.

Pfaller, R. (2017). *Interpassivity: The Aesthetics of Delegated Enjoyment.* University of Edinburgh.

Phillips, A. (2020). COVID-19: Demand for Underground Bunkers Soars Over Fears of Coronavirus Pandemic. Sky News. 13 December. https://news.sky.com/story/covid-19-demand-for-underground-bunkers-soars-over-fears-of-coronavirus-pandemic-12156996

Pieper, J. (1998). *Leisure: The Basis of Culture.* St. Augustine's Press.

Pistor, K. (2019). *The Code of Capital: How the Law Creates Wealth and Inequality.* Princeton University Press.

Portman, R., & Carper, T. (2020). *The Art Industry and U.S. Policies that Undermine Sanctions.* United States Senate Permanent Subcommittee on Investigations, Committee on Homeland Security and Governmental Affairs. https://www.ballardspahr.com/-/media/files/senate-report-on-art-and-ml.pdf

Postman, N. (1993). *Technopoly: The Surrender of Culture to Technology.* Vintage Books.

Power, M. (1997). *The Audit Society: Rituals of Verification.* Oxford University Press.

Pryor, R. (2016). *Crime and the Art Market.* Lund Humphries.

Putin, V. (2014). Address by President of the Russian Federation. President of Russia. 18 March. http://en.kremlin.ru/events/president/news/20603

Rascouet, A. (2022). The Rich Are Spending on Luxury Goods Like It's 1999. Bloomberg. 20 October. https://www.bloomberg.com/news/articles/2022-10-20/luxury-goods-still-sell-big-even-as-recession-fears-grow

Raymen, T. (2016). Designing-in Crime by Designing-Out the Social: Situational Crime Prevention and the Intensification of Harmful Subjectivities. *The British Journal of Criminology*, 56(3), 497–514.

Raymen, T. (2021). The Assumption of Harmlessness. In P. Davies, P. Leighton, & T. Wyatt (Eds), *The Palgrave Handbook of Social Harm* (pp 59–88). Palgrave Macmillan.

Raymen, T. (2022). *The Enigma of Social Harm: The Problem of Liberalism.* Routledge.

Raymen, T., & Smith, O. (2017). Lifestyle Gambling, Indebtedness and Anxiety: A Deviant Leisure Perspective. *Journal of Consumer Culture*, 20(4), 381–99.

Raymen, T., & Smith, O. (2020). Gambling and Harm in 24/7 Capitalism: Reflections from the Post-Disciplinary Present. In S. Hall, T. Ø. Kuldova, & M. Horsley (Eds), *Crime, Harm and Consumerism* (pp 73–89). Routledge.

Redhead, S. (2011). *We Have Never Been Postmodern: Theory at the Speed of Light.* Edinburgh University Press.

Redhead, S. (2017). *Theoretical Times.* Emerald.

Reyburn, S. (2022). Why the Global Explosion of Billionaires Will Keep Auction Houses Afloat – For Now. The Art Newspaper. 11 November. https://www.theartnewspaper.com/2022/11/11/why-the-global-explos ion-of-billionaires-will-keep-auction-houses-afloatfor-now

Rid, T. (2020). *Active Measures*. Farrar, Straus and Giroux.

Roberts, J. (2019). Secret Spaces of Luxury: Ignorance, Freeports and Art. In J. Roberts & J. Armitage (Eds), *The Third Realm of Luxury: Connecting Real Places and Imaginary Spaces* (pp 159–76). Bloomsbury.

Robinson, W.I. (1996). *Promoting Polyarchy: Globalization, US Intervention, and Hegemony* (Vol. 48). Cambridge University Press.

Rosa, H. (2021). *The Uncontrollability of the World*. Polity.

Roubini, N. (2022). *Megathreats: Ten Dangerous Trends that Imperil Our Future and How to Survive Them*. Little, Brown and Company.

Ruiz, C. (2016). Panama Papers Expose Art World's Offshore Secrets. The Art Newspaper. 8 April. https://www.theartnewspaper.com/2016/04/ 08/panama-papers-expose-art-worlds-offshore-secrets

Rushkoff, D. (2022). *Survival of the Richest: Escape Fantasies of Tech Billionaires*. Scribe.

Sakhnin, A. (2021). How a Russian Nationalist Named Alexei Navalny Became a Liberal Hero. Jacobin. 31 January. https://jacobin.com/2021/ 01/alexei-navalny-russia-protests-putin

Sakwa, R. (2010). The Dual State in Russia. *Post-Soviet Affairs*, 26(3), 185–206.

Sakwa, R. (2015). Is Russia Really a Kleptocracy? Times Literary Supplement. https://www.the-tls.co.uk/articles/public/is-russia-really-a-kleptocracy/

Sakwa, R. (2021). Heterarchy: Russian Politics between Chaos and Control. *Post-Soviet Affairs*, 37(3), 222–41.

Sampson, S. (2005). Integrity Warriors: Global Morality and the Anti-Corruption Movement in the Balkans. In D. Haller & C. Shore (Eds), *Corruption: Anthropological Perspectives* (pp 103–30). Pluto Press.

Sampson, S. (2015). The Anti-Corruption Package. *Ephemera: Theory and Politics in Organization*, 15(2), 435–43.

Sargent, D. (2014). Oasis in the Desert? America's Human Rights Rediscovery. In J. Eckel & S. Moyn (Eds), *The Breakthrough: Human Rights in the 1970s* (pp 125–45). University of Pennsylvania Press.

Sauer, P. (2023). Alexei Navalny in 'Critical' Situation after Possible Poisoning, Says Ally. *The Guardian*. 14 April. https://www.theguardian. com/world/2023/apr/14/alexei-navalny-in-critical-situation-after-possi ble-poisoning-says-ally

Schuilenburg, M. (2011). The Securitization of Society: On the Rise of Quasi-Criminal Law and Selective Exclusion. *Social Justice*, 38(1/2), 73–89.

Schüll, N.D. (2012). *Addiction by Design: Machine Gambling in Las Vegas*. Princeton University Press.

Schwartz, M., & Carrier, A. (2023). Revealed: Vladimir Putin's Secret Black Sea Bunker. Business Insider. 17 May. https://www.businessinsi der.com/revealed-vladimir-putins-secret-black-sea-bunker-russia-krem lin-palace-2023-5

Schwarzkopf, S., & Backsell, J.I. (2021). The Nomos of the Freeport. *Environment and Planning D: Society and Space*, 39(2), 328–46.

Searcey, D. (2022). Russia Fights Efforts to Declare It an Exporter of 'Blood Diamonds'. *The New York Times*. 16 August. https://www.nytimes.com/ 2022/08/16/climate/russia-conflict-diamonds-kimberley-process.html

Sennett, R. (1977). *The Fall of Public Man*. Cambridge University Press.

Service, R. (2009). *The Penguin History of Modern Russia: From Tsarism to the Twenty-First Century*. Penguin Books.

Shankar, P., & Savage, J. (2023). Ukraine Confronts Two Enemies: Russia and Corruption. Al Jazeera. 14 February. https://www.aljazeera.com/ news/2023/2/14/ukraine-confronts-two-enemies-russia-and-corruption

Shaxson, N. (2012). *Treasure Islands: Uncovering the Damage of Offshore Banking and Tax Havens*. Pan Macmillan.

Shea, A. (2018). Shooting Fish in a Bliss Bucket: Targeting Money Laundering in the Art Market. *Columbia Journal of Law & the Arts*, 41(2), 665–87.

Shore, C. (2003). Corruption Scandals in America and Europe: Enron and EU Fraud in Comparative Perspective. *Social Analysis: The International Journal of Social and Cultural Practice*, 47(3), 147–53.

Shore, C., & Wright, S. (2015). Audit Culture Revisited: Rankings, Ratings, and the Reassembling of Society. *Current Anthropology*, 56(3), 421–44.

Shore, C., & Wright, S. (2018). How The Big 4 Got Big: Audit Culture and The Metamorphosis of International Accountancy Firms. *Critique of Anthropology*, 38(3), 303–24.

Shotwell, A. (2016). *Against Purity: Living Ethically in Compromised Times*. University of Minnesota Press.

Sikka, P. (2016). Big Four Accounting Firms: Addicted to Tax Avoidance. In J. Haslam & P. Sikka (Eds), *Pioneers of Critical Accounting: A Celebration of the Life of Tony Lowe* (pp 259–74). Palgrave Macmillan.

Simes, D.K. (1978). Détente, Russian-Style. *Foreign Policy* (32), 47–62.

Simpson, B.R. (2013). Self-Determination, Human Rights, and the End of Empire in the 1970s. *Humanity: An International Journal of Human Rights, Humanitarianism, Development and Change*, 4(2), 239–60.

Slaughter, J.R. (2018). Hijacking Human Rights: Neoliberalism, The New Historiography, and the End of the Third World. *Human Rights Quarterly*, 40(4), 735–75.

Slobodian, Q. (2018). *Globalists: The End of Empire and the Birth of Neoliberalism*. Harvard University Press.

Smith, B. (2021). How Investigative Journalism Flourished in Hostile Russia. The New York Times. 21 February. https://www.nytimes.com/2021/02/21/business/media/probiv-investigative-reporting-russia.html

Snyder, T. (2022a). Ukraine Holds the Future. *Foreign Affairs*, 101(5), 124–41.

Snyder, T. (2022b). We Should Say It. Russia Is Fascist. The New York Times. 19 May. https://www.nytimes.com/2022/05/19/opinion/russia-fascism-ukraine-putin.html

Solomon, J.M. (2010). New Governance, Preemptive Self-Regulation, and the Blurring of Boundaries in Regulatory Theory and Practice. *Wisconsin Law Review*, 591–625.

Sousa, J., & Moser, A. (2020). Data and Databases in Provenance Research. In A. Tompkins (Ed), *Provenance Research Today: Principles, Practice, Problems* (pp 85–96). Lund Humphries in association with IFAR.

Stakun, R. (2017). *Terror and Transcendence in the Void: Viktor Pelevin's Philosophy of Emptiness*. University of Kansas.

Stallybrass, P., & White, A. (1986). *The Politics and Poetics of Transgression*. Methuen.

Stark, L., & Hutson, J. (2022). Physiognomic Artificial Intelligence. *Fordham Intellectual Property, Media and Entertainment Law Journal*, 32(4), 922–78.

Steinberger, M. (2023). The Fed May Finally Be Winning the War on Inflation. But at What Cost? New York Times Magazine. 10 January. https://www.nytimes.com/2023/01/10/magazine/inflation-federal-reserve.html

Stephens, B. (2021). Dissidents First: A Foreign Policy Doctrine for the Biden Administration. The New York Times. 25 January. https://www.nytimes.com/2021/01/25/opinion/navalny-biden-russia.html

Stevenson, C.L. (1960). *Ethics and Language*. Yale University Press.

Strathern, M. (Ed). (2000). *Audit Cultures: Anthropological Studies in Accountability, Ethics and the Academy*. Routledge.

Supiot, A. (2017). *Governance by Numbers: The Making of a Legal Model of Allegiance*. Bloomsbury.

Sutela, P. (1991). *Economic Thought and Economic Reform in the Soviet Union*. Cambridge University Press.

Swain, A. (2006). Soft Capitalism and a Hard Industry: Virtualism, The 'Transition Industry' and The Restructuring of The Ukrainian Coal Industry. *Transactions of the Institute of British Geographers*, 31(2), 208–23.

Swain, A., Mykhnenko, V., & French, S. (2008). Performing Corruption in Ukraine. Fourth Annual Danyliw Research Seminar in Contemporary Ukrainian Studies, University of Ottawa.

Swain, A., Mykhnenko, V., & French, S. (2010). The Corruption Industry and Transition: Neoliberalising Post-Soviet Space. In K. Birch & V. Mykhnenko (Eds) *The Rise and Fall of Neoliberalism: The Collapse of an Economic Order* (pp 112–32). Bloomsbury.

Szulecki, K., & Wig, T. (2022). The War in Ukraine Is All about Democracy vs. Dictatorship. RevDem: Review of Democracy. 9 April. https://rev dem.ceu.edu/2022/04/09/the-war-in-ukraine-is-all-about-democracy-vs-dictatorship/

Tansey, O. (2016). The Problem with Autocracy Promotion. *Democratization*, 23(1), 141–63.

Tayan, B. (2019). The Wells Fargo Cross-Selling Scandal. Harvard Law School Forum on Corporate Governance. 6 February. https://corpgov. law.harvard.edu/2019/02/06/the-wells-fargo-cross-selling-scandal-2/

Taylor, M.C. (2011). Financialization of Art. *Capitalism and Society*, 6(2), 1–19.

Telleria, J. (2020). Policies without Politics: The Exclusion of Power Dynamics in The Construction of 'Sustainable Development'. In G. Koehler, A.D. Cimadamore, F. Kiwan, & P.M.M. Gonzales (Eds), *The Politics of Social Inclusion: Bridging Knowledge and Policies Towards Social Change* (pp 99–114). Ibidem.

Tepper, J., & Hearn, D. (2019). *The Myth of Capitalism*. Wiley.

Thompson, C. (2004). How to Make a Fake. New York Magazine. 20 May. https://nymag.com/nymetro/arts/features/9179/

Tilman, R.O. (1968). Emergence of Black-Market Bureaucracy: Administration, Development, and Corruption in the New States. *Public Administration Review*, 28(5), 437–44.

Tokar, D. (2022a). Sanctions Turn into New Priority for Justice Department. The Wall Street Journal. 27 April. https://www.wsj.com/articles/sancti ons-turn-into-new-priority-for-justice-department-11651097156

Tokar, D. (2022b). Treasury Targets Russia, Oligarchs as Part of Plan to Combat Illicit Finance. The Wall Street Journal. 13 May. https://www. wsj.com/articles/treasury-outlines-strategy-for-tackling-illicit-finance-thre ats-11652464812

Tombs, S. (2016). 'After' the Crisis: Morality Plays and the Renewal of Business as Usual. In D. Whyte & J. Wiegratz (Eds), *Neoliberalism and the Moral Economy of Fraud* (pp 31–43). Routledge.

Tombs, S., & Whyte, D. (2015). *The Corporate Criminal: Why Corporations Must Be Abolished*. Routledge.

Tompkins, A. (2020). *Provenance Research Today: Principles, Practice, Problems*. Lund Humphries in association with IFAR.

Transparency International (TI) (2017). *Tainted Treasures: Money Laundering Risks in Luxury Markets*. Transparency International. https://images.tran sparencycdn.org/images/2017_TaintedTreasures_EN.pdf

Tsingou, E. (2018). New Governors on the Block: The Rise of Anti-Money Laundering Professionals. *Crime, Law and Social Change*, 69, 191–205.

Tsoukas, H. (1997). The Tyranny of Light: The Temptations and Paradoxes of the Information Society. *Futures*, 29(9), 827–43.

Tudor, K. (2018). Toxic Sovereignty: Understanding Fraud as the Expression of Special Liberty within Late-Capitalism. *Journal of Extreme Anthropology*, 2(2), 1–15.

Underkuffler, L.S. (2013). *Captured by Evil: The Idea of Corruption in Law*. Yale University Press.

United Nations (UN) (1997). *Corruption Is Evil and Insidious*. Press Release SG/SM/6318.

Vadi, V., & Schneider, H.E.G.S. (Eds) (2014). *Art, Cultural Heritage and the Market: Ethical and Legal Issues*. Springer.

Vaishnav, M. (2017). *When Crime Pays: Money and Muscle in Indian Politics*. Yale University Press.

Veblen, T. (1970). *The Theory of the Leisure Class: An Economic Study of Institutions*. Unwin Books.

Veggeland, N. (2009). *Taming the Regulatory State: Politics and Ethics*. Edward Elgar Publishing.

Veggeland, N. (2010). *Den nye reguleringsstaten: Idébrytinger og styringskonflikter*. Gyldendal Akademisk.

Velthuis, O. (2005). *Talking Prices: Symbolic Meanings of Prices on the Market for Contemporary Art*. Princeton University Press.

Verhage, A. (2011). *The Anti Money Laundering Complex and the Compliance Industry*. Routledge.

Verkhovsky, A. (2016). Radical Nationalists from the Start of Medvedev's Presidency to the War in Donbas: True till Death? In P. Kolstø & H. Blakkisrud (Eds), *The New Russian Nationalism: Imperialism, Ethnicity and Authoritarianism, 2000–2015* (pp 75–103). Edinburgh University Press.

Virilio, P. (2007). *The Original Accident*. Polity.

Vogl, F. (2021). *The Enablers: How the West Supports Kleptocrats and Corruption – Endangering Our Democracy*. Rowman & Littlefield Publishers.

Von Groddeck, V., & Schwarz, J.O. (2013). Perceiving Megatrends as Empty Signifiers: A Discourse-Theoretical Interpretation of Trend Management. *Futures*, 47, 28–37.

Voronkov, K. (2011). *Алексей Навальный: Гроза жуликов и воров (Aleksei Naval'nyi: A Threat Against Scoundrels and Thieves)*. EKSMO.

Walters, W. (2008a). Anti-Policy and Anti-Politics: Critical Reflections on Certain Schemes to Govern Bad Things. *European Journal of Cultural Studies*, 11(3), 267–88.

Walters, W. (2008b). Editor's Introduction: Anti-Policy and Anti-Politics: Critical Reflections on Certain Schemes to Govern Bad Things. *European Journal of Cultural Studies*, 11(3), 267–88.

Watson, P. (1997). *Sotheby's: Inside Story*. Bloomsbury.

Watson, P., & Todeschini, C. (2006). *The Medici Conspiracy: The Illicit Journey of Looted Antiquities From Italy's Tomb Raiders to the World's Greatest Museums.* Public Affairs.

Way, L. (2016). The Authoritarian Threat: Weaknesses of Autocracy Promotion. *Journal of Democracy*, 27(1), 64–75.

Wedel, J. (2014). *Unaccountable: How the Establishment Corrupted Our Finances, Freedom and Politics and Created an Outsider Class.* Pegasus Books.

Weeks, S. (2020). A Freeport Comes to Luxembourg, or, Why Those Wishing to Hide Assets Purchase Fine Art. *Arts*, 9(87), 1–15.

Wei, S.-J. (1999). Corruption in Economic Development: Beneficial Grease, Minor Annoyance, or Major Obstacle? Policy Research Working Paper Series 2048. World Bank.

Westad, O.A. (2007). *The Global Cold War: Third World Interventions and the Making of Our Times.* Cambridge University Press.

Whitaker, A. (2019). Art and Blockchain: A Primer, History, and Taxonomy of Blockchain Use Cases in the Arts. *Artivate*, 8(2), 21–46.

White House (2021a). Interim National Security Strategic Guidance. https://www.whitehouse.gov/wp-content/uploads/2021/03/NSC-1v2.pdf

White House (2021b). United States Strategy on Countering Corruption. https://www.whitehouse.gov/wp-content/uploads/2021/12/United-States-Strategy-on-Countering-Corruption.pdf

White House (2022). National Security Strategy. https://www.whitehouse.gov/wp-content/uploads/2022/10/Biden-Harris-Administrations-National-Security-Strategy-10.2022.pdf

White House (2023). National Cybersecurity Strategy. https://www.whitehouse.gov/wp-content/uploads/2023/03/National-Cybersecurity-Strategy-2023.pdf

Whitmore, B. (2016). Corruption Is the New Communism. Radio Free Europe, Radio Liberty. 12 April. https://www.rferl.org/a/corruption-is-the-new-communism/27669638.html

Whitson, J.R. (2013). Gaming the Quantified Self. *Surveillance & Society*, 11(1/2), 163–76.

Whyte, D., & Tombs, S. (2015). *The Corporate Criminal: Why Corporations Must be Abolished.* Routledge.

Whyte, D., & Wiegratz, J. (2017). Neoliberalism, Moral Economy and Fraud. In D. Whyte & J. Wiegratz (Eds), *Neoliberalism and the Moral Economy of Fraud* (pp 17–30). Routledge.

Whyte, J. (2019). *The Morals of the Market: Human Rights and the Rise of Neoliberalism.* Verso.

Wiktor-Mach, D. (2019). Cultural Heritage and Development: UNESCO's New Paradigm in a Changing Geopolitical Context. *Third World Quarterly*, 40(9), 1593–612.

Winlow, S. (2014). Trauma, Guilt, and the Unconscious: Some Theoretical Notes on Violent Subjectivity. *The Sociological Review*, 62(2), 32–49.

Winlow, S., & Hall, S. (2013). *Rethinking Social Exclusion: The End of the Social?* SAGE.

Winlow, S., & Hall, S. (2016). Criminology and Consumerism. In P. Carlen & L. Ayres França (Eds), *Alternative Criminologies* (pp 92–109). Routledge.

Wintour, P. (2023). High Stakes for Ukraine as Clampdown on Corruption Comes Under Scrutiny. *The Guardian*. 18 April. https://www.theguardian.com/world/2023/apr/18/high-stakes-for-ukraine-as-clampdown-on-corruption-comes-under-scrutiny

Wright, R. (2022). Why Sanctions Too Often Fail. *The New Yorker*. 7 March. https://www.newyorker.com/news/daily-comment/why-sanctions-too-often-fail

Yablokov, I. (2018). *Fortress Russia: Conspiracy Theories in the Post-Soviet World*. Wiley.

Yakouchyk, K. (2016). The Good, the Bad, and the Ambitious: Democracy and Autocracy Promoters Competing in Belarus. *European Political Science Review*, 8(2), 195–224.

Yakouchyk, K. (2019). Beyond Autocracy Promotion: A Review. *Political Studies Review*, 17(2), 147–60.

Ylönen, M., & Kuusela, H. (2019). Consultocracy and Its Discontents: A Critical Typology and a Call for a Research Agenda. *Governance*, 32, 241–58.

Zanda, E. (2013). *Fighting Hydra-like Luxury: Sumptuary Regulation in the Roman Republic*. Bloomsbury.

Zarobell, J. (2020). Freeports and the Hidden Value of Art. *Arts*, 9(4), 1–12.

Zedner, L. (2007). Pre-Crime and Post-Criminology? *Theoretical Criminology*, 11(2), 261–81.

Zelikow, P., Edelman, E., Harrison, K., & Gventer, C.W. (2020). The Rise of Strategic Corruption: How States Weaponize Graft. *Foreign Affairs*, 99(4), 107–20.

Žižek, S. (1989). *The Sublime Object of Ideology*. Verso.

Žižek, S. (1993). *Tarrying with the Negative: Kant, Hegel, and the Critique of Ideology*. Duke University Press.

Žižek, S. (1997). *The Plague of Fantasies*. Verso.

Žižek, S. (2000). *The Ticklish Subject: The Absent Centre of Political Ontology*. Zero Books.

Žižek, S. (2008). *Violence*. Picador.

Žižek, S. (2012). *Less Than Nothing: Hegel and the Shadow of Dialectical Materialism*. Verso.

Zuboff, S. (2019). *The Age of Surveillance Capitalism: The Fight for a Human Future at the New Frontier of Power*. Profile Books.

Zucman, G. (2015). *The Hidden Wealth of Nations: The Scourge of Tax Havens*. Chicago University Press.

Index